AUTOCOURSE

Sports Sponsorship

A PROFESSIONAL'S GUIDE

icon
PUBLISHING LIMITED

Sports Sponsorship

A PROFESSIONAL'S GUIDE

By **Brian Sims** –
One of international sport's most experienced and successful
exponents of sponsorship acquisition.

Sports Sponsorship –
A professional's guide

is an *Autocourse* imprint and is published by:

Icon Publishing Limited
Regent Lodge, 4 Hanley Road
Malvern, Worcestershire
WR14 4PQ, United Kingdom

Tel: +44 (0)1684 564511

Printed in the United Kingdom by
Butler Tanner and Dennis Ltd
Caxton Road, Frome
Somerset, BA11 1NF

→ ISBN: 978-1-905 334643

Acknowledgment

SPORTS SPONSORSHIP – A professional's guide, by Brian
Sims, is a completely revised and updated version of the
previously published *Sports Sponsorship: Getting your
share* by Brian Sims. Published by Hazleton Publishing in
January 2005 (ISBN-10: 1903135478).

Credits

Publisher: Steve Small
Email: steve.small@iconpublishinglimited.com
Commercial Director: Bryn Williams
Email: bryn.williams@iconpublishinglimited.com
Text Editor: Ian Penberthy

Design and production: Damion Chew Design
Tel: +44 (0)1723 871500
Mobile: +44 (0)7810490074
Email: info@damionchewdesign.com

**Photographs in this book have kindly been
supplied by:**
Brian Sims

Distributors

UNITED KINGDOM
Gardners Books, 1 Whittle Drive
Eastbourne, East Sussex, BN23 6QH
Customer Care Tel: +44 (0)1323 521777
Customer Care Fax: +44 (0)1323 521666
Email: sales@gardners.com

NORTH AMERICA
Quayside Distribution Services
400 First Avenue North, Suite 300
Minneapolis, MN 55401, USA
Tel: +1 612 344 8100
Fax: +1 612 344 8691

Contents

Introduction

When I negotiated my first ever sponsorship deal, back in 1974, little did I realise that it would lead me to a life-long career in sports marketing.

Although I enjoyed an 11-year career as a professional race driver, I wasn't good enough to make it to Formula 1. I did get there eventually, however, not as a driver, but as the marketing director of two Formula 1 teams. More importantly, having got there, I was able to make the most of the opportunity and became successful in initiating and securing many high-profile, multi-million-dollar sponsorship deals, as well as many others of lower value that often were just as complex to structure.

I recently worked out that during my career in sport, I've negotiated nearly 70 meaningful sponsorship deals, worth in total almost £60 million, at all levels of motorsport, as well as in professional rugby union and the charity sector.

As a marketing tool, sponsorship has come a long way since I started. Not only has it grown in use on a global scale, but also it has changed significantly to keep pace with the dramatic developments in communication technologies, as well as with modern business practices.

There is one factor, however, that hasn't changed over the years. In fact, it's the common thread that runs through virtually all of the sponsorship deals that I've managed to bring to fruition. That factor is very straightforward: it's the opportunity for achieving measurable, sustainable business development.

If you can demonstrate to a company a way in which it might be able to develop specific new business or increase its market share in a measurable way, through your proposed sponsorship programme, you'll find that this normally outweighs by far the benefits that traditional brand awareness, hospitality or PR opportunities will bring.

Sadly, I must admit that motorsport has too many stories about sponsors who have had their fingers badly burned, although I'm sure that this applies to many other sports as well. To add to that, all too often, sponsorship is looked upon as nothing more than a form of charity, merely a way of getting someone else to pay for a person's own pleasure.

I've also come across far too many people who think that sponsorship is their right and that because they're good at a particular sport, it's the responsibility of the business sector to support them in fulfilling their dreams. These individuals really do need a reality check.

The tough reality is that businesses are interested in making a profit. If they don't, they won't last long. In the difficult economic times in which we now live, why should companies spend money without there being a viable return on their investment? If you can't show how your sponsorship proposal can help a company achieve that, why would you expect that company to take any interest in your proposal?

The good news is that there is a very positive aspect to this. In such difficult times as we are now experiencing, if you can show a business how you can help generate more sales of their products or services, they are far more likely to take notice of you than they might when business is pouring in without too much effort. What you will find now is that sponsors will be far more demanding than perhaps they used to be. Every penny counts.

I've written this book to provide what I feel is much-needed encouragement and guidance for anyone who has to undertake the quest for sponsorship, for whatever reason. I know that it's not an easy task, but I genuinely believe that if you take the trouble to approach the task in a planned way, there's no reason why you shouldn't be successful.

The book's content is based very much on my own experiences in securing sponsorship: from my first ever deal back in 1974, to the most recent that I have put together, 37 years

later. Many deals were for my own motor racing career, some were for a variety of teams, including Formula 1, while the rest were for other sports and even a charity. The principles are very much the same.

It's true to say, however, that in motorsport, probably more than in any other sport, the need for significant sponsorship starts at a very early age. Without a kart, racing or rally car, how are you going to compete? The cost of buying or even hiring these, let alone running them competitively, is beyond the reach of most people. Therefore the need to learn, at an early age, how to obtain sponsorship is extremely important to anyone wanting to compete at any level of the sport.

Maybe you're an individual sports competitor seeking sponsorship, or you have been given the task of securing funds for your local football team. Perhaps you're the parents of a young sports person and are finding that the struggle to support your child is becoming too much for your own pocket. It could be that you're embarking on a career in sports marketing with an agency, or already work for a sports association that requires sponsorship for one of its championships. Whatever your reason for wanting to learn more about sponsorship, I hope that some of the experiences that I've related will strike a chord and maybe offer a different approach for you to try.

One thing is for sure: after a lifetime spent in this business, I'm still learning. I hope that by passing on to you many of my experiences in seeking sponsorship, both successful and unsuccessful, they will help you to not only find those much needed sponsors, but also to understand the importance of looking after the sponsor, so that you develop a mutually beneficial long-term relationship. Believe me: keeping an existing sponsor is much easier than looking for a new one.

↗ **BRIAN SIMS**
SEPTEMBER, 2011

01

Believe in yourself

I doubt if there's another word in the English language that has seen a greater increase in use over the last four decades than 'sponsorship'. Even five-year-olds understand what it means, thanks to their teachers encouraging them to find sponsors for various fund-raising activities at their schools.

It's not only in sport that commercial sponsorship has become commonplace. Sponsorship is equally popular in education, the arts, charities, fashion, broadcasting, music and conservation, to name just a few areas.

It's sport, however, that most people think of immediately when they talk about sponsorship. Think Formula 1, Premiership football, the Olympics, Champions League, the Grand National and the Rugby World Cup, and you can't help but associate them with high-profile corporate sponsors. Can you imagine a Formula 1 car that isn't emblazoned with brand names? It would look totally out of place on the grid. It wasn't always like that, however.

When I first started watching motor racing in Britain, back in the mid-sixties, the only names that you saw on racing cars were those of trade suppliers, such as Dunlop, Castrol, BP and Shell.

Grand prix cars were usually painted in the national colours of the manufacturers — red for Italy, British racing green and the blue of France. Today, only Ferrari and the Lotus F1 team stick to that principle.

Commercial advertising was taboo in most other sports at that time. Football shirts simply carried the club's badge, while the mere prospect of commercial branding on the side of a yacht would have sent many a sailing club commodore into an apoplectic fit.

In 1968, however, just about everyone in sport took notice when Colin Chapman, the legendary boss of Lotus, took advantage of a change in the rules that governed motorsport in Europe and negotiated a lucrative sponsorship deal for his Formula 1 team with tobacco giant John Player and Sons.

That year, Chapman entered two drivers, Jim Clark and Graham Hill, in the Formula 1 World Championship. Their cars were painted red, white and gold to look like cigarette packets on four wheels. The team was renamed Gold Leaf Team Lotus, promoting the Player's brand of the same name. For nearly 40 years after that momentous deal, the tobacco industry was the primary sponsor of the majority of Formula 1 teams, pumping in hundreds of millions of pounds in return for high-profile branding on the cars, drivers and just about everything else that could be seen during a grand prix race weekend.

That has changed in recent years, of course, and visible tobacco sponsorship has disappeared from Formula 1, as it has done in most other sports. Only Marlboro is still involved, albeit without branding, as a Ferrari sponsor, but for how much longer that will

be allowed remains to be seen. Nevertheless, the impact and positive effect of tobacco sponsorship on attitudes to sports marketing across virtually all sports should never be underestimated. It changed the face of sport.

❝ **In the UK, at the time of writing (2011), the sponsorship industry is worth an estimated £500 million per year, and it is growing.**

Today, sponsorship has effectively become the lifeblood of the majority of sports, but don't think that this happens only at a professional level. I'm sure that those of you who have children involved in sport, even at a very junior level, will know only too well about the ever increasing costs of equipment, training, and even travel to and from events. The only

↗ The example that all others would follow – Gold Leaf Team Lotus, 1970

↗ The 1997 Benetton F1 car, displaying Gillette and FedEx branding. These deals were personally initiated and secured by Brian.

option for many parents is to seek help via a company's marketing budget. In other words, they need sponsorship.

In the UK, at the time of writing (2011), the sponsorship industry is worth an estimated £500 million per year, and it is growing. It's only when you look at the large number of sports that are seeking their share of the sponsorship cake, that you realise the incredible competitiveness of the situation.

It wasn't long ago that sponsorship was regarded as the poor cousin of advertising. That situation has changed dramatically, and specialist sponsorship agencies and consultancies have sprung up all around the

world. Just about every aspect of sponsorship management, commercial exploitation and implementation is now on offer. Some of these agencies have become major global corporations. One of the most famous is IMG, started by the late Mark McCormack. IMG specialises in the management of international sports stars and the promotion of international sports events, where more often than not they own the commercial rights.

Many other agencies offer a range of niche skills. Some work with companies to help them extract a viable commercial return from their sponsorship investment, while others provide a service for measuring the impact of sports sponsorship expenditure. In the process, they will analyse every aspect of TV viewing statistics and print-media exposure. This provides sponsors, sports teams and associations with essential information for measuring how well sponsorship programmes are performing.

I'm sure you're saying to yourself, "That's great if you're a sponsor or if you have a sponsor who needs assistance and expertise in making the sponsorship work. But what about the task of finding sponsors in the first place? Where does the help come from to do that?" Unfortunately, this is where matters become a little more difficult.

I would estimate that less than ten per cent of all sponsorship-related agencies and consultancies are able to offer assistance in terms of finding sponsors. In other words, 90 per cent of these businesses do not employ sales personnel. At best, if you approach them with a sponsorship opportunity, they will present it to the companies that they already represent. If those companies aren't interested, that's usually as far as it will go.

So why is it difficult to find agencies or consultants that are interested in selling sponsorship opportunities on your behalf? The answer is surprisingly straightforward. Selling sponsorship is considered by most sports marketing agencies to be extremely difficult and very risky, particularly when a meaningful regular income can more easily be earned managing a client's sponsorship portfolio or consulting on behalf of a sports association or team. The income that can be generated from the commission on a sponsorship deal might be extremely lucrative, in some cases up to 20 per cent of the sponsorship fee obtained, but there are no guarantees that the deals will be done. Not only that, but often there is a long delay between an agency concluding a deal and receiving the commission due. This is because sponsorship fees are usually paid by instalment, and agency commission is normally only paid by the sponsored party on receipt of each instalment.

Also it's not unusual for a high level of expenditure to be incurred throughout the sales process. This is particularly true with international sponsorship deals, where sales personnel's travelling expenses and international phone calls can quickly build up, as can the costs incurred in creating and producing a presentation and other sales material to a professional standard.

The majority of those agencies or consultancies that are prepared to look for sponsors on behalf of an individual, team or organisation will almost certainly insist on a monthly retainer being paid, irrespective of success, and will usually expect all of their expenses to be covered. In addition, of course, they will take a commission on any sponsorship that they secure. Many people would object to paying a retainer, but I don't see why they should. It's a notoriously tough market to be in, and to expect a salesperson who has a track record of delivering sponsorship to work on a commission-only basis is rather unrealistic. Why should the salesperson carry all of the risk?

I have to say that, in my experience, a large number of motorsport teams and drivers do expect something for nothing in this respect. They're not prepared to go out and find their own sponsorship, but they moan continually that businesses aren't supporting them. Ask a driver to find £1,000 for a new helmet that supposedly gives them an aerodynamic advantage, and somehow they'll come up with the money, even though there is no guarantee that it will actually improve their performance. Some of them will find the money to acquire a luxurious motorhome to spend time in at the track. However, if you ask them to pay a reasonable retainer to a specialist with a proven track record in securing sponsorship, the very lifeblood of all their activities, they will come up with every reason in the book as to why they shouldn't do so. Of course, it's a very short-sighted practice. In my experience, it is the teams and drivers who are either willing to put in the effort themselves, or who are prepared to invest sensibly in securing the services of a professional sponsorship sales consultant or agency, who ultimately will secure long-term, meaningful sponsorship.

But what if you can't afford to employ a professional agency or consultant? What if you are an individual competitor, team or association who just doesn't have that type of budget? What if you don't have an in-house marketing team to work on your behalf?

There's a simple answer – do it yourself. Although obtaining sponsorship is not easy, it is not beyond the capability of anyone who is prepared to go about it in a logical manner and who is prepared to put in a great deal of effort. I should stress that you must also be able to cope with rejection, because for every success, there will be a multitude of failures. If you can't take this, you really should think very carefully before getting involved in this business.

It might surprise some of you to learn that the principles that form the basis of all good campaigns to obtain sponsorship are very similar, regardless of whether the amount sought runs to a few thousand pounds or millions. I've tried to make this book as applicable to the parents of a youngster who perhaps needs a few hundred pounds to take part in a junior championship event, as to the marketing manager of, say, a sports stadium who is seeking significant sponsorship for a new international event.

It's my belief that if you're prepared to take the time to read this book and are willing to put into practice some of the ideas and suggestions it contains, there's no reason why you shouldn't be successful in securing meaningful sports sponsorship.

I must warn you, however, not to expect some magic formula that will guarantee success. If there is one, I certainly haven't found it! What I have found is a systematic approach to obtaining sponsorship that has worked well for me over many years. I know that if you give it a chance, it can greatly improve your odds of being successful, provided you are willing

to accept that there is no substitute in this business for hard work. I can't guarantee that you will get out what you put in. What I do know, however, is that if you're not prepared to accept new ideas and to put in a huge amount of effort, you have little chance of being successful.

Summary

→ Sponsorship is the life-blood of many sports.
→ At all levels of sport, there is an increasing demand for sponsorship.
→ Very few good agencies or sponsorship consultants will work on your behalf to find sponsorship for you, without a sizeable financial retainer being paid.
→ The skills needed to succeed in obtaining sponsorship can be learned. We can all sell. It's simply a case of enhancing the style that you feel most comfortable using.
→ There is no reason why you shouldn't become a competent exponent of sponsorship acquisition, if you understand the basic reasons why companies use sponsorship as a marketing tool.
→ It will involve a lot of hard work and more than a little heartache.

02

A professional approach

If you're going to be successful in securing meaningful sponsorship in such a highly competitive market, you've either got to be incredibly lucky or you need to develop some effective professional selling skills.

I can imagine many of you immediately panicking. Calm down! It doesn't mean you have to become a foot-in-the-door salesperson or a 'Del Boy'. Far from it!

It does mean that first you will need to develop an understanding of just what constitutes a saleable sponsorship opportunity. Then, and only then, will you need to find an effective way of presenting this to potential sponsors.

Looking at my own background, I consider myself fortunate that before I moved into professional sport, I'd enjoyed a successful sales career in the corporate world. This included working for Rank Xerox whose own internal sales training programmes were so highly regarded at the time that they launched a company to market them to other businesses, Xerox Professional Learning Services. I think I learned more about selling during my time at Xerox than at any other company where I worked.

After Xerox, I went on to become the UK sales training director for the global ITT Corporation, which at that time owned many high-profile companies, such as Koni Shock Absorbers, Rimmel Cosmetics, Sheraton Hotels and Avis Car Rentals.

I derived a great deal of satisfaction and enjoyment from training people in the skills necessary to present business opportunities in a professional and effective manner. I always work on the basis that everyone has their own style of inter-personal communication. The key is to help them understand the ways in which that style can be most effectively used. It's not to try to mould them into clones, all quoting the same spiel.

When I first started looking into ways of finding sponsorship for my own racing, there was very little help available. I remember trying to buy books on the subject without any success. Then eventually I discovered Mark McCormack's excellent *What They Don't Teach*

You at Harvard Business School. I still have that book, which I am proud to say the great man signed when he hosted a seminar that I attended in Johannesburg, South Africa. It's still a worthwhile read and I learned a great deal from it.

To this day, rather surprisingly, the amount of material available to help sponsorship seekers is extremely limited, which is one of the reasons why I developed and continue to run training courses on the subject. The first of these was at the superb Williams F1 Conference Centre in 2003. Following on from that, I was invited to run bespoke courses for several sports organisations, including the British Horse Racing Board, the Race Track Association and the British Speedway Promoters' Association. Having received positive feedback from those who attended the courses, it seemed a logical progression to write the first edition of this book, back in 2004.

> **It's often said that salespeople are born, not made. I don't subscribe to that at all.**

It's often said that salespeople are born, not made. I don't subscribe to that at all. It makes no more sense than saying that car drivers are born, not made. I accept that some people are more naturally gifted than others in their driving capabilities, but there are very few people who can't be taught to become a competent driver. The same applies to selling sponsorship opportunities. How successful a person ultimately becomes will have a great deal to do with other qualities. As in sport, your levels of dedication, focus, perseverance and hard work will play major roles in determining your ultimate success.

At this point, a lot of you will be thinking that you're not the type to be a salesperson and that you've never really been able to sell. Please don't put this book down just yet! I want you to forget for a minute about the business world. I want you to think about your own private life. We're all salespeople, like it or not.

Have you ever asked a person to go on a date? Have you ever asked your bank manager for a loan? Have you been successful at a job interview? Have you ever talked your spouse or partner into going to a holiday resort that perhaps they weren't keen on visiting? If the answer to any of these questions is "Yes", then don't tell me that you can't sell. You can! Most people sell themselves all the time: to friends, relatives, boyfriends, girlfriends, potential employers and even to prospective husbands and wives. What you really mean when you say that you can't sell is that you don't feel confident about doing it on a business basis, particularly with strangers and especially in an unfriendly environment. That I can understand.

There are several reasons for this lack of confidence, but with most people, the main ones are:

➔ Fear of rejection.
➔ Fear of the unknown.
➔ Fear of failure.

These same fears prevent a lot of people from succeeding in a variety of activities. Don't worry about admitting that they apply to you. They apply to about 95 per cent of the population, and it's only if they *don't* apply to you that you should start worrying. Even top sports performers will tell you that if they don't get really nervous before the start of their particular competitive event, they rarely perform well. I've known several who were so scared that sometimes they were physically sick. James Hunt, the late Formula 1 world champion, was one of them.

The difference is that they have learned to overcome these fears and channel their nervousness in a beneficial way, giving an extra edge to their performance. What they will also tell you is that their nervousness and fear of failure are balanced by the confidence that comes from knowing that they have prepared as well as possible.

This is no different to selling. If you have the confidence that comes from knowing that you've prepared in a professional manner and followed a clearly planned strategy, just as the athlete adheres strictly to a training schedule, then you will have gone a long way to reducing your fears. For a start, you will know what to expect when you make contact with your potential sponsor. Your level of confidence will grow considerably once you discover that you can genuinely provide a solution to his or her needs. This book is all about finding the most effective ways of doing just that.

Think about your own buying habits. When you go out to buy a TV, a sound system or perhaps even a car, take a careful note of how the salesperson acts. Do they give you confidence that they know what they're talking about, or do you buy despite them? What is it that makes you feel that you are buying from them, rather than being sold to? What perhaps causes you to resent buying from a particular salesperson? Do they generate your respect as being professional? You can learn a great deal by observing how people try to sell to you, noting what works and what doesn't.

It's a fact that in this highly competitive world, more and more people are developing a resistance to being sold to. We are constantly being bombarded by sales campaigns. Nothing is more irritating than being interrupted in the middle of your evening meal by a tele-salesperson, whatever the product or service they are offering. You advertise with *Auto Trader* and you immediately receive half a dozen calls from their competitors, trying to switch you to their online service or publication. In the same way, a lot of people dislike being approached at a motorway service centre by a salesperson trying to foist yet another credit card on them. As if they haven't got enough already!

With the huge increase in online commerce, people are becoming more and more accustomed to buying in this way, rather than being sold to. Theoretically, a company could buy a sponsorship opportunity online. Indeed there are some online agencies offering just that. Despite this, I believe that it will be a long time before that becomes the norm, if ever. Successful sponsorships are normally based on productive personal relationships, and long may that be the case!

Perhaps the words 'selling' and 'salesperson' are the real problem. To many people, they conjure up an image of a smooth, fast-talking, forceful, persistent individual of the type you associate with second-hand car lots. The major skill attributed to them is 'gift of the gab', and there are still plenty of such individuals around. The problem is that if you want to be successful at securing commercial sponsorship, those traits won't get you very far.

> ❝ **You can learn a great deal by observing how people try to sell to you, noting what works and what doesn't.**

Before you think that I'm maligning salespeople, let me dispel that idea. I have always been proud to call myself a salesman, whatever my official title may have been. I also happen to believe that while the skills needed to be a professional salesperson might have changed, the need for high-quality, professional salespeople hasn't.

Imagine a world without salespeople. You are thinking about buying a digital camera for the first time. Of course you can go online and read all of the information about the products available, but that doesn't always answer all of your questions. Don't you feel more comfortable if, before making a decision, you can talk face-to-face with someone who really knows the products inside out, and who can answer questions that actually relate to you and your needs? No, you don't like being sold to, but you do want to learn as much as you can about the best choice for your particular circumstances. Surely what you want is for that salesperson to determine exactly what you want the camera to do and also your budgetary constraints, then to demonstrate to you the models that will best suit your needs. Done professionally, isn't that better than simply choosing from a brochure? It's still selling, but selling in a way that most people find acceptable.

What really brasses people off is the salesperson who doesn't listen to what you want and who is more interested in his need to sell the product than in finding the most suitable product for your needs. Instead of listening to what you are saying, he is busting a gut to get on with what he wants to say.

A contributory factor is the commission schemes that so many sales people are on. It doesn't take long to work out that they are trying to steer you towards a particular product or service because there is a bonus or increased commission on it.

Marketing a sponsorship opportunity is no different. You won't get far if you try to 'hard-sell' the opportunity and don't listen to the prospect (the potential buyer). You need to identify a company's marketing objectives and then demonstrate that your sponsorship opportunity can help that company achieve some of those objectives in a cost-effective manner – no more and no less than that. If your opportunity isn't right for them, that's not a problem. You simply ask them if they can introduce you to any business contacts for whom it might be appropriate and then leave, creating in the process a professional image so that you can always go back if another opportunity presents itself that better suits their requirements.

So, relax. As I said before, I don't want to turn you into another 'Del Boy'!

Over the years, I've been very fortunate in negotiating many sponsorship deals, but I have to admit to being unsuccessful on far more occasions. Very often, what I had to offer simply didn't match the company's needs at the time. That's very much the name of the game. You have to recognise this and not let it get you down. Hopefully, however, by taking on board the information in this book, you'll be able to improve your own personal performance level and learn something useful from my experiences, both successful and unsuccessful.

Summary

➔ You sell every day of your life.
➔ It is not correct to say that salespeople are born, not made.
➔ People dislike selling because they fear:
  ➔ Rejection.
  ➔ The unknown.
  ➔ Failure.
➔ Increasingly, everyone is developing a resistance to intrusive salespeople.
➔ Fortunately, the old 'foot in the door' style has had its day. People want to buy, as opposed to being sold to.
➔ Professional sponsorship selling requires a high level of integrity and a genuine belief that you will only recommend your sponsorship if you know that it is capable of helping the company achieve its stated objectives.

03

You don't need to be a champion

The very first time that I watched a motor race was at Brands Hatch in Kent, on a freezing cold Boxing Day, far too long ago to remember the exact year. I had been invited by some friends, and I recall standing on a frozen grass bank, thinking to myself what heroes the drivers were. Tyres screaming, cars spinning, the crowd cheering and stacks of adrenalin in the air. Yes, I thought, I could really get to like this.

In those days, it wasn't as easy as it is today to experience the thrills of driving on a racetrack. Red Letter Driving Experience Days hadn't been invented, and racing schools were few and far between. Track days were virtually unheard of. Nevertheless, a few years after that first taste of motor racing, I managed to get the cash together to pay for a trial lesson at the Brands Hatch racing driver school, which was appropriately called Motor Racing Stables. I remember being taken around the circuit by the late former grand prix driver Peter Arundell, in a TVR Vixen, before eventually being let loose behind the wheel myself for a couple of laps in a Formula Ford. This was a single-seater racing car, like

a smaller version of a Formula 1 car. It was an experience that was beyond my wildest dreams, although I didn't exactly cover myself in glory – I spun the car.

That was all it took, though. I was definitely going to become a racing driver! Of course, at that age you don't ask yourself silly questions such as where the money is going to come from to buy and maintain a racing car. So for the next couple of years, I had to be content with making my road cars look and sound as competitive as money would allow. I shudder with embarrassment at the thought of that now.

It was in 1972 that I finally decided to go for broke and enrol at the famous Jim Russell Racing Driver School, which then was based at Snetterton in Norfolk. My instructor, John Kirkpatrick, had just started at the school. Eventually he went on to own the business, and he became a very good friend of mine. Some 16 years later, he came to my own racing driver school in South Africa as a judge in our annual competition, the Camel Rookie of the Year Challenge, which I had created to identify our top pupil.

While attending my first course at the Jim Russell School, I used to stay at a small hotel in the vicinity of Snetterton, called Bunwell Manor. It was owned by another of the school's instructors, Alf Lilford, and I spent many a happy evening over supper discussing with him and a few other wannabe Formula 1 stars, the technicalities of race car driving. I remember thinking at the time that there was nothing I wanted more than to become a professional racing driver.

> **The philosophy within Xerox was that everyone who came into contact with the outside world was effectively a salesperson and should be trained properly.**

Even in those days, however, unless you had a fair amount of money, it was difficult to get started in racing. At the time, I was working as a salesman for the Goodyear Tyre Company, selling earthmover and truck tyres. Despite winning the Goodyear Sword of Honour as the company's top UK salesman, I still wasn't earning anywhere near enough money to contemplate buying my own race car. A sword doesn't make up for a lack of money. It certainly doesn't pay the mortgage!

A chance meeting with a girl at a party helped change that situation. She told me that she worked for the photocopier company Rank Xerox and that the company was looking for new sales people. At first I wasn't interested

in the idea of selling photocopiers for a living. Then she told me how much commission their sales force personnel were earning – it was nearly three times what I was getting at Goodyear, so I went along for an interview and was lucky enough to become a Xerox salesman. Little did I realise that this decision would eventually play a vital role in helping me build a career in Formula 1.

My Xerox employment started with a three-week course at the company's residential sales training school in Newport Pagnell, which was very close to the David Brown Engineering works where Aston Martins were built. In those days, even the Rank Xerox secretaries, engineers and customer-relation officers were sent on sales training courses. The philosophy within Xerox was that everyone who came into contact with the outside world was effectively a salesperson and should be trained properly.

Xerox was a great company to work for. At that time they had over 1,000 UK salespeople, and each year we all attended a sales conference in London. One year in particular sticks in my memory. After the sales conference, we all went to the Grosvenor Hotel in Park Lane for the official dinner. The entertainment was provided by a surprisingly flat Ronnie Corbett, who I recall was booed off the stage and pelted with bread rolls by some of the most vociferous of the sales team. He was followed on stage by Pan's People, the regular dance troupe on *Top of the Pops*, who could best be described as real stunners. They were still quite naive, however, because they had to run for their lives after being foolish enough to ask if a few of the 1,000 sales staff, of whom about 85 per cent were male, would like to dance with them on stage!

For me, the abiding memory of the evening was the traditional speech by the chairman, in which he ecstatically praised the sales force for delivering the company's best ever results. At the end of this rousing oration, it was common practice for him to allow a few questions from the floor. One brave salesman stood up: "If we are such a superb sales team and have made the company so much money, I would like to know why we have to drive 1100cc two-door Ford Escorts as our company cars?"

As quick as a flash, the chairman replied, "Because I haven't yet finalised the deal with Ford to build one-door Ford Escorts!"

Within two years of joining Xerox, I'd saved enough to buy a racing car. It was a modified Ford Escort, which I bought from Nick Whiting, a highly talented race driver and one of the three Whiting brothers. Charlie Whiting went on to work for Bernie Ecclestone at the Brabham F1 team, before eventually becoming Formula 1's technical director. Poor Nick, a talented touring car racer, was the victim in an unsolved murder case. The youngest brother, Andy, ran the family motorsport accessories business opposite the main entrance to Brands Hatch.

I dabbled with the car for a couple of months, practising mainly, before realising that I really wanted to drive a single-seater, similar to the one that I had driven at my very first session at Brands Hatch. In the seventies, Formula Ford 1600 offered by far the best opportunity for an aspiring young driver, so I traded in my saloon car for a second-hand Crossle Formula Ford, complete with a trailer. Now I had a car, but the problem was that I didn't have the budget to run it competitively.

What I needed was a sponsor, but I had already convinced myself that this was impossible, as I hadn't built up any sort of track record in racing. Then one day, I really took myself to task: "Brian, you call yourself a salesman, you've sold a lot of photocopiers for Xerox and you've had some superb sales training. If you want to race competitively, get out there and find a sponsor!" For once, I spoke some sense. It took me just over a month to achieve my goal. I'll explain how.

I'd realised that due to work commitments, I would only have the time that year to race at my local track, Brands Hatch. Therefore

I decided that it would be appropriate to approach companies in that specific area. I tried about half a dozen, generating absolutely no interest. Then one day, on a business trip to Ashford, I was driving along the old A20 when I passed what looked like a building site. A large sign caught my eye:

"**New Night Club opening on March 1st**".

I drove on to my meeting, storing the information in my mind.

Over the weekend, I did a little research. Remember, this was in the days before mobile phones and the Internet, so research was a lot more difficult than it is now for sponsorship seekers. What I found out was interesting. The new club was to be called Victoria's, and it would target the 21–45 age group, providing them with a luxurious restaurant, dance floor and bar. Membership wasn't too expensive, putting it within the range of a wide variety of people. I recall sitting in a Happy Eater with a note pad, writing down what I thought might be Victoria's likely marketing needs, with a view to attracting new membership. Then I developed my strategy.

> ❝ A week later, I towed my Formula Ford on its trailer to Victoria's car park and positioned it prominently across the front entrance to the club.

A week later, I towed my Formula Ford on its trailer to Victoria's car park and positioned it prominently across the front entrance to the club. As I had hoped, quite a few people were already arriving for lunch. I'd confirmed previously that the owner was likely to be there that day, so I walked in and asked if I could talk to him about an idea for generating membership subscriptions. When eventually he came through to the reception area, I simply asked him to look out of the window.

As I had anticipated, a group of people had gathered around the racing car, having a good

Brian's first ever sponsorship deal was with Victoria's Nightclub; it was achieved before he had ever raced, showing that you don't have to be a champion to secure a deal.

nose at it, as often happens when you pull up in a crowded place. I waited for a couple of seconds before posing the question: *"Can you imagine what would happen if we put that car, emblazoned with Victoria's branding, in the middle of Maidstone shopping centre on a Saturday morning?"* That was all it took to achieve my objective, which was a subsequent meeting with him. The aim of that meeting was to identify ways in which my racing programme could:

→ help him sell more memberships.
→ help develop a potential customer database.
→ introduce the motor racing fraternity to his club.
→ create awareness for the club through the local media.

The outcome was that I succeeded in negotiating my very first sponsorship deal. With some of the budget that was agreed, I had the car and my helmet painted in the aubergine and gold livery of Victoria's, and had hundreds of car stickers printed. I also generated a fair amount of media coverage for his business by organising a press launch at the club to announce the sponsorship.

That season, through the use of shopping-centre displays, as well as county show promotions, I was able to introduce a lot of new members to the club, each providing me with commission, which was part of the sponsorship deal. More importantly, I had learned a very important lesson. Not once during the negotiations did the owner of Victoria's ever ask me how good I was as a race driver, how quick the car was or my ambitions in racing. He was only interested in finding out what the use of a racing car as a marketing tool could do for his business.

I see many sponsorship proposals that are based almost entirely on the level of success achieved in a particular sport by the presenter. While performance standards can often play a major role in the decision making process, normally this only happens when a high-profile club or individual is involved, or when a company will be basing its marketing strategy specifically on a competitor's performance, as in the case of a sports shoe manufacturer for example. For the majority of sponsorship seekers it is, at best, only a minor consideration and usually is looked at only in the final stages of a negotiation. The harsh reality is that most sponsorship decisions are based on the benefit to a company's bottom line, not on the competitor's achievements.

Summary

→ You don't have to be a winning competitor or team to obtain sponsorship.
→ Your level of performance is less important than the potential for a business return that your sponsorship opportunity offers.
→ You need to be creative and bold if you are going to interest companies in looking at your sponsorship opportunity.

04

What can sponsorship offer a business?

It shouldn't come as a huge surprise to learn that for a sponsorship proposal to be of interest, it has to meet at least some of the real, not the assumed, marketing needs of a company.

So why is it that when I talk to many of the decision makers in the corporate world about the standard of sponsorship proposals they receive, they nearly all agree on one major point? A high percentage of the many hundreds of these proposals display a total lack of understanding as to what the company is likely to look for as being beneficial to their marketing objectives. In other words, there is no research, just assumption.

This is such a fundamental and crucial part of the sponsorship sales process that unless you have a proper understanding of it, everything else that is covered in this book will be a waste of time. If you don't appreciate the range of reasons why a company considers sponsorship a valuable part of its marketing mix, you'll find it incredibly difficult, if not impossible, to demonstrate how your

sponsorship opportunity can deliver any worthwhile benefits.

I think it's fair to say that if you were to conduct a survey among sponsorship seekers, asking if they could list the main reasons why companies sponsor, the majority of people would give three reasons:

→ Brand awareness.
→ Hospitality.
→ Public relations (PR).

Without doubt, these are very important criteria for many sponsors. If you rely on only these three factors, however, you'll struggle to interest many companies.

Imagine going to a restaurant and finding that there are only three choices on the menu. What if you don't really fancy any of them? What will you do? Go somewhere else, of course. It's the same with only offering brand awareness and hospitality to a potential sponsor. If none of the three major entitlements really turns a company on, they won't spend a great deal of time trying to find out what else you could offer. They will simply go somewhere else, to a person or organisation that offers a sponsorship opportunity capable of meeting their real needs.

The list of reasons why companies become commercial sponsors is almost endless. To simplify the task, however, I will identify the factors that I've found to be the most common. I should stress that these aren't in any order of importance and also that the list is far from complete. I've usually found that it is a combination of many of the following factors that results in a sponsorship agreement being reached.

Brand awareness

There is no doubt that brand awareness is extremely important to certain categories of company in deciding whether or not to use sponsorship as a marketing tool. In recent years, undoubtedly the most blatant business sector to use sponsorship as a way of increasing brand awareness has been the tobacco industry, which paid premium prices for its brands to be seen at televised sporting events. These have included Formula 1, snooker, motorcycle racing and yachting.

While there are many other business sectors that seek high levels of brand awareness, such as the fast moving consumer goods sector, mobile phones, IT, soft drinks and clothing, there are many types of business to whom it is less important. A management consultancy, for example, or a company that sells expensive industrial cutting equipment typically would not see the need to spend huge sums of money promoting their name to a wide audience. The public at large are not their target market, so why spend money promoting the company name in that way? However, from the following list, you'll see that there are many other ways

in which such companies can effectively benefit from the use of sports sponsorship.

Hospitality

The same companies that I have just shown as probably not being interested in brand awareness may well see the importance of certain types of hospitality being included in your sponsorship proposal. The opportunity to invite clients or prospective clients to join their management team at a sporting event can be very effective for a company. In Formula 1, for example, on the Sunday of a grand prix, the VIP Paddock Club is full of company directors, many of them involved as sponsors. Many others are prospective or existing clients who have been invited by sponsors. The opportunity to spend seven or eight hours together, without the interruption of phones and other office distractions, can be highly rewarding from a business perspective. This can apply just as effectively with various levels of hospitality. It doesn't have to be at the level at which Formula 1 operates for the concept to work well for a company.

It's important to bear in mind, however, that it is very easy to fall into a trap. Sports hospitality is a booming and highly competitive industry in its own right, and companies are being approached all the time to buy hospitality at major sporting events. Favourite hospitality venues include Wimbledon, Wembley, Twickenham and Ascot. Many sponsorship proposals that rely too heavily on the provision of corporate hospitality are rejected because a company decides that it can achieve the same objective by booking the corporate hospitality itself, without the added expense of a sponsorship involvement.

It's also important to mention a new development that is already having a significant impact on the use by companies of hospitality as a marketing tool, the *Bribery Act*. The UK Act, which was passed just before the General Election in 2010, creates two general offences of bribery, a specific offence of bribery of a foreign public official and another offence of failure by a company to prevent a bribe from being paid on its behalf. It is already being mooted by some professional race teams, and individuals in other sports, that race tickets and entertainment packages could be viewed as a 'currency of bribery'. This will mean that corporations will enter into sponsorship agreements with a lot more caution, which could impact on sponsorship revenues.

I'm sure that there will be clarification of this thorny issue in future, but it is well worth being aware of it.

Image transfer

This is an important aspect of sponsorship that is commonly overlooked. Very often, companies will respond to your proposal, which highlights brand awareness, by informing you that they can guarantee the same or an even higher level of awareness through conventional advertising. Why, they will ask, should they take the risk with sponsorship?

There is one very important factor that can be used to answer such an objection. It's a prime reason why many companies become involved in sponsorship. It is known as 'image transfer'. What does that mean? I'll use Formula 1 as an example. Think for a minute of the various qualities or images that you might associate with the Formula 1 World Championship. I'm not saying that there aren't some negative emotions as well, but think of all the positive ones. Here are just a few that you might come up with:

→ Aspirational
→ Global
→ Hi-Tech
→ Glamorous
→ Colourful
→ Exciting
→ Competitive
→ Skilful

→ Fast
→ Teamwork
→ Powerful
→ Trendy
→ Fashionable
→ Dynamic
→ Elite

Now, put yourself in the shoes of the marketing director of a company that you are approaching for sponsorship. There are many qualities with

which he would like his company or brand to be associated. He considers it important to project these qualities to his target market in some way. If he can be convinced that the qualities Formula 1 projects match a high number of those that he is looking to promote, it creates a very powerful reason for him to consider sponsorship opportunities within Formula 1.

For example, if he wants his brand of male toiletries to be perceived as being expensive, macho and elite, Formula 1 might be a very good platform for him. The perceptions of Formula 1 can be shown to match those qualities. It could be argued that boxing, for example, would not provide such perceptions, although it has other qualities that might suit a different company. By being involved in Formula 1, his company could benefit from the image transfer that comes from people mentally linking the qualities of grand prix racing to his company's brand of male toiletries.

Conventional advertising might be able to create brand awareness for that company, but what it can't do as well as sponsorship is to create the emotive response that comes from being associated with the qualities that we identified as being important.

So if you can list all of the qualities that could be associated with your specific sport, you can build a very good case to put forward. When you talk to your prospect, ask him to list some of the qualities that he or she would equate with their brand. You can then draw examples from the list that you've mentally compiled and equate the two.

There is a final matter about image transfer that I would like to bring to your attention, and that relates to 'perception'.

Throughout my career in motorsport, I have seen many ups and downs in the economy. When times are tough, when the economy is in a bad way, companies not only have to decide whether or not they can *afford* to enter into a sponsorship agreement, but also whether they can afford to be *seen* to be entering into a sports sponsorship agreement. This is particularly true in what are often seen as elite sports, such as motor racing, powerboat racing and the like.

In other words, what worries companies is the perception that they are seen to be spending money on elite sports while perhaps making staff redundant or not offering pay rises to staff.

Bearing this out, Tesco recently embarked on a powerful poster campaign in the area where I live. It depicts a heavily branded Formula 1 car. Beneath the picture is a caption, something along the lines of: "While some companies spend their money sponsoring race cars, we prefer to pass on price reductions to our customers."

You'll see later in this chapter how you can help to overcome the issue of negative perception if it is raised by a company.

PR

Public relations is yet another important factor when looking at the reasons why companies sponsor. The trouble with the term 'PR' is that too often it conjures up the image of a young girl handing out drinks at a business function. When asked by someone what her job is, she tells them that she "does PR".

So just what is meant when we talk about public relations? According to the Institute of Public Relations:

Sponsorship can play a vital role in providing a company with worthwhile PR opportunities. It is true to say that conventional advertising can be highly effective, otherwise companies wouldn't continue to spend hundreds of millions of pounds on it. The problem with advertising, however, is that it is perceived by the public to be just that, paid-for advertising, and there is no hiding the fact. While it might do its job in creating awareness, there will always be a slight reluctance on the part of the public to believe everything that it states.

On the other hand, if a newspaper carries a feature article about the product or the company, the people who read that article will be far more convinced that what is being said is closer to the truth.

Sponsorship, used creatively, has the ability to provide a high level of feature-style media coverage. Imagine, for example, that as a result of some effective PR work by the marketing department of an international motorsport team, an article appeared in an in-flight airline magazine about Team Nasamax, explaining how it had become the first team ever to complete the world famous Le Mans 24-hour race using a wholly renewable fuel, bio-ethanol, produced from sugar beet and potatoes. This would prove far more beneficial for the team's sponsors than if they had simply placed an advertisement in that publication.

PR can also play a pivotal role in helping to promote the image transfer that I have identified as being important to so many

> **Public Relations is about reputation – the result of what you do, say and what others say about you. Public Relations is the discipline which looks after the reputation, with the aim of earning understanding and support and influencing opinion and behaviour. It is the planned and sustained effort to establish and maintain goodwill and mutual understanding between an organisation and its public.**

sponsors. Take the previous example. The airline magazine article on Team Nasamax would create the perception that 'environmental awareness' is of importance to the sponsors of that team. This would be a direct result of image transfer. The team is concerned with the environment; therefore the sponsors of that team must also be concerned. This has been promoted because of the PR activity that enabled the article to appear in the airline magazine.

Other ways in which sponsorship can provide a host of excellent PR opportunities include:

→ Media relations
→ Newspapers (both national and local)
→ TV, radio and magazines
→ Online: websites, Facebook and Twitter
→ Corporate print: internal newsletters, press releases and reports
→ Special events: conferences, exhibitions, product launches
→ Photography: websites, brochures

Promotions

The opportunity for a sponsor to create and implement special promotions, using the sponsorship as a platform, can often prove very important. These can range from in-store merchandising promotions to participative events linked to the sports programme itself.

I remember Blackthorn Cider, the main sponsor of Bath Rugby in the Zurich Premiership, devising a superb promotion a few years ago, called the Blackthorn Golden Boot Competition. It took place on a regional basis, and its objective was to find the best goal kicker in each region, outside of professional rugby. The heats took place at rugby union clubs throughout the country, with the final taking place at half-time during one of Bath Rugby's televised matches at the Rec. The competition was promoted widely through all of the major retail outlets and supermarkets that stocked Blackthorn products.

The great thing about creating innovative promotions on the back of a sponsorship is that

for a sponsor, they take away much of the risk factor that comes from relying totally on the performance level of the sponsored team or individual.

When I ran my own motor racing school at the Kyalami Grand Prix Circuit in South Africa, I negotiated a sponsorship deal with Camel, the cigarette brand. The way in which I put this together is detailed later in the book. What it provided was the opportunity for Camel to run consumer promotions through many major retail outlets, offering the public the chance to win places at the school and to participate in the Camel Rookie of the Year Challenge. Through this, they could win a test drive with the professional Paul Stewart Racing team in the UK. It proved very popular.

The important thing to realise is that promotions don't have to be the sole preserve of large companies. Creating the opportunity of an innovative promotion for your local hardware store can be just as effective. Suppose the store agrees to sponsor a show jumper in a local event and has a product stall in place at the venue. By running a competition for a prize, comprising a course of riding lessons, with coaching from the sponsored rider, the store could generate a useful database of names to whom later they could send special product offers and promotions.

The opportunities that sponsorship provides for creating and implementing innovative promotions are endless, which is why this is a very important factor for companies when deciding whether or not a sponsorship is cost-effective.

Case study development

This is one of the least known reasons why a company will decide to become a sponsor, yet I have seen it used extremely effectively by several companies.

One of the first examples of this that I came across was in 1995, when Andersen Consulting (now Accenture) became an official sponsor of the Williams Formula 1 team. Accenture is a global management consultancy, technology services and outsourcing company. Not the type of organisation you immediately think of as a typical Formula 1 sponsor. At that time, Williams were looking to move from their HQ at Didcot to a new state-of-the-art facility at Grove, near Wantage. This is not an easy thing for a Formula 1 team to achieve without major disruption. Andersen Consulting saw an innovative opportunity to co-ordinate the move and help design the new factory to work at maximum efficiency. That provided the platform on which a 14-year partnership programme was built. I say partnership and not sponsorship, because that is really what it was.

More and more, the word sponsor conjures up a one-way relationship. It's only by developing a win-win, two-way partnership that both parties, the sponsor and the sponsored, are able to derive the maximum benefit from the relationship.

The effectiveness of the project management and lack of disruption caused by the move, was demonstrated when Williams F1 cars finished first and second in the season's opening race, going on to win both the drivers' and constructors' championships.

In turn, Andersen's project management of the factory move provided them with the perfect opportunity to produce a case study, explaining the various aspects of its involvement with a high-profile F1 team. The case study could then be used to promote those project management abilities to potential new clients. Add to that the opportunity for their senior personnel to meet executives from other businesses in the F1 Paddock Club over a race weekend, and it was easy for Andersen Consulting to justify the expenditure of becoming a sponsor, or rather a partner.

It's not only in Formula 1 that such case studies can be effective. The concept can be used for sponsorship at any level.

Take a small accountancy firm for example. It might benefit from developing a case study on how it sponsors the local football team. This could show how it was able to introduce a far more effective way of handling the club's tax matters, saving it hundreds of pounds a year. The local high profile of the team might prove an effective point of interest for the firm to use the case study to generate new business in the area.

The opportunity that a sponsorship can provide to develop powerful case study material is one that should not be overlooked. With a little bit of imagination, you should be able to come up with a number of possibilities for the use of this facet of sponsorship.

Business-to-business

The opportunity to generate business as a result of a sponsorship programme is a powerful reason for companies to participate in this form of marketing.

Never forget that the business world is fiercely competitive. Whatever the message that companies might like to portray, most of them are only interested in one thing – generating profit. It shouldn't come as a surprise then, when I tell you that in my experience most companies won't part with a penny of sponsorship money unless it directly or indirectly benefits their bottom line. Why should they? They have separate charity budgets for good causes. Sponsorship has to be justified for business reasons.

Unfortunately there are a lot of people who still think that sponsorship is their right. Because they have won a particular championship or done well in their sport, they think that it is incumbent of companies to help them turn professional and make a career out of their sport. Although they will deny it until they are blue in the face, in effect what they are doing is seeking charity. You even hear it in some of the media interviews with the parents of talented young sports participants: "It's not fair, overseas youngsters get the backing of big business. We have to fork out money from our own pocket because companies here don't want to help." WRONG!

What these people really mean is that they don't know how, or can't be bothered, to design a sponsorship proposal that shows a company the ways in which it can potentially generate business through the use of a well-thought-out sponsorship programme.

I'm sure that many of you will know people who look upon sponsorship in this way. Unfortunately, their primary objective is only too clear. They want to race a yacht during Cowes Week, and they want someone else to pay for it, or they might want to row across the Atlantic single-handed, but want to do so at someone else's expense. The problem is not with this demand for sponsorship in itself, it's with the fact that so often scant regard or recognition is given to the sponsor's need for a commercial return.

I've seen this happen even at the top level of sport. Just after rugby union became professional, the management of a well-known professional rugby club looked upon sponsors as a necessary evil. They didn't want to give up the way that the club had been run in the amateur days, but nevertheless were more than happy to receive the income that came with commercial sponsorship. Rightly or wrongly, what came across was the perception that the least they had to do for the sponsors, the better.

I remember seeing the team run out on to the pitch for one match at which the club's primary sponsor was hosting a large hospitality function for their business clients. To the astonishment of everyone in that suite, the players were wearing shirts without the sponsor's branding. It was an unforgivable error that could have resulted in a lawsuit. Of course mistakes can happen, but the fact that no one at the club really understood why the sponsor was so upset typified the problem.

Having talked about the need for a meaningful commercial return, this conveniently brings me to one of the most compelling reasons why a company decides to become a commercial sponsor, and that is the opportunity that it presents for securing meaningful business-to-business revenue.

Put very simply, if it can be shown to the board members or owner of a company that by spending £25,000 on a sponsorship programme with a sports team, the company should be able to generate at least £50,000 of business from other commercial sponsors of the team, the proposal will most likely be of some interest. Needless to say, it isn't always that straightforward, but the principle is important. Every company looks to expand its customer base, and to increase turnover and profit. If it doesn't, it will soon go out of business.

If you can show the senior executives of a company that through the innovative use of sponsorship, they can generate additional business, you stand a good chance of at least securing a meeting. In a later chapter, we'll look in depth at how this can be put into practice in a number of different ways.

As a simple example, however, imagine you are the marketing manager of a cricket team. You're seeking a sponsor for an overseas tour in the off-season. Your team already has a major sponsor in place. It's a company called Markhams, specialising in building and civil engineering. Markhams won't extend its sponsorship agreement to cover the proposed tour, but after a conversation with the managing director, you gain agreement for a strategy that might pay dividends in identifying a company that will.

Your first step is to approach your local motor dealership and meet with the sales director to present the tour sponsorship opportunity. In the process, you mention that following a discussion with the MD of Markhams, the club's existing sponsor, it has come to light that the company runs a fleet of 15 company cars, which it buys from a dealership in another region. These vehicles are normally changed every two years.

You go on to explain to the sales director that even if his dealership decides to sponsor the tour, there is no way that you can guarantee that it will secure this future vehicle business from Markhams. However, what you can guarantee is that if the sponsorship is agreed, the Markhams MD will immediately set up a meeting with the dealership's sales director to discuss the potential future purchase of cars.

In other words, what you are offering is the guarantee of a meeting at the right level, but not a guarantee of business. That will only come if the dealership is able to put forward a convincing business case at the meeting. However, it does present the dealership with that very real business opportunity of sitting in front of the key decision maker, in a favourable environment, with both parties keen to do a deal. If presented in that way, it might be enough, in addition to the other sponsorship entitlements, to persuade your target to see the benefit of agreeing to your proposal.

This is a very simplistic example. As you will see later, there are many variations on this theme. The main point is that you are offering a potential business-to-business opportunity, which uses the sponsorship as a catalyst. It should not be difficult to understand why business-to-business is a major factor in the decision making process of many companies.

One of the largest sponsorship deals that I ever generated was with FedEx, whom I secured as a major sponsor for the Benetton Formula 1 team. I was able to show this company the tremendous business opportunities that could open up within the Benetton Group if they became a sponsor of the F1 team. In addition, there would be other opportunities to meet the key decision makers of some of the other 40-odd sponsors and suppliers of the Benetton F1 team. Although it wasn't the only reason they duly signed up, it

was by far the most important to them in their decision making process.

If you can show a potential sponsor how they can do extra business as a direct result of the introductions that can be facilitated through the sponsorship, you're in with a good chance of gaining their interest.

One thing that I should emphasise is that you should never promise potential business. As the example showed, normally the most that you can offer is the chance of a meeting with key personnel who would be in a position to make decisions. In most cases that is enough. Companies will recognise that then it is up to their own sales skills to secure a business relationship. The chance of a meeting at the right level, in favourable circumstances, can be a tempting opportunity.

Community involvement

Many companies are keen to build a good relationship with the local community in which they operate and use sponsorship for this purpose. They realise the importance this can have in terms of recruitment, as well as perhaps maintaining a good working relationship with the local council, which can help in such matters as future planning applications.

I have found this to be the case on many occasions. I negotiated a substantial sponsorship with Virgin Mobile on behalf of Bath Rugby, based on the fact that the Virgin Mobile head office was in the same geographical region and employed over 1,400 people from that area. They saw the importance of being involved with a team that enjoyed the support of many of their workforce and which, in addition, was involved in working with the local community through its schools programme.

For many years, the football team that I have always supported, Wolverhampton Wanderers, was sponsored by the Goodyear tyre company. At the time, its head office was at Bushbury, about five miles from Wolves'

Molineux Stadium. Goodyear even had their own hospitality suite at Molineux so that they could entertain their staff and their families at matches, in addition to their corporate hospitality activities.

The opportunity for a company to be seen to play a role in the local community can be high on their list of reasons for becoming a sponsor.

Sales incentives

Although some companies use sponsorship for this reason, I am surprised that this hasn't been taken on board by a lot more.

I mentioned previously that I had worked for Rank Xerox. They were great believers in innovative sales-incentive programmes to motivate their substantial sales force. On one occasion, along with the other 999 Xerox salespeople, I was invited to a sales conference at the Drury Lane Theatre in London's West End. At the conference, an announcement was made about the sales-incentive programme for the forthcoming year. It was to be called the Race of Champions and was based on a Formula 1 Grand Prix season. The opportunity existed for salespeople to win interim prizes at different stages of the 12-month programme. These prizes normally involved trips to UK motor races and some to overseas grands prix.

Following this, the chairman announced the top prize, which would go to the overall winner of the Race of Champions at the end of the 12-month competition. To everyone's amazement, motor racing legend Stirling Moss drove it on to the stage. It was a brand-new MGBGT V8. At that time, it was worth a lot of money.

A well-structured sponsorship programme can be used as a highly effective platform for the design and implementation of such an incentive programme for a company's sales force. If you have targeted a company that employs a reasonably high number of salespeople and you can build an innovative sales-incentive programme into your sponsorship proposal, you will immediately be head and shoulders above your competitors. For the right company, sales-incentive programmes are extremely important. Providing an opportunity for them to create a scheme around the catalyst of a sports sponsorship can be highly attractive.

This can be even more effective in the austere times in which we are now living. One of my recent sponsorship deals was based on exactly this concept. Sales are hard to come by for most businesses, and anything that will encourage their sales personnel to find new business should be of some interest to a company, if presented in the right way.

Personal appearances by sports personalities

One of the factors that contribute to a company sponsoring an individual or team is the opportunity that it presents to invite a sports personality to major business events. These might be sales conferences, exhibitions, product launches, media conferences, client presentations or even an exclusive business dinner with a VIP client.

It is fair to say that the bigger the name, the more attractive this is, but don't underestimate the value that any level of sportsperson might offer a company. It is relative to the size of a company and the importance of that person to its target market. For example, the chance for a company to invite the winner of a local, but high-profile cycle race to open a new shop may be very important. Alternatively, the opportunity to invite a VIP client to play a round of golf with the captain of the local football team can also be very effective.

If a sponsor is able to build into a sponsorship agreement the right to a specified number of days' use of either the sponsored individual or a member of the team, it can provide a significant reason for going ahead with the proposed deal.

Brand value through advertising

Many companies will consider sponsorship because of the opportunity that it provides to further demonstrate their brand values through the use of that sponsorship in their conventional advertising. In America, this has been used extensively for much longer than in the UK. Sponsors in the NASCAR championship are particularly attracted to this opportunity, and you will see their print media advertising as well as TV commercials using their sponsorship involvement to add power to the brand.

What sponsorship can do is provide a powerful and more personal communication link between a company's advertising and their target market. The sponsorship of a major sporting event, for example, will make the public feel closer to the sponsoring company and vice versa, in a way that doesn't happen with conventional advertising. This can be an important consideration in the use of sports sponsorship.

Merchandising

For an appropriate company, the opportunity to develop a range of branded merchandise, such as T-shirts, caps and bags, can be very attractive. This form of marketing is often used to help promote the launch of a new product or brand. An innovative sports sponsorship programme can provide an effective platform for this to generate a higher degree of interest than if it were simply product based. Although this is perhaps more effective for larger companies, there is no reason why merchandising can't play an important role in any level of sponsorship.

It is quite normal for sponsors to insist on the right to use the team's or association's badge/brand in conjunction with their own brand identity on a range of merchandise. The more well known the badge, the more effective this link becomes for the sponsor.

Product sampling

This can be a very powerful marketing tool for a company. Suppose that you are staging a sporting event at a stadium. Provided you have the right to do so, you can show a potential sponsor that they can hand out free product samples to each person who goes through the turnstiles. This can be very effective for a company producing soft drinks or biscuits, or anything that they want to put straight into the hands of the general public. On its own, it won't be the reason why they sponsor, but in addition to other factors, it can be a very important issue.

In Chapter 15, you'll see how product sampling played a major role in helping me secure the sponsorship deal that allowed me to turn professional as a race driver. The company in question was SodaStream, a big name back in the 1970s

Recruitment

I remember at the time being very surprised when two global companies, with whom I worked closely, told me that one of the major reasons they used motorsport sponsorship was to promote recruitment. In a highly competitive market, they wanted to attract the very best graduates, and they found that their involvement in motorsport was very often a powerful influence. They discovered that it showed the graduates that the company was forward thinking and young in nature, qualities that were perceived as being important. The two companies were Honda and Nissan, and what I learned stayed in my mind as a possibility for helping create appropriate sponsorship proposals.

By way of example, I have outlined the way in which a well-known insurance company, RIAS, used sponsorship as a cost-effective part of its recruitment programme. Although the specific deal in question is no longer in place, it fully achieved its objectives at the time, which is why I have included it.

THE RIAS SPONSORSHIP DEAL

RIAS is one of the UK's leading general insurance intermediaries. Its impressive corporate head office is situated in Poole, Dorset. The company focuses on the over-50s age profile. Its main lines of business are home, garden, motor, travel, caravan, legal expenses and personal accident.

In 2004, the company undertook a major re-branding exercise to increase customer awareness and recognition within its local community.

RIAS didn't have a previous history of any kind of sports sponsorship. The company was growing at the rate of 35 per cent, year on year, to the point where it employed around 1,000 staff in its two geographical sites. The managing director recognised that this growth was creating some exciting new challenges for the company. These included the need to recruit high-quality personnel, in line with its growth, as well as the equally important need to retain and motivate existing personnel. In the catchment area for staff recruitment, the situation was extremely competitive. With an unemployment rate of less than two per cent, it wasn't easy to attract the quality of people that RIAS required, mainly for their call centre. Their experience showed that in the past such personnel usually came from two age groups: 20–28 and over 50.

In addition, it was recognised that there was an ongoing need for brand awareness, not only in the region, but nationally. In such a competitive business sector, a high-profile brand was seen as being very important.

The Poole Pirates speedway team competes in the Sky Elite League, which is British speedway's top-flight competition, sponsored by Sky TV. The team was and, at the time of writing, still is one of the most successful in the country. At the time of this situation, 2003/04, they had won all three of speedway's major trophies: the Sky Elite League and the sport's two primary knock-out cup competitions. They enjoyed very good spectator attendance of between 3,000 and 6,000 per meeting, which for a local sport of this kind was very high.

Speedway has increased in popularity at a rapid rate, not only in the UK, but also internationally. The Speedway Grand Prix Championship comprises rounds in nine countries, including the UK, where it is held annually in the Millennium Stadium, Cardiff, attracting over 45,000 spectators.

Sky TV statistics in 2004 showed that it was their third most watched sport.

The Sponsorship

Following a number of meetings between Poole Pirates board members and the RIAS managing director, agreement was reached that RIAS would become the official title sponsor of the highly successful Poole Pirates speedway team.

There were three primary objectives on which the sponsorship agreement was based:

1. Staff recruitment.
2. Staff retention.
3. Brand awareness.

↘ Staff Recruitment

Because of the difficulties in recruiting staff in the region, this was the most important of all the considerations in progressing this sponsorship.

The region had a labour shortage. RIAS was a relatively new company, only having operated then for ten years. It was competing in the recruitment market against many high-profile, big-name companies that had been in the region a long time. Many of these were well-known national financial institutions, which were, and still are, equally prominent in the region.

RIAS considered itself a labour-intensive business, as customers and potential customers in the insurance business need to talk to people. Thus recruitment was very important.

It was the company's intention to move RIAS up the list of choices available to job seekers and job movers in the region. The target age groups for recruitment were 20–28 and 50+.

Sponsorship of a high-profile local sports team seemed a good way of promoting awareness of the company as a high-quality employer of people. There were only two choices in the Bournemouth and Poole region that would have provided a sufficiently high profile. One of these was Bournemouth AFC Football League team; the other was Poole Pirates speedway team.

An alternative was to consider the two south-coast Premiership football teams: Southampton and Portsmouth. However, these were considered to be too far away geographically in respect of hitting the target job market. They were also deemed too expensive.

The deciding factor between the two options within the region came down to the excellent relationship that the Poole Pirates promoters had built with the regional media, particularly *The Echo*, which is the paper that was considered by RIAS as being exceptionally important from a recruitment advertising point of view. In addition, the coverage received by the high-flying speedway club on both regional TV and radio news programmes helped the decision.

It was decided that Poole Pirates would provide the best route for achieving the objectives in respect of staff recruitment.

Staff Retention

The need to motivate and retain existing staff was also seen as a key factor in the decision to use sports sponsorship. This was particularly important if a campaign was to be mounted to recruit new staff.

Part of the deal that the company negotiated with Poole Pirates was that twice a year, RIAS would be able to take all of its staff, together with their families, to the speedway. This would include the opportunity to visit the pits, meet the riders and build a unique relationship with the team.

It was considered important in building not only existing staff ties, but also in promoting the company to young people. In addition, this provided a benefit to the team inasmuch that a lot of people who went to watch speedway for the first time with RIAS decided that they enjoyed it and returned as paying spectators.

Another way of involving staff was that each week the company provided 20 tickets as a staff incentive to recognise outstanding work effort.

Brand Awareness

Sky TV coverage of the Elite League was exceptionally popular. It had a wide range of viewer demographics. Many of the TV viewers were people in the 45–65 age group, who had been fans of the sport since its previous heyday of the 1950s and 1960s. It could also be shown that a lot of young people were attending and watching speedway, having witnessed the rapid growth of the sport in the last decade.

As triple champions, it was likely that Poole Pirates would have eight league matches at the home track televised live during the first year of the sponsorship. This would involve a high number of post-race interviews, with the RIAS brand on the interview area backdrop featuring prominently, as well as on the race-bibs of the riders.

Period of Agreement
It was decided that an initial two-year agreement would be the most beneficial for both parties. The first year would allow RIAS time to identify the most effective ways in which the sponsorship could be exploited commercially. It would also allow the relationship between the two organisations to develop in a more relaxed way than if it had only been for a one-year period.

Another consideration in agreeing a two-year deal was that it would give the target market time to become fully aware of the relationship. It would have been unrealistic to expect the full benefits of the programme to be achieved in one short burst of activity.

Measurement
RIAS was aware of the importance of measuring the cost-effectiveness of the sponsorship programme. It put in place methods of assessing the number of people who made contact with the company through its call centres as a result of the Poole Pirates sponsorship activities and promotions.

In respect of the primary objective, recruitment, incoming correspondence from job seekers was monitored carefully. Three months after the season started, it was seen that in the month of June alone, 17 new employees resulted from unsolicited letters, expressing a desire to work for RIAS, as opposed to people responding to advertisements for specific jobs. Before the Poole Pirates sponsorship, this averaged one or two a month at most.

That immediately saved the company the normal cost of advertising, which was amortised at £2,000 per application. In June alone, this effectively saved the company over £34,000.

In terms of staff retention, 60–70 per cent of the staff turned out for the first speedway meeting, to which all the RIAS personnel were invited. In a high number of cases, they brought family with them, further cementing the relationship between RIAS, their staff and the speedway.

All media coverage was carefully monitored, providing RIAS with an indication of the brand awareness that resulted from the Pirates' success.

Conclusion
RIAS showed that sports sponsorship can provide a benefit to companies that is not widely recognised, that of enhancing its recruitment activities in a cost-effective way.

The need to recruit high-quality personnel in a highly-competitive labour market was a vital requirement for the company. Through an innovative link-up with the region's most successful sports team, Poole Pirates, RIAS demonstrated that sports sponsorship can play an important role in achieving this objective.

This particular deal also highlights the importance of fully understanding and appreciating what is important to a company, rather than making assumptions. The choice of a speedway team as the sponsorship vehicle for a company that targets the over-50s age group might have seemed strange. However, as you can see, this was a well-thought-out sponsorship programme, based on sound research, vision and an in-depth knowledge of the target market.

As I stressed at the beginning of this chapter, what I am setting out are just some of the many reasons why a company will consider including sponsorship as a major part of its marketing mix. It's rare for there to be only one factor that generates interest, and most sponsorship deals are concluded through a combination of several of these.

It's important to be aware of these factors. You can then develop your sponsorship opportunity to provide a range of entitlements that will build a much stronger case than if you simply do what the majority of sponsorship seekers do – rely on those old favourites brand awareness, PR and hospitality.

❝ You need to show that you recognise their concerns; don't try to argue with them.

Vital as these three criteria can be for many prospective sponsors, believe me when I say that in their search for sponsorship, many of your competitors will almost certainly be focusing only on these. By expanding the list of what sponsorship can do for a company, you separate yourself from most of your competitors. This can make a great difference to a company's interest in wanting to find out more and then hopefully accepting your proposals.

There are more to come.

Database generation
As can be seen from the SodaStream deal in Chapter 15, sponsorship can be very effective in helping a company to generate detailed databases of individuals who either buy their products or services, or show an interest in them. This is becoming an increasingly valuable requirement within marketing programmes.

Social responsibility
I mentioned earlier that in tough economic times, companies are more than ever concerned about the perception created by sponsoring sport, and in particular motorsport,

↗ A deal is done: Benetton F1 boss Flavio Briatore signs the deal that Brian had secured with FedEx. FedEx Marketing Director Paul Evans and European President Bob Elliott were present.

which is seen by many people as elitist. This is a reality, and while some of you may disagree with that view, what matters is that many companies are now taking this stance.

Tesco recently ran a poster campaign to publicise the fact that unlike companies that spend money on sponsorships such as Formula 1, they would rather pass on cost cutting opportunities to their customers. Powerful stuff! You can scoff at what they say, but don't ignore its impact.

While some of the companies that you approach might simply be using this attitude as a way of fobbing you off, there will be an increasing number who are genuinely keen on many aspects of the sponsorship programme that you are proposing, but are concerned by the 'perception' issue. You need to show that you recognise their concerns; don't try to argue with them.

Then you need to try to help the person you are dealing with to put forward a constructive argument for proceeding with the proposed deal. They need help to counter any negative opposition within their own company. What you can do in this case is to offer additional activities/entitlements in your proposal that might help the person overcome his or her concerns. These might take the form of 'social responsibility' entitlements.

An example might be to add the opportunity for a company to link the provision of educational bursaries to the sponsorship programme. Another idea is to include environmentally related entitlements. You need to research what would be a good fit for the company, in line with its activities.

Whatever you decide to offer must not be seen as a gimmick, but should be carefully thought out and researched to add meaningful value for the recipients of the programme.

Customer interface

A well-planned sponsorship programme can allow a company to get 'face to face' with its customers, so often a vital ingredient in the marketing strategy. For the right company, this can provide a valuable opportunity to supplement its conventional advertising schedule. Advertising is a proven way of promoting products or services, but invariably it is a one-way communication. Sponsorship, particularly of an event or a team, allows the company's personnel to come into direct contact with its customers and offers great opportunities for interaction.

Summary

If you don't understand the reasons why companies use sports sponsorship as an important part of their marketing strategies, you will find it extremely difficult to match the features of your sponsorship opportunity to their marketing requirements.

Although the need for brand awareness and hospitality are two important reasons why companies sponsor, there is a long list of other factors that can be equally, if not more important.

The more options you have to offer, the more likely you are to structure a sponsorship proposal that will meet a company's needs.

There are many reasons why companies sponsor. Here are some of the main ones:

→ Brand awareness.
→ Hospitality.
→ Image transfer.
→ PR opportunities.
→ Promotional opportunities.
→ Case study development.
→ Business-to-business opportunities.
→ Community involvement.
→ Sales incentives.
→ Personal appearances.
→ Integration with advertising.
→ Merchandising.
→ Product sampling.
→ Recruitment.
→ Social responsibility.
→ Customer interface.

05

Creating a saleable sponsorship property

Those of you who like cooking will be only too aware that the key to producing a successful meal lies in the standard of preparation that you undertake. The same rule applies equally to the business of securing a new sponsor. The better the quality of your preparation, the more likely you are to be successful.

It doesn't matter whether you're looking for £500 or £500,000. If you put in the right amount of quality groundwork, you'll not only develop so much more confidence in your ability to interest companies in what you have to offer, but you'll also save yourself a lot of time further down the road.

If you want an analogy within sport, you only have to look at Michael Schumacher. His achievement in winning a record number of seven Formula 1 world championships was quite extraordinary, but he would be the first to admit that it was not based solely on his superb ability to drive his Ferrari at race-winning pace. It was a combination of a number of factors: very often it was the Ferrari race strategy that helped Michael win races, supported by

his ability to put in incredibly quick laps to make the strategy work. A lot of his success was due to the team's ability to adapt a race strategy more quickly and effectively than his rivals. This can be put down to the tremendous amount of preparation that both Michael and his team undertook, to provide themselves with a wide range of options when it really mattered.

Seeking sponsorship is very similar. The reaction of companies to a sponsorship proposal can be extremely unpredictable. As a result, you need to prepare for as many eventualities as you can. It's rather like setting out on a long journey in your car. You can't always predict major traffic hold-ups, emergency road works or accidents, but if you have a SatNav or a map with you, it's usually

By adopting this approach, it'll be far easier to find features of your sponsorship property that can actually satisfy the needs of the sponsor. This is particularly true when it becomes apparent that brand awareness and hospitality will not be enough on their own. What you are doing is creating a far more saleable product.

There is another very important reason for putting together such a list. It will help you arrive at a realistic valuation of the sponsorship opportunity that you are marketing. That is extremely important and is a practice that a lot of sponsorship seekers ignore.

So often I've heard people talk about the fee that they have placed on their opportunity and yet when they are asked how they arrived at that fee, they haven't got a clue. The usual response is to embark on a list of all the costs that they will incur during the delivery of that sponsorship.

If it costs them £50,000 to compete in the World Karting Championships, then that must be the value of the sponsorship opportunity. That's not the right way to go about it! This is so important that I want to spend more time examining this vital part of creating a saleable property.

Valuation

Have you ever sold a car? I don't mean a new one, but one that you've owned yourself for a while. When you decided to advertise it, can you remember the price that you set? How did you arrive at that figure? I would hazard a guess that it was probably with the help of the price guides that you find at the back of magazines such as *What Car* or *Auto Trader*, or through online services. In other words, you checked the going rate for your particular model, taking into account the mileage and its condition. You may have had to come down slightly on the price that you expected to close a deal, but the chances are that if you did your homework carefully, you wouldn't have found it too difficult to sell.

Now you have to do exactly the same with your sponsorship opportunity, if you are to have a saleable property. If you don't set the price fairly accurately, one of two things will happen:

→ You'll never sell it.
→ You'll sell it for much less than it is worth.

The problem is that while you can fairly easily find the market value of your car, it's far more difficult to arrive at a market value for your sponsorship property. That's probably the primary reason why it's not often carried out by sponsorship seekers.

Imagine that you have succeeded in setting up a meeting with a company to present your sponsorship proposal. Into the boardroom walk two people. One is the marketing director and the other is the financial controller. After you have run through your initial presentation and had a reasonable discussion with the marketing director, he asks you about the sponsorship fee. You provide him with the figure that you have decided upon. Nothing too difficult as yet, you're thinking.

So often I've heard people talk about the fee that they have placed on their opportunity and yet when they are asked how they arrived at that fee, they haven't got a clue.

For the first time, the financial controller asks a question: "How did you arrive at that figure?"

Unfortunately this is where a lot of people start to defend their position by explaining how expensive it is either to run their race car or travel to all the rounds of their clay-pigeon shooting championships, or whatever.

What you are doing by adopting this approach is confusing the cost of fulfilling the sponsorship programme with its value. There is a critical difference between the two, although sometimes they might both have the same monetary amount. Let me explain.

Two speedway riders, Grant and Darren, of similar ability on the track, have made the decision that they are going to compete in all nine rounds of the Speedway Grand Prix Championship, which involves racing in nine different countries. They are both seeking sponsorship for the task. They've put together proposals and decided on the fees that they will be expecting.

Grant's operational plan for the season includes staying at five-star hotels, flying to each venue, and employing six mechanics to service his bikes and transport them from event to event. He has costed the season at £150,000, so that is the fee that he has attached to his sponsorship proposal.

Darren, on the other hand, has decided to use a camper van and make do with just four mechanics. He has costed the season at £90,000, which is the fee that he decides to ask for.

❝ One phone call to the MD of the previous sponsor could spell disaster for your chances of being successful.

Both riders contact the same company and submit their proposals. So what do we have from a sponsor's point of view? Same series, same opportunities and entitlements, same media coverage, same hospitality, but two fees that vary by a huge amount, simply because of the different levels of cost involved. They can't both be correct.

After carefully looking at the opportunity and involving his sponsorship evaluation personnel, the prospective sponsor decides that it is worth around £75,000 to his company, based on other comparative sponsorship opportunities that exist in the market place and comparisons with conventional advertising. Then the question is asked as to why two almost identical opportunities should vary so much in respect of the fee expected.

The answer is very simple. They vary because both riders have misunderstood that what is important to the potential sponsor is not what it costs them to compete in the championship, but what the value of that opportunity is to the company. Their predicted costs of participation have varied greatly, but the value of the sponsorship opportunity to the company in question is exactly the same in both cases.

At this point, I am sure that many of you will take the view that the value of the sponsorship property is whatever you can get for it. For example, if you can get a £75,000 fee for a sponsorship programme that should be valued at around £40,000, isn't that a great deal? The answer to that question depends on whether you are looking to the very short-term or whether you are keen to build a long-term relationship with a sponsor.

What is likely to happen if you do secure this type of deal? However unlikely you may think it is, there is a very strong chance that at some stage in the season your sponsor will fall into conversation with another sponsor in the same sport. Being business people, the subject of value for money will probably arise. When your sponsor realises that he has paid over the odds for what he is getting, he will not be too happy and the chances of him ultimately renewing the agreement will be very slim. If you do lose that sponsor, you will also have lost a good point of testimonial reference for the future. Companies that you might contact to replace that sponsor at the end of the agreement will most likely want to know how the previous sponsorship worked out and why that company didn't continue its relationship with you. One phone call to the MD of the previous sponsor could spell disaster for your chances of being successful.

If you want to work on that basis, that's up to you, but remember people talk, and if you develop a reputation for not giving value for money, it will harm your future prospects.

So if the value of the sponsorship to a company does not necessarily correlate with the cost of participation, how do you arrive at that valuation? There's no simple formula to provide this. The good news, however, is that the work you have done in preparing a list of all the entitlements that you are able to offer will play an important role.

What you need to do is work your way through that list and identify all the entitlements that you can put a price on. For example, if you are offering hospitality for six people at each event, you can put a specific figure against that, based on what it would cost the company if they had to pay for it themselves. Similarly, you may have included a one-page advertisement in the official programme for each event. You can find out what that would cost the sponsor if it had to be paid for. In case you're thinking that this is the same as working out what it would cost to deliver, it's not.

This is working out market values for the entitlements that you are offering. That's not the same thing. For example, your cost of hotel accommodation and flights is not an entitlement to the sponsor.

After applying this to all the 'priceable' entitlements, you need to look at what remains and try to estimate a value for these items. Suppose that you have guaranteed a feature article in the local newspaper. You should be able to determine an approximate value for this based on what it would cost the company to place an advertorial of the same size. The paper's sales department will give you the price for this. As another example, you might have included in your sponsorship proposal, an entitlement for one of your team's star players to attend three business functions during the year for the sponsor. You should be able to ascertain what this would cost by contacting a professional speaker agency and asking what their fee would be for a speaker of similar status to attend a similar type of function. These don't have to be precise figures, but if you can get a fairly accurate estimate, it will

help you arrive at a realistic valuation for your sponsorship property.

The next step is to try to compare your sponsorship opportunity with others that are either currently available, or that have been successfully implemented. Obviously this will involve finding out the fee that was paid in each case. This isn't always easy, but it is important if you are going to pitch your opportunity at the right level. You need to know what is being paid by companies for similar sponsorship deals.

❝ **There are also many publications that specialise in sports marketing and provide details of many of the sponsorship deals as they are negotiated.**

Your sport's governing body or association may well be able to give you some guidance as to realistic sponsorship fees within your own sport. There are also many publications that specialise in sports marketing and provide details of many of the sponsorship deals as they are negotiated. These include *SportBusiness International* and *Sports Pro*, as well as specialist sports media magazines and websites relating to your own sport.

Although some of your fellow competitors may be willing to advise you on what they have secured in sponsorship, be careful, because egos will come into play and you may be given highly exaggerated claims.

If you have any friends in the advertising or marketing businesses, ask them for help. Outline your sponsorship opportunity and ask them to have it valued for you. It might come as a shock when they tell you the real value, but it's better to know at this stage than when you are sitting in front of your sponsorship prospect.

If you adopt the approach that I've just outlined, you should be able to arrive at a reasonable estimate of the true value of your sponsorship opportunity. It is a blend of the actual entitlement values and the value that comes from all of the qualities that sponsorship is able to offer that in general can't be derived from conventional advertising. It's difficult to put a value on qualities such as 'aspiration' or 'team building', which we've seen under the heading of Image Transfer. Don't worry too much about that. The very fact that you have identified that there is a value for these qualities, over and above the value placed on all the other entitlements, shows that you have structured the fee in a professional, not haphazard manner. As a result, you will be far more likely to gain the respect of that financial controller when he asks you how you arrived at your sponsorship fee.

You've now created a sponsorship property that should have a wide appeal, with a comprehensive range of entitlements, and which is priced both competitively and realistically. The first step in developing your sales strategy is now in place.

Summary

→ The phenomenal success of Michael Schumacher was not only due to his exceptional driving talent. It was also based on the design of and adherence to a carefully planned strategy that was flexible and capable of maximising his skills.

→ Knowing what you are doing at any stage of the sponsorship sales process will increase your confidence greatly and reduce your fear of the unknown.

→ The first step in the sales strategy is to make sure that you create a sponsorship property that is saleable, through the inclusion of a wide range of potential benefits to the market that you are targeting.

→ The sponsorship fee should be based on market value and not on the cost of participation. It needs to be competitive and realistic.

→ Unless you know how you have arrived at your sponsorship fee and can justify it to a potential sponsor, you are going to run into problems in the presentation of your sponsorship opportunity.

↗ An innovative request from Brian to BBC newsreader Richard Baker resulted in the latter hosting the launch of his Perivan Colour Print sponsorship.

→ Identifying the entitlements (features) that will provide the specific company to whom you are presenting with a benefit, *as confirmed by them*.

Example:

→ **Feature**: 20 days' use of a full-size replica display car.
→ **Advantage**: this can provide an attention-grabbing display at a show.
→ **Benefit**: the company to whom you are talking are exhibiting at the *Ideal Home Exhibition* in March, and a display car would allow it to offer visitors to the exhibition the opportunity of having their photographs taken sitting in the car, after which they can sample the company's new confectionary brand.

Prior to a meaningful discussion with that prospect, the entitlement of being able to use a display car is only a feature of your sponsorship property. Yes, its advantage is the opportunity to use it as a crowd-puller, but only if the company confirms that it would indeed be helpful to them does it become a benefit.

If you present your sponsorship opportunities in terms of benefits, as opposed to advantages, you will increase your success rate quite dramatically. You can only do this by asking the right questions, listening to the answers and then selecting only those features that are most likely to offer a benefit to that specific company.

I strongly believe that a lot of time can be wasted trying to flog the proverbial dead horse; it is much better to adopt a realistic attitude if you recognise that what you have to offer doesn't meet the needs of your prospect in any way. If you genuinely don't believe that your sponsorship opportunity is capable of delivering what the prospect is looking for, be honest and admit it. Don't confuse persistence with stubbornness.

→ If you think that you can help the prospect, persistence is a valuable quality.
→ If you know in your heart that you can't help, but you don't want to accept the fact, that is stubbornness.

Summary

→ It is important to fully understand the difference between:
  → Features
  → Advantages
  → Benefits
→ Features of your sponsorship property are essentially facts.
→ Advantages demonstrate how those facts *might* become a benefit.
→ Benefits are only derived when the potential sponsor confirms that the features and advantages suit their specific needs.
→ It is important to remember that what is a benefit to one company might be a disadvantage to another.
→ If you present features and advantages, and then ask questions to determine if these are potential benefits, you'll be faced with far fewer objections than if you try to present everything as a benefit.
→ Until your prospect confirms which of the features are beneficial, they are never anything other than features.
→ The more benefits that you identify, the greater your chance of securing a sponsorship deal.

Multi-dimensional planning

The next logical step in the sponsorship acquisition strategy would be to identify the companies that you want to approach. However, before we set about that task, which I'm sure you'll agree is one of the most difficult aspects of the entire sponsorship process, I want to introduce you to something that you might not have come across before.

It's a way of adding greater value to your sponsorship property and is employed quite extensively. If used correctly, it can make it a lot easier to attract companies into a meaningful discussion.

Instead of simply sitting down at the computer and browsing the internet, trying to create a list of companies that you feel could be potential sponsors, I want to show you another option. If I had to put a name to it, I think I would call it 'multi-dimensional planning'. It's a method that I have used for many years, and it has helped me to secure some extremely worthwhile sponsorship deals at all levels, from a few thousand pounds to a few million.

Some of you may be familiar with the technique already, but even if you are, please don't ignore this chapter. It can play such a vital role in the successful negotiation of a meaningful sponsorship programme that I don't think you will be wasting your time by going through it again. If the method is new to you, believe me it is well worth making sure you fully understand its implications before moving on.

Multi-dimensional planning means that instead of targeting companies one by one, you devise various strategies that allow you to link together a number of companies that potentially can each benefit from the involvement of the others. It can incorporate the increasingly popular practice of business-to-business marketing, but we'll be looking at that particular aspect separately.

I think that the most effective way of explaining what I mean when I talk about multi-dimensional planning is by giving some examples.

Back in the real heyday of American IndyCar racing, before the CART/Indy Racing League split, a couple of sponsorship deals were negotiated that were so successful that they both stayed in place for more than 15 years. One of them is still going strong as this book goes to print. The deals involved two well-known retail store groups in the United States, One was Kmart and the other was Target. The companies have stores in most major towns across the country and online, both selling a range of products from baby apparel to home electronics, and from food to motor oil.

At the time, the leading team in the IndyCar Championship was Newman-Haas Racing, for whom the Andrettis drove, both father and son. Hollywood star Paul Newman was a partner in the team and one of the most natural people you could hope to meet. I consider myself very fortunate to have met him on several occasions during visits I made to the United States while working at Lola Race Cars. Carl Haas, boss of the team, was the North American agent for Lola, hence my reason for being there on many occasions. Some of you may recall that, in 1993, Nigel Mansell went to America and won the IndyCar (CART) Championship at his first attempt, driving for the Newman-Haas team, the year after he had been crowned Formula 1 world champion for the Williams team.

The Newman-Haas team was a well-funded operation, helped considerably by a multi-dimensional deal that involved the Kmart store group.

Another leading team in the same championship was Ganassi Racing, run by Chip Ganassi, a legendary figure in the sport. Ganassi negotiated a deal with the huge Target store group that was not dissimilar to the Kmart deal.

The first of the two sponsorship deals to which I refer, Kmart, was brokered by a colleague of mine in the USA, on behalf of Newman-Haas Racing. The first part of the deal was fairly standard, and it worked like this:

→ Kmart would become the title sponsor of the Newman-Haas team.
→ They would be allocated a large amount of space on the cars and drivers' suits.
→ There would be Kmart branding on the sides of each car and on the rear wing.
→ There would still be spaces left over that Kmart had been allocated, but had not used.
→ The team's cars and drivers would be made available to Kmart for promotional purposes in selected stores when there was an IndyCar race nearby. This would be publicised by Kmart in the local press in advance, guaranteeing a large turn-out of people at the store to meet the drivers, see the cars and obtain autographs.
→ Kmart would be able to use images of the team and drivers in its advertising.

Now comes the innovative part:

→ Obviously a significant sponsorship fee would be involved.
→ Kmart approached several key suppliers and proposed that these suppliers should also become sponsors of the team, paying Kmart a sponsorship fee. In return for agreeing to this, they would receive a number of entitlements:
  → Branding on the cars in the spaces still owned, but not used by Kmart.
  → Prime merchandising opportunities in-store.
  → Participation in Kmart exclusive promotions and mail drops.
  → The right to promotional activities when the team cars and drivers were in-store.
  → Participation in exclusive Kmart advertising activities based on the sponsorship of the team.
  → A range of other entitlements that were added to these main points.

In this way, Kmart effectively enjoyed being a major sponsor of one of the sport's most high-profile and successful motor racing teams, with virtually the entire sponsorship fee being paid by several of their key suppliers. Companies taking up this unique opportunity included Gillette, Dirt Devil, Havoline and Energiser. For them to have continued for nearly 15 years shows that it must have been well worth their while in respect of a business return.

The Target deal with Ganassi Racing was put together in a very similar way.

You can see Ganassi's Target sponsored cars for yourself by watching NASCAR and IndyCar races on TV. Juan-Pablo Montoya drives one in NASCAR, while Dario Franchitti does a similar job in the Indycar series.

This is just one example of what I call multi-dimensional planning. Had the broker originally approached Kmart with a straightforward sponsorship deal, not involving any other companies, there may have been some interest, but it would have been a hard sell. However, by approaching them with this strategic-alliance concept, he was able to show them all of the benefits that could be derived, together with a highly effective way of recouping their sponsorship fee. It really was a win-win situation, because everyone involved benefited. The suppliers were happy because it gave them all the normal benefits of a sponsorship programme, but in addition, it secured for them an exclusive relationship with one of their biggest customers.

Let me describe another example of a multi-dimensional deal, this time from another sport, rugby union. It approaches the task of securing sponsorship from a different angle.

Without doubt, Bath Rugby is one of the most famous rugby union clubs in the UK. Once the top amateur club, Bath now plays in the highly professional Aviva Premiership. Very shortly after the game turned professional, the club's primary shirt sponsor was a famous cider brand, Blackthorn. The Blackthorn brand was owned by the Matthew Clark Group. Within the Premiership regulations, a team was only allowed to display three sponsor brand identities on players' shirts. In 2001, Bath Rugby only had Blackthorn, the club's title sponsor, on its team shirt, and I was given the task of securing two additional high-value sponsorship deals.

> **For them to have continued for nearly 15 years shows that it must have been well worth their while in respect of a business return.**

I should explain that the reason I was involved with Bath Rugby was very simple. I had been the marketing director of the Benetton F1 team until it was sold to Renault in 2000. It had been announced that Flavio Briatore, who'd been 'asked to resign' by Benetton a few years previously, was to return as the new CEO of Renault F1. Putting it bluntly, I had no more desire to work for Briatore than I'm sure he had for me to work for him. I never did like his style of doing business and I still don't. Thanks to him, the API agency, for whom I was working when I first started doing deals for Benetton, lost considerable commission on a deal with which I had been involved. I found Briatore to be a rude and a totally egotistic individual. On top of that, it had become blatantly obvious that he liked to surround himself with 'gofers', not people capable of securing the major deals. He liked to control those himself.

I've never understood how he could have been the boss of Renault F1 and yet manage drivers in other teams (eg. Mark Webber). It's a huge conflict of interest and shouldn't have been permitted. Can you imagine that happening in football? Alec Ferguson of Manchester United being the agent of a Chelsea player?

Having negotiated a good severance deal with Benetton F1, I thought it would be a challenge to see if I could be as successful at securing sponsorship in another sport, as I had been in motorsport. A friend of mine was, and still is, the managing director of Leicester Tigers RFC. He suggested that I should take a look at rugby. My view was that I knew very little about the sport. His response was that it would probably stand me in good stead, as I would have no preconceived ideas. He mentioned that Premier side Bath RFC were looking for someone to become marketing director and that my F1 experience would almost certainly be invaluable to them.

The outcome was that I joined Bath Rugby.

❝ Instead of approaching random companies that might be interested in becoming sponsors of this top-flight club, I used multi-dimensional planning to focus my approach.

Instead of approaching random companies that might be interested in becoming sponsors of this top-flight club, I used multi-dimensional planning to focus my approach. What I set out to do was to create a strategy that would provide the three permitted sponsors and Bath Rugby with a way of potentially doing meaningful business together, in addition to the benefits that each sponsor would normally expect to generate.

I decided to target companies from various business sectors that not only might benefit from an association with Blackthorn, the primary sponsor, but also that might be able to provide valuable expertise in their specific field of operation to Bath Rugby, as a business. The two business categories that I identified as offering the greatest potential for this were information technology and mobile communications. I found that this immediately made the task of targeting companies a lot easier.

Having determined what I wanted to achieve, my next step was a vital part of the multi-dimensional plan. During that year, I had developed a good relationship with the Blackthorn managing director, Rob MacNevin.

Prior to joining Blackthorn, he had held a senior marketing position with Guinness, and had been involved in putting together and exploiting the Kaliber sponsorship of the Ford team in the British Touring Car Championship. He really understood the various ways in which sponsorship could be cost effective for a company. I put forward a proposal as to how he could help me bring in another two sponsors.

"Why would he want to do that?" I can hear some of you asking.

Well, it was in Blackthorn's own interest that we secured two appropriate-level sponsors. As you can imagine, they wouldn't have been very keen on an association with companies that projected the wrong image. This is an important point to remember. If you secure a sponsorship deal with a major brand, it will not be appreciated if then you announce that you have also secured a sponsorship agreement with a local fish-and chip-shop (no disrespect intended to fish-and-chip shops!). The 'fit' would be all wrong.

I arranged a meeting with Rob MacNevin to present my ideas. I described why I needed to introduce an IT partner and a mobile communications partner to Bath Rugby. I went on to explain that in addition to a sponsorship fee, an IT partner could equip the club with urgently required IT hardware and also provide the expertise to set up such processes as online ticketing, computerised stock control in the club's retail shop and so on. He was happy to hear this, as he quickly realised that it would also enhance the potential for Blackthorn to further promote its own brand.

Then I asked him if he would make it possible for me to offer a very important entitlement to any potential IT and mobile communication sponsors that I identified. What I wanted was to be able to offer a company the opportunity to do business with the Matthew Clark Group. The company spent a considerable amount on its IT infrastructure, which included a call centre in addition to many other areas of operation.

January 2002 Issue 1

BATH RUGBY MEANS
BUSINESS

INSIDE THIS ISSUE

| 2 Marketing Viewpoint | 2 Youth Academy | 3 Round & About | 4 Seen at Bath Rugby |

Bath Rugby Business Partners: BLACKTHORN · Virgin mobile · adidas · ↑northgate · HAMPTONS

Bath Rugby really does mean business

↗ While acting as Bath Rugby's head of marketing, Brian introduced a regular business publication to provide further coverage for the sponsors that he had secured, including Virgin Mobile and Northgate Information Systems.

It also provided a high number of staff with mobile phones.

I wasn't expecting Rob to offer a guarantee that they would do business with any company that I introduced to them. That would have been totally unrealistic; no company would entertain that notion. What I wanted from the Blackthorn MD was a guarantee that if I was in discussion with an IT or mobile phone company, I could offer that company a meeting with the purchasing director of the Matthew Clark Group, but *only* after they had signed up to become a sponsor of Bath Rugby. No more than that. Then it would be up to the company's sales personnel to conduct a normal presentation of their product range. Whether or not they eventually secured business would be down to their own sales skills and Matthew Clark's discretion.

The chance to secure such a meeting, in a favourable environment, is an attractive prospect to the right company.

Rob saw no problem in concurring with my proposal and even introduced me to the purchasing director to make sure that he was in agreement. He turned out to be a huge F1 fan, and when he found out my background from Rob, we got on like a house on fire.

By adopting this method of approach, I was able to secure a major sponsorship deal for Bath Rugby with a leading IT company, Northgate Information Systems, who became the club's official IT partner. As part of the sponsorship agreement, Northgate conducted an IT audit at Bath Rugby, and subsequently designed and supplied a new IT infrastructure for the club.

As it turned out, the second deal was with a mobile phone company, Virgin Mobile. Again, the potential business-to-business opportunities that were presented were attractive and played a major role in Virgin Mobile's decision to become a sponsor. In addition, there was the opportunity to market Bath Rugby branded phones through the team's retail shop in the centre of Bath. The community involvement aspect was also an important benefit for Virgin Mobile, as its head office was within a few miles of Bath, and many of its workforce came from that city.

There was another reason why I was keen to secure Virgin Mobile as a sponsor for Bath Rugby. The average age of Bath Rugby supporters at that time was quite high, and it was apparent that the club needed to attract more youngsters. I knew that the Virgin Mobile brand appealed more to a younger audience than some of the other mobile phone companies. I also knew that Virgin Mobile would be a very pro-active sponsor, which was just what I needed.

I remember the shock waves among some of the more elderly and staid members of Bath Rugby when the first Virgin Mobile advertisement appeared in the official programme. It showed the face of a very attractive young woman, whose tongue was sticking out in what can only be described as a rather sexy manner. The caption read, *"Virgin Mobile, sponsors of Bath Rugby…lick 'em boys!!"*

" By adopting this method of approach, I was able to secure a major sponsorship deal for Bath Rugby with a leading IT company.

The sponsorship proved a huge success for several years, and it certainly succeeded in attracting the interest of many more young people to Bath Rugby.

The Junior Supporters Club was a bit of a joke at that time. The main membership benefit was a tacky monthly newsletter, hardly exciting for kids brought up in this high-tech age. I did a deal with the local Disney store to become sponsor of the Junior Supporters Club and also set up a website for the youngsters. It wasn't difficult, but it made a huge difference and for very little outlay. The Disney store ran a number of events for the members that added huge value to the subscription.

Returning to the two sponsors that I had introduced to Bath Rugby, having secured signed agreements, I set about creating the strategic alliance that I had offered them, enabling them to enter into business discussions with Blackthorn. My objective was to strengthen the bond with the club through a powerful business-to-business relationship between the three primary sponsors.

I decided that the best way to bring this about quickly was to invite the CEOs of the three companies to lunch. I felt that if they could meet each other and explore ways in which they might be able to do business together, using Bath Rugby as the catalyst, it would work well. By starting this process at the very top level of each company, I knew that the three MDs would pass down an instruction to their sales and marketing personnel to start looking at ways to make it happen.

As you can easily check out, the relationship did materialise and remained in place for several years, working really well.

These are just a couple of examples of how you can create a multi-dimensional plan to approach the task of finding sponsors. By looking for ways to create a possible alliance between companies and using the sponsorship programme simply as a catalyst around which this can be developed, you will be able to add considerable extra value to the proposals that you are making to prospective sponsors. It is well worth spending some time looking for ways to achieve this. It's important to remember, however, that although this method can add value to the sponsorship opportunity, you will still need to build a very strong case for sponsorship in the normal way for each company that you approach. Don't rely only on the strategic alliance to produce results.

The two examples that I have related are by no means the only way of using this method. You need to be somewhat creative, but you will soon get used to thinking in this way. Take the following three categories of business, for example, and see if you can create a way of bringing them together around a sponsorship opportunity.

1. Business equipment distributor.
2. Office furniture supplier.
3. Insurance company.

I want you to work this out for yourselves, but let me point you in the right direction. A business equipment distributor:

→ employs salespeople,
→ owns several company cars,
→ has a large office and showroom,
→ has a potential need for insurance,
→ has a potential need for office furniture.

Now do the same for the other two and you'll be able to put together a possible strategy for creating an interesting potential alliance.

If you start thinking about the situation in this way, you'll be surprised at how relatively easy it becomes to apply any of these examples, and your own ideas, to your particular sponsorship opportunity. The principle can be applied to any situation, no matter what size of business or sponsorship is involved. The Kmart example could work just as well for your local hardware store and some of its suppliers.

One of the most important benefits that I've derived from using this system is that it helps me identify which companies I should be approaching. That alone is a great help. After you've used this method for a while, difficult as it may be in the early stages, you'll soon find that it almost becomes a habit.

In the next chapter, I will expand on the subject of multi-dimensional planning and look at some of the other ways in which sponsorship deals can be constructed.

Summary

→ If you devise strategic sales plans, which use your sponsorship property as a catalyst for business development, it can help you identify the companies that might offer a higher level of potential.
→ Strategic sales plans need to be creative and practical.
→ If you can involve a group of companies in a strategic sales plan, it will increase the value of the sponsorship opportunity for each company involved.
→ Companies will be more receptive to sponsorship opportunities that demonstrate how they might improve their bottom line as a result of participation.
→ The primary reason for a company being in business is to make a profit. If you can bring together like-minded companies to help them develop new business opportunities, your sponsorship proposals will be more likely to gain their attention and interest.
→ The more creative and innovative your strategic sales plan, the more likely it is to be successful.

08

Media as a selling tool

I know I'm repeating myself, but I want you to be aware that there is no magic formula that I can disclose to you that will make you more successful in securing sponsorship. I wish there was such a thing. However, although it's not a formula, there are common threads that run through many of the sponsorship deals that I have put together over the years.

In the last chapter, I outlined the system of multi-dimensional planning that I use a great deal. I also mentioned that I would disclose some other ways of applying this method. That's what I want to do now.

As we've seen, one of the many reasons that companies use sponsorship is to be able to generate a higher and more effective level of media coverage than relying purely on conventional paid-for advertising. It's been my experience that, in general, most companies like positive media coverage and are always looking for cost-effective ways of creating it.

The problem with many of the sponsorship proposals that I see is that they refer blandly to the fact that their sport, or their championship or their team generates a high amount of media coverage and then leave it at that.

This may be true, but it is fairly meaningless when you think about it.

Instead of coming up with such a bland statement, what if you could inform a potential sponsor that in the next 12 months, there are going to be three specific TV programmes that will feature you or your sports activity, as well as two major features in a high-circulation Sunday newspaper? Would that not add considerable value to your proposal? I'd be surprised if it didn't.

The problem is that media coverage doesn't work that way. You're probably already thinking that unless you're Andy Murray, playing at Wimbledon, or Arsenal playing in Europe, you won't get any substantial guaranteed media coverage.

You're right! Under normal circumstances, you can't guarantee this. There is a way, however, to do just that. I'll show you how. If you can build in a high level of guaranteed powerful media coverage, you have a head start over many of your rivals when you are looking for a share of that sponsorship cake.

There are several ways of going about building guaranteed media coverage, but I want to look at two specific strategies that I use a great deal of the time. I can honestly state that they work for me more often than not.

I think that the best way to demonstrate how I use this method is to look at a brief case study of a deal that I put together in South Africa.

Example 1

In the late eighties, Group C Sportscar racing was at its peak. Basically, these were the cars that raced in the top class at the world-famous Le Mans 24-hour race in France. The series was extremely well supported and included many famous teams. Among the most high-profile of these were the Rothman Porsches, driven by Jochen Mass, Stefan Bellof, Jackie Ickx and Derek Bell. These cars were capable of speeds well over 220mph.

Traditionally, at the end of the international Group C season, the teams would compete in an endurance race at the Kyalami Grand Prix Circuit in South Africa. It was normal for a few of these international teams to offer selected South African drivers the opportunity to join their driver line-ups. Attractive as this was for the drivers in question, there was a slight problem. In most cases, they would be required to bring along a certain level of sponsorship for their team. If you don't follow motor racing, you're probably thinking that this is a very strange way of going about participating. It is! In how many sports does that happen?

In 1987, I was driving for the works Honda production car team in South Africa and relished the idea of competing in this televised

international race at the end of the season, the Yellow Pages 500. As it happened that year, there were going to be two races, over two successive weekends. I was delighted to be invited by one of the overseas teams to drive for them in both events and set about securing the fairly substantial amount of sponsorship that I would need. I remember well that I had exactly six weeks to find an amount that today would equate to around £50,000. It was a lot of money to find in such a short time. I knew that I would have to be very creative in coming up with an attractive strategy. This is how I set about the task.

First of all, I contacted the *Sunday Times* newspaper, South Africa's largest-circulation paper. I explained that this prestigious international race was coming to South Africa and went on to suggest that the readers of the paper might find it interesting to learn how the business of sponsorship in motor racing worked. My own search for sponsorship would provide a good example. When they learned that I wasn't looking for sponsorship money from them, neither was I expecting them to write a feature about my performance in the race, they took a little more notice than at first.

> " When they learned that I wasn't looking for sponsorship money from them, they took a little more notice than at first.

What I proposed was that I would write a feature article for them about the business of hunting for sponsorship in motor racing. In return, I *would not* expect a fee. What I did ask was for the editor to guarantee me a three-page feature in their highly popular colour magazine, included with the paper. In addition, I asked that he would include a large colour photograph of the racing car, carrying the livery of whichever sponsor I was able to secure by the deadline date for the magazine to go to print. After quite a lot of discussions about this, eventually they came back to me and confirmed that they liked the idea. A deal was struck.

↗ The powerful use of media partners has been an important strategy in Brian's sponsorship sales. This article in the *Sunday Times* colour supplement helped him secure the GBS Wang sponsorship deal and a drive in a Group C race at Kyalami.

The problem was that I still had no money and had to find the sponsor, otherwise I would have nothing to write about.

Then I doubled my problem by offering a similar opportunity to another publication. This time it was South Africa's top selling lifestyle magazine, *Style*, a high-quality, glossy, full-colour monthly that covered all the glitzy social activities within the Transvaal, as Gauteng Province was then known.

In this case, I had to take a different approach, since it was a very different type of publication. I was able to convince their editor that although we were talking about a motor race and *Style* didn't cover sport, the international event was set to be a big social occasion with lots of personalities and glamorous people attending. That was very much more up their street.

This time, I suggested that they had their branding on the car, in return for a major feature on the lifestyle of a professional racing driver, namely one Brian Sims! To my astonishment, they really jumped at the opportunity. Once I had gone back to the *Sunday Times* and got their agreement that there was no conflict of interest, we agreed a deal. Now I had two media deals.

The difference was that I didn't have to write the *Style* feature. The editor dispatched a reporter to a poolside breakfast at my house, with both my wife and myself, to find out all sorts of things about my lifestyle as a racing driver.

On the sponsorship front, by now I was getting nervous, as I still hadn't approached a single potential fee-paying sponsor. Nevertheless, I knew that sticking to my strategy was my only chance of putting this together.

My next step was to make contact with the SABC, the South African equivalent of the BBC. I spoke to the producer of a programme called *Graffiti*, hosted by Penny Smythe, who was as popular then as Fiona Bruce is in the UK today. *Graffiti* was a programme not unlike the BBC's *One Show*, with guests from various walks of life. I explained to the producer that it might be interesting for the viewers to discover the ways in which a driver, who was not a big-name star, had to secure a drive in this much-heralded international race that was taking place in South Africa.

She liked my idea and arranged a date for me to appear on the programme.

At this point, I realised that I would have some pretty serious egg on my face if I couldn't deliver a fee-paying sponsor. I was in the position of having three extremely high-profile media organisations building me into their schedules and I still didn't have a penny to pay for the drive that I had been offered.

It was time to get on the phone and start contacting companies in search of that £50,000. It took me no fewer than 60 calls before eventually I hit the jackpot!

Based on the guaranteed high level of media exposure that I was able to offer the company, in addition to all the other entitlements that came with the sponsorship, I was able to conclude a deal. It was not quite what I had expected, but at least it enabled me to secure the drive.

The company in question was called GBS Wang, the Wang computer distributors for South Africa. I had managed to arrange a meeting with the chairman of the company, who fortunately had the vision to see the potential for his company and was able to make a fast decision. GBS Wang agreed to sponsor me for about 60 per cent of the total that I required, but were happy for me to secure another sponsor for the second weekend's race.

That meant I had to go back to the phone. A few more calls were made and I found the required sponsor for the second weekend. This time it was a South African retail jewellery chain called Sterns, not dissimilar to H. Samuel in the UK.

So, with just ten days to go, I had managed to put not one, but two sponsorship deals together. It had been touch and go, but I had the confidence that my strategy would pay dividends. As I said at the beginning of this book, confidence breeds success.

The main reason that I had been successful was that I had put together a programme of guaranteed media activities that made the deal attractive. I had stressed to both sponsors in my proposals that this media coverage negated the very real risk that exists in motor racing: that I could crash out on the first lap of both events. What I had promised them, not literally, was that they would have had full value for money by 6.00pm the evening before the race. Whatever happened on race day was a bonus, the icing on the cake. It's a statement I like to use a great deal, because it makes sponsors less nervous about all the things that can go wrong on race day.

As to the media coverage that these three sources gave me, I have to say that it was better than I could have expected. The *Sunday Times* article, which was titled 'Executive Behind the Wheel', appeared over three pages in the centre of its colour supplement. A sideways view of the racing car, resplendent in GBS branding, was spread across the front two pages. On the third page, a smaller, but effective photo of the car in Sterns livery appeared, I was also able to explain in the feature why both companies had decided to become involved in the events. This ensured them a really good profile.

Style magazine approached it from a totally different angle, but the coverage was superb and even included a photo of the GBS chairman sitting in the car. This appeared in the

↗ Another of the effective media partners that Brian enlisted for his Group C drive was the South African lifestyle magazine *Style*.

magazine's society pages, in which everyone normally stands with a glass of champagne in their hand, smiling uneasily at the camera. In addition, the three-page feature, which had the title 'Wanna Race My Motor, Baby?' was humorous, totally inaccurate, but very effective. It included some great photos of the racing car in GBS and Sterns branding.

The TV programme went well and I was able to talk about both sponsorships in some detail during my five-minute interview, outlining how I had put the deals together.

Finally, the race itself went to plan and there was considerable TV coverage of the car. The corporate entertaining that was organised proved to be very successful. All in all, it proved to be a win-win situation for each of the parties involved in the sponsorship programme, and it showed another example of successful multi-dimensional planning.

It demonstrated that by developing a strategy that secures a guaranteed level of media coverage, there is far more likelihood of generating interest when you make your initial sales approach to a potential sponsor. It will also help you in your targeting of companies. By knowing the markets that the media sources appeal to, you can direct your sales efforts towards companies that have similar target markets.

Example 2

Another sales strategy that involves the use of the media is often referred to as a media barter deal. This is rather more simplistic, but can be quite effective. It involves approaching a media source such as a commercial radio station or regional newspaper, although it can apply to any media source that carries commercial advertising, including online activities.

The initial approach to the media organisation should take the same form as the presentation of a sponsorship proposal to any prospective company. The difference is that when, as so often happens, the media organisation informs you that they don't have a budget for conventional sports sponsorship, you offer them an alternative way of funding the programme.

What you propose is that in return for a certain amount of branding and/or other sponsorship entitlements, they provide you with the following:

→ An agreed amount of advertising space or airtime, which you can either sell on or use for your own purposes.
→ A guaranteed number of feature articles or programmes relating to your sponsorship property.

If they accept the proposal, what have you actually achieved? For a start, you have some guaranteed media coverage in place. Secondly, you have an amount of advertising space or airtime that has a specific value, which you can use to your advantage.

What I would normally do with this is immediately include that space in a sponsorship proposal to a company that I might expect to consider the publication or radio station important. This will add value to your sponsorship proposal and help you justify your fee to the prospective sponsor.

This is how it works. Assume that you have a sponsorship proposal, which you would normally value at £50,000. Thanks to your media sponsorship deal, you have an amount of advertising space, which is valued at £20,000 (being calculated at the lowest rate available to a major advertiser). You can now include that space in your proposal. It would make sense to increase that sponsorship fee, but not by the full value of the media space. Instead you decide to add only 25 per cent of the true value of that space, making your sponsorship fee £55,000.

That represents good value for the potential sponsor, assuming that your original valuation was correct. The sponsor is now being offered £20,000 worth of advertising for only £5,000, and this is in addition to all the other entitlements that the sponsorship brings, as well as the benefit of the guaranteed media features that you secured as part of your agreement.

From your point of view, it's a good deal, provided that you didn't give away a silly amount of entitlements to the media sponsor, and provided that you can afford to allocate them an area of branding. Normally this should be an area that you would not expect to sell anyway. What you have succeeded in doing is bringing on board a new sponsor and a new media partner, and you have gained £5,000 in the process.

Summary
→ The use of the media as a powerful sales tool is very effective.
→ By offering a guaranteed level of media coverage to potential sponsors, in addition to that which would normally be expected within the sponsorship programme, you are adding meaningful extra value.
→ You need to plan this carefully and have the confidence that the media partners you bring on board will appeal to the companies that subsequently you will approach.
→ There are two ways of working with the media in this way:
  1. One is to secure media partners, using the guaranteed features to attract other sponsors.
  2. The other way is to enter into media barter deals. These provide you with a guaranteed level of media advertising space or airtime, which you can use within a sponsorship proposal to increase its value. It may be possible to include a small level of feature coverage into these barter deals as well.

09

Where do you start?

I'm not sure exactly how many registered companies there are in the UK, but I believe it's in excess of 1.6 million. Now add in all of the smaller, non-incorporated businesses and you have a market that surely can provide you with at least one sponsor. After all, that works out to just 0.0000625 per cent of the total number of companies that theoretically you can contact. Not that difficult is it, when you look at it that way?

Once you've found your sponsor and secured your budget, you can get on with the business of doing well in your particular sport.

If only it were that easy! Of course, we all know that life doesn't work like that. Deciding which companies to contact is one of the most difficult parts of the sponsorship seeking process. With so many out there, it's a daunting task. It's rather like a child being let loose in a huge chocolate factory and told that they can choose any bar they like, but only one!

Many of you might be thinking that instead of talking about which companies to contact, the next logical step in the marketing strategy should be the design and creation of a sponsorship presentation. I know that a lot of people do just that at this stage in the sales

strategy, and it's not for me to say that this is wrong. Personally, however, I feel that there is an advantage to be gained from holding back on this, until you've finalised the plans that will determine which companies you approach. By doing so, you'll have a far better idea of the companies that you are going to target and will be able to design a modular presentation that you can 'mix and match' to suit the industry sector that they are in. As a result, it will be more effective. So I'm asking you to bear with me on this and leave the design of a presentation until later in the process.

There are two main ways of targeting the 1.6 million or so companies that exist.

The first is referred to as the 'shotgun approach'. What this means is that you compile a list of a large number of businesses from a source such as a local trade directory or perhaps you even purchase a database from one of the many companies offering this service. Then you contact as many of these companies as you can, on the basis that the Law of Averages dictates that ultimately you'll find one that will be interested.

This is an extremely common approach and obviously it works for some people. The problem it presents for me is that it rules out doing any meaningful research on the companies before you make contact. The time needed to do this would be very considerable and, in most cases, prohibitive. By adopting this shotgun approach, you really are stabbing in the dark: it comes down largely to luck as to whether you happen to hit the right company, at the right time and your proposal lands on the right person's desk.

This type of approach also makes meaningful follow-up almost impossible. For follow-up to be effective, it should be done within 2–3 days of the proposal or communication being sent. If you send out a large number at virtually the same time, there is little chance of you having the time to do this properly.

The other option is to adopt what is best described as the 'rifle approach'. This is the careful identification of companies that match certain criteria that you have set out prior to making contact. It usually involves being in contact with no more that a dozen companies at any one time. In this way, you will be able to research the companies, ensuring that they match your pre-set criteria, and follow them up in a meaningful manner. It will also allow you to follow up each contact within the desired period of time.

I would never totally rule out the use of a shotgun approach. There are occasions when it is feasible perhaps to send out a mail shot, offering a specific sponsorship opportunity to a known database. It might be, for example, that a sports venue is seeking a small amount of sponsorship for a forthcoming event. To mail all the venue's existing advertisers, corporate hospitality clients and local business contacts could make sense, as undoubtedly there will be a degree of interest in your venue if these companies are already in regular contact.

" I have always found that in the majority of cases, a carefully planned approach to specific companies is far more successful.

I must admit, however, that although sometimes the shotgun approach works, I prefer the other, more precise method. I have always found that in the majority of cases, a carefully planned approach to specific companies is far more successful. This approach is also far more effective when you are looking to develop strategic alliances between companies from specific sectors, as we saw in the last chapter.

Think about it. For most people, from a time point of view, it's quite difficult to conduct in-depth research into more than a couple of dozen companies at a time. Even with the aid of the Internet, securing the range of background information that will help you put together an approach that relates to a company's genuine marketing needs takes considerable time.

In my opinion, the best way to go about targeting is to adopt the rifle approach and spend your time effectively. It ensures that you have the time to research and subsequently follow up each contact that you make. Incidentally, I've always found that research has another major benefit if you go about it the right way. It can be an extremely effective door opener. When we look at what to many people is the scariest part of the sponsorship sales process, getting a meeting with a company, you'll appreciate how useful this ploy can be.

With so many companies out there, the first thing you need to do when devising your targeting strategy is to establish some initial selection criteria. This will immediately help you to home in on companies that hopefully will provide a realistic 'fit' for your opportunity and eliminate the rest.

A very simplistic example of this might be a women's football team that is looking for a shirt sponsor. The team plays in a local league. The problem facing the person responsible for finding sponsorship is to know which companies to approach.

How should that person go about the task? For a start, it is highly unlikely that a major national brand would find the opportunity of interest, as it wouldn't provide the geographical coverage that is essential. It would seem logical, therefore, that only companies that are situated within the county would be worth approaching. This would be the first criterion that could be set.

Criterion 1: Must be based in the county.

Next question: what is the most important entitlement that this women's team has to offer? Probably the opportunity for a sponsor to have it's branding shown prominently on the team shirt, which would offer a potential sponsor the likelihood of reasonable local media coverage. It would make sense, therefore, for the team to introduce a second qualification factor, which states that of the companies situated within the county border, only those whose target market is situated in the county would be appropriate. In other words, a company that is based in the county, but that specialises in export sales probably would not find the local media coverage important.

Criterion 2: Target market must be within the county.

There are many more criteria that might be applied in this way, to narrow down the targeting exercise. One might include the type of business that would be most likely to show interest. For example, if brand awareness in the local media is the primary entitlement for the sponsor, it's not very likely that this will excite a company that manufactures church organs. To a shop that sells women's toiletries, on the other hand, it may well be of interest.

Criterion 3: Brand awareness is important to the company.

By continuing to apply this train of thought to the process of establishing which companies will be worth approaching, you will find that what initially looked quite a daunting job will become much more manageable.

Before you suggest that by doing this, I am pre-judging companies, which earlier I stated you should never do, I want to point out that we are not excluding or pre-judging any company. All we are doing is creating a starting point, based on companies that would appear to be most likely to fit your criteria. If you have no joy with the companies you target initially, you should extend the criteria slightly to include some of those that weren't selected. If you continue to do this, eventually you'll cover virtually all possibilities.

In this way, you will discover that it isn't too difficult to list companies that one could assume might find your sponsorship opportunity relevant to their marketing activities. You need to narrow your targeting to a number of companies that you can find the time to approach individually and follow up in the manner that is necessary to bring them on board. The criteria that you apply will vary from situation to situation, but it is well worth taking some time to draw up such a list. If you don't, you'll find yourself wasting a great deal of time further down the road.

This brings us to another targeting process that I have always found to work extremely effectively, and which can be easily combined with what we have just covered. It's called 'targeting by sector'.

Targeting by sector

There are many benefits to be gained from identifying specific categories of business and focusing your efforts on those sectors. The FedEx deal that I mentioned earlier came about as a direct result of my decision to target the international courier and freight transportation industry. This included such companies as UPS, TNT, FedEx and DHL.

Within the space of four months of making my first 'cold call' to both FedEx and one of its competitors, I was in the enviable position of having potential multi-million-dollar deals on the table from both companies. The eventual outcome was that within six months of that first call, the Benetton Formula 1 team appeared at the British Grand Prix at Silverstone in 1997 with FedEx branding proudly emblazoned on the side-pods of its two cars. FedEx remained a major Benetton F1 sponsor until it moved to Ferrari and subsequently on to the Williams BMW team.

I found that by focusing on a specific industry sector in this way, there were several key benefits:

→ It saved a great deal of time on research.
→ It helped me understand the needs of companies in that sector.
→ It helped me learn about the competition within the industry.
→ It helped me discover the key players.
→ It helped me learn which were the up-and-coming companies.
→ I found out what key events take place within that industry sector, such as exhibitions, conferences, etc.
→ I better understood the problems facing the industry sector.
→ I was soon able to talk the language of the companies operating in that sector.
→ I was able to generate greater respect because of this.

Targeting by sector can be very helpful when you sit down to plan your contact strategy. It can also play a useful role in developing multi-dimensional sales plans, which offer the advantage of effective business-to-business opportunities for participating companies.

There is no doubt that the whole business of targeting and research has become so much easier today than it was for much of my career. The reason for that is the availability of the Internet. Instead of having to wade through trade directory after trade directory at your local library, as most of us did in those days, now you can work from the comfort of your own home in a far quicker and more effective fashion.

Where this comes in really helpful is in collating all of the news articles that appear in the business pages of newspapers and magazines. These are vital leads for you when it comes to selecting the companies that you will approach.

Most publications today have an online version, which carries many of the headlines and major stories. If you choose the right media sources to match your targeting criteria, you can soon compile a highly effective list of potential sponsors.

Whether you are targeting on a local, national or international basis, the principle is the same. Look for stories that could provide useful information. One area that I refer to a great deal is 'people on the move' within the business sections of newspapers and magazines. If you see that your local furniture store has a new branch manager, there is a good chance that he will want to introduce some new ideas for promoting increased sales. That means he might be receptive to the idea of a creative sponsorship opportunity.

You read about a company opening their first new branch in your area. Maybe they will be looking for promotional ideas. It's worth a try, and it should be possible to identify some aspects of your sponsorship opportunity that might be perfect for a company in that situation.

Other sources of inspiration for compiling your target list could include:

→ Marketing magazines.
→ Sports marketing publications.
→ Chamber of commerce newsletters.
→ Trade associations (for targeting by sector).
→ Business exhibitions.
→ Advertisements.
→ Employment advertisements (Informs you of company expansion).
→ Existing sports sponsors.
→ Sports arena advertisers.
→ Personal referrals from friends and families.
→ Websites.
→ TV commercials.

If you approach the business of compiling your target list in a systematic manner, aimed at quality rather than quantity, you will soon reap the benefits; that I can promise you. I usually target 8–10 companies at a time, finding that this gives me the best chance to research and follow up on an individual basis. As a company drops out, for whatever reason, you can just replace it with another that meets your criteria. In that way, you keep the project manageable.

Once you have compiled a list of companies that match your criteria, you will need to find out some fairly fundamental information about them before making your initial sales approach. In the next chapter, I'm going to look at the sort of information that will help you to gain an insight into what is important to them from a marketing viewpoint.

Unless you can really get under the skin of a company and appreciate how they look at the marketing of their products and services, you'll always battle to convince them even to speak to you, let alone set up a meeting.

Summary

→ There are hundreds of thousands of potential companies to approach.
→ You have a choice of adopting a shotgun or a rifle approach to targeting potential sponsors.
→ The problem with the shotgun approach is that although it allows you to communicate with perhaps hundreds of companies at a time, it will not be quality contact. You will not have the time to research these companies effectively to find out anything about their marketing objectives and structures. Neither will you have the time to follow up these companies in a meaningful way.
→ By adopting a more focused approach, you will be able to conduct some vital research into each company before making contact, increasing the chances of securing their attention.
→ You will find that you can manage the task of follow-up much more efficiently if you only have 10–12 contacts on the go at any one time.

10

The value of research

I find it a sobering thought that I had already left school when the sports sponsorship revolution started back in 1968, when Colin Chapman negotiated that famous Gold Leaf Team Lotus sponsorship deal.

I'm often asked what I think has been the most significant change during the intervening years that has made the sponsorship acquisition process so much harder. I find it quite a difficult question to answer, as it's not easy to identify just one area. There have been so many changes over that period of time, including the incredible amount of competition that you face from every other sport and from the charity, arts, educational and conservation sectors.

I think that if I were really pushed to come up with an answer to the question, it would have to be the barriers, both human and technical, that have been put in place by companies to discourage personal communication from external sources. Let me explain what I mean by this. I always used to find it relatively straightforward to phone a company, speak to an appropriate person and, within the space of a few minutes, establish whether there were grounds for progressing my proposals. That is no longer the case; now it is one of the most difficult aspects of the job.

Forgetting sponsorship for a moment, I think that it is a very sad reflection of our society in general that more and more obstacles are being put in the way of personal communication in so many areas of our lives. Yes, I know all about Facebook, which does have some good points about it, and Twitter, which personally I find incredibly 'lightweight' and banal. I know there are many more, but I still retain the same viewpoint.

I'm sure that you've all suffered the interminable process that occurs when you phone many large companies today. You experience an endless pre-recorded selection of menus before being forced to listen to mindless musical overtures in the vain hope that somewhere at the end of this debilitating process, you might be lucky enough to reach a human being.

Have you ever tried phoning back a second time and asking to speak to the person with whom you had started to share an understanding of your problem, some 30 minutes before? You have more chance of winning the Lottery! The sad result is that you often have to start from scratch again.

In so many ways in our lives, personal communication is being discouraged and eroded. As a result, the levels of frustration we endure on an almost daily basis are increasing rapidly. From conversation with friends, family and business colleagues, it has become apparent that there are many people who are sick and tired of the way in which these impersonal systems are being forced on us. So why do we let it happen? Why do we let companies dictate to us in this way? Perhaps that's the subject of another book!

" **There are far too many marketing personnel within companies who have an inflated opinion of their own importance.**

Let me put the soapbox away and get back to the sponsorship sales process! Those of you who are currently involved in marketing sponsorship opportunities must surely agree that the task of actually speaking to a meaningful contact within a business is becoming more difficult by the day.

It's so easy for people in companies to hide behind voice-mails and e-mails that it comes as quite a surprise when someone actually takes your call. Of course, I'm not so naive as to ignore the difficulties facing companies if they were to take every call that came in, but I feel that too many of them have taken it to extremes. In the process, they are missing out on some very innovative and powerful business opportunities that they may be totally unaware of.

It always reminds me of a much-publicised cartoon, showing King Harold in his tent, cleaning his sword, on the eve of the Battle of Hastings in 1066. A messenger walks in and advises the King that a travelling merchant is

outside. He has something to show him that he feels could help win the battle.

Harold's reply, that he is far too busy cleaning his sword to be disturbed, is relayed back to the merchant, who shrugs his shoulders and loads the machine gun back on to his cart!

I recall a great example of the difficulty that can exist in making contact with a company. A few years ago, I read in the trade press that a well-known company that produces a high-volume brand of mineral water had appointed a new marketing director. At the time, my company represented a very high-profile international sports association that was offering the exclusive soft drink pouring rights at one of its major events. This meant a potentially high level of revenue for the right company. Of course, there was a level of sponsorship involved as well, but with comprehensive TV coverage, it certainly wasn't an opportunity that could be called insignificant.

I phoned the company to ask for the e-mail address of the new director, thinking that it would be more polite to introduce myself briefly by e-mail and outline my reason for wishing to speak to her. "Sorry, we don't give out e-mail addresses," the switchboard operator informed me. Perhaps I could speak to her PA to explain the purpose of my call, I suggested? No, she doesn't accept phone calls. Could I e-mail her? No, you have to send a fax! Accordingly, I dusted off my now little used fax machine and sent through a one-page letter, requesting a conversation about the potential revenue-generating opportunity.

A week went by with no response. I decided to follow up by phone to see if the fax had been received and read by the person in question.

I explained to the switchboard operator that I had sent in a fax, as requested. Could I now speak to the PA to check that it had arrived and been read by the director?

"Hold on." A long wait ensued. "No, she doesn't know who you are, so she won't take your call." How can I find out if the fax has been read, I asked? I was told that I must send in another fax, asking if my previous ones had been read!

I put together another communication, politely enquiring whether the fax had been read and if there was an interest in finding out more detail. Guess what? No response. To this day, I still don't know whether my faxes were read.

How long would it have taken for that PA to send out a one-line e-mail, thanking me for the opportunity, but declining the offer, or telling me that they hadn't had time to look into the matter as yet? Twenty seconds maximum.

Call me old-fashioned, but I think that the way in which this was handled simply displayed a lack of manners. It wasn't as though this was an insignificant association on whose behalf I was making the approach, and most certainly it was not an insignificant revenue generating opportunity for the company. Sadly, manners in many businesses seem to be very much in decline, and I have to assume that it emanates from the top. These days, I find that there are far too many marketing personnel within companies who have an inflated opinion of their own importance, who feel that bad manners are acceptable. I believe that we all have a job to do, and if we treat people as we ourselves would like to be treated, it would make all of our lives easier and more pleasant.

The worst are people who spend half the time telling you how incredibly busy they always are. I'm sure you've come across some of those. It's as though no one else has an idea of what it is to be busy. There are people in companies who are so busy that they can't even find 20 seconds to ask their PA to send off a short e-mail or letter, regretting that they will not be pursuing the opportunity that you have sent to them. They consider that it is far easier just

↗ In 1984, Brian worked at the South African F1 Grand Prix with Williams F1 sponsor Denim, helping to activate their high-cost involvement with the team. Jacques Laffitte is in the car.

to ignore your communications and hope that you'll go away. I don't think that it does them any favours.

These very same companies are quite happy to thrust their own advertising in our faces, to bombard us with pop-ups on the Internet, and to send us junk e-mails and direct mail by the ton. Why then, do they take offence when people want to make contact with them and try to sell them something? If we have no time for manners or respect in business, I think we are going backwards.

Fortunately, there are many companies that do recognise that if they relied totally on ideas generated internally, they could be missing out on some great opportunities. As a result, they treat people who contact them with respect.

Recently I had reason to make contact with one of the country's largest power generators, to put forward a sponsorship opportunity that I felt was appropriate. It was declined eventually, but the company's brand development manager, with whom I had been dealing, took the trouble to e-mail me with a bullet-point list of the various reasons that had led her and her colleagues to this decision. She even offered to introduce me to someone in a different geographical part of the company whom she felt might have been interested in what I was offering. I immediately wrote back and thanked her for this.

> **This ability to be able to talk to relevant personnel within a company is of prime importance.**

What a difference to my previous example. Of course, the cynical among you might say that it doesn't matter how, or even if, you are told "No". You could say that what mattered was that I didn't get a "Yes". I'm sorry, but I totally disagree! Not only was I able to take on board the points that this person made, which helped me with my next approach, but also now I had another contact within that company. In addition, a relationship had been established,

which means that if another opportunity comes along, I feel confident that I can approach her again. Her attitude also enhanced my opinion of her company.

I would like to say that the difficulty in establishing communication with companies is a rare occurrence. Unfortunately, I can't. This policy of isolation is an increasing trend in the business world. It is something that we have to find a way of managing.

Fortunately, as I have shown, there are still many companies whose senior personnel will, if approached in a professional manner, communicate with you in a pleasant, helpful way. They are aware that you are simply doing a job, just as they are. They may also have heard the King Harold story that I related earlier in this chapter and be thinking that the next caller might just be the merchant offering a machine gun! Perhaps your proposal will be just what the company has been looking for.

If I had to pinpoint the one skill that I have developed that has stood me in good stead throughout my career, I would say that it has been my ability to find a way around these barriers and initiate contact with a company at the right level. I'll be sharing my methods with you later, when we look at the subject of making contact.

The feedback that I get from a high number of people who attend my training courses and others, to whom I have spoken, shows that this is the aspect of the sponsorship acquisition process that they find the most difficult.

This ability to be able to talk to relevant personnel within a company is of prime importance. Whether it is to research a company, or to make contact for the purpose of setting up a meeting, you will need to be proficient at this form of communication.

Crucial research

In the previous chapter, we looked at ways of selecting the companies you should approach with your sponsorship opportunity. With any luck, you should be able to do a considerable amount of the initial research necessary to determine whether or not a company meets your pre-set criteria on the Internet, where you will also find helpful company reports and trade directories. Once you have identified a manageable number of companies that you feel potentially meet your criteria, however, you will still need to do more research.

This time, it will be research to provide you with the information that can help get you a meeting, or at least a phone conversation, with personnel at a senior level in those companies.

Thorough research can help you to create a powerful attention-grabbing sales approach, one that is capable of generating enough interest at the right level within a company. If you take the time to work your way through a company website, you can often unearth a great deal about its business aims and philosophy, and in the process find a possible fit with your sponsorship opportunity.

A statement such as "It's the intention of the ABC company to develop our European business growth by establishing offices in France and Italy," can provide an opportunity for you to approach the company with a sponsorship deal that could provide a high profile for its services in those countries. Similarly, you might discover in the recruitment section of the company website that it's expanding its sales force. What a good opportunity to offer a sponsorship programme that includes the creation of a sales-incentive programme, based on its primary activity.

Research not only helps you develop ways of approaching a company, it can also provide you with another benefit.

If you go about it in the correct way, through your research activities it's quite feasible to develop a significant relationship with someone in that company, such that you will be able to ask them to set up an initial meeting with the appropriate decision maker. In other words, the research process can help you find an ally within the organisation.

That ally may be someone far removed from the sponsorship decision making process, but if they can help you with the information you are seeking, and then facilitate a meeting, what an added bonus for you.

> " Thorough research can help you to create a powerful attention-grabbing sales approach.

This is what I did in a couple of the Formula 1 deals that I put together. I found an ally within each company who would answer my questions and point me in the right direction. What this meant was that when eventually I made my initial sales contact with the company, I had enough information not to waste the person's time and subsequently would gain their respect for having done my homework. Such an ally can be invaluable, but it is important to respect their confidentiality. Another thing: don't forget to thank them and keep them informed of progress.

Having stressed its importance, when you start your research process, what is it that you need to find out?

For a start, I always like to know if the company has been involved in sponsorship before. If so, how did it work out? This information can do two things for you. First, it can save you a great deal of pain. You might discover, for example, that recently they sponsored a sports team that became insolvent mid-way through the season and was unable not only to fulfil its sponsorship obligations, but also to refund any part of the fee. Armed with this information, you can avoid a very unpleasant surprise. You can also highlight the financial soundness of your sponsorship opportunity and turn that to your advantage (assuming, of course, that it is financially sound). One way of doing this would be to build in a stage-payment plan, demonstrating in the process that your sponsor remains in control of the financial situation.

On the other hand, you might find out that the company has been involved previously in quite a successful sponsorship, which came to an end purely because of a change in the direction of their own marketing strategy. Very often, a company will decide that after a certain period of time, a sponsorship programme has delivered as much as it can, and it is time to look at new opportunities, no matter how successful it may have been.

Either way, it's important to know as much about the situation as possible.

You also need to understand the geographical marketing structure within a company. For example, is the UK marketing department responsible for marketing activities in Europe, or is that done by a separate European office? Very often you'll find that within a large organisation, each country will have its own marketing budget and decision making process. You need to know this, particularly if you are selling a sponsorship property that includes events in other European countries as well as the UK.

> **Very often you'll find that within a large organisation, each country will have its own marketing budget and decision making process.**

If you are selling an international or even a global sponsorship property, it becomes even more critical to understand just how decisions are reached and budgets allocated, within any global corporations that you target. You need to know how an international company that commits to a major sponsorship in a sport such as Formula 1 will finance the deal. Very often, it is

through mandatory contributions from the budgets of their operations in each country.

I remember carrying out an interesting sponsorship consultancy for the Unilever Group in South Africa. It came about as a direct result of this method of a global company financing a sponsorship.

Elida Gibbs, a Unilever company, took the decision to promote sales of Denim, the male toiletry brand, through sponsorship of the Williams F1 team. Each Elida Gibbs operation around the world had to contribute to the sponsorship fund. That was fine for the European countries within the group, as they could leverage (commercially exploit) the sponsorship across several European grands prix. This could be done quite easily, because of the geographical proximity for entertaining VIP guests and for running promotions within retail stores. For example, Denim in France would benefit from the European media coverage of the French, Italian, German, Monaco, Belgian, Spanish and even the British races, and could also use these as a basis for sales promotions and possible entertaining. In this way, they might amortise their expenditure across up to half a dozen grands prix.

For Elida Gibbs in South Africa, however, it was far more difficult to justify the financial investment, as its marketing department had to make the most of their commercial mileage from just one event a year, the South African Formula 1 Grand Prix at the Kyalami circuit.

I was retained by Elida Gibbs to help the company design and implement a strategy that would help them generate as much brand awareness as possible while the Williams F1 team was in South Africa for the grand prix. This involved the creation and implementation of a number of innovative promotions, media events and sales-incentive programmes. I also had to ensure that we made full use of the team's two drivers at that time, Keke Rosberg and Jacques Laffite. The work that I did gave me a good insight into some of the issues facing a company when it is considering what amounts to an international sponsorship.

I hope that this will demonstrate to you the importance of finding out as much as you can about the geographical structure of a company and the way in which it involves its individual satellite operations to put together a budget. If you are aware of how international sponsorships are often funded, you will be better prepared to show ways in which all the contributors can derive value from their contribution.

What else might be important to find out about a targeted company? The following are some of the information categories that I try to build into my research activities.

What are the primary target markets? (Age, gender, social status, etc)

If you don't discover this, you can waste a great deal of time and end up looking very amateurish. For example, it's unlikely that Saga Holidays (for the over-50s) would be interested in becoming sponsors of a skateboarding competition. On the other hand, they could be perfect as sponsors of a bowls championship. By assessing the target audience accurately, you can save yourself a lot of unnecessary effort.

When is the marketing budget prepared, submitted and approved?

This is really critical, particularly if you are seeking a fairly large sponsorship fee. If you can work to a company's budget timetable, you are far more likely to be successful.

Who are the prospect's major competitors?

Why should this be important? Well, if you can ascertain what major marketing activities their competitors are involved in, it can often prove helpful. You'll find that many companies will try to take a different approach to that of their competitors. This can mean that if their

main rival is already involved in sponsoring the sport in which you are involved, it's better to be aware of this and try to counter it than be totally unprepared.

Does the company use a sponsorship evaluation agency?

Increasing numbers of large companies use the services of a sponsorship agency to evaluate, advise and recommend sponsorship opportunities. If you can find out if this is the case, it will be an important factor in developing your approach strategy. It may be advantageous to approach the agency first of all to get them on your side.

Which are the major media sources that the company considers important?

If you can identify which publications or TV and radio programmes are important to a company, it will help greatly with the way in which you position your sponsorship opportunity. Time and again, I have found the innovative use of the media within a sponsorship sales strategy to be a very powerful tool. If you know in advance which media sources are likely to impress a potential sponsor, it can help you to create an innovative proposal of the type that I outlined previously.

Does the company have a sales force and how is it incentivised?

One of the most underrated ways in which sponsorship can be used is as a platform for measurable sale-incentive programmes. It will help you a great deal to find out the size of a company's sales force, whether the company uses sales-incentive programmes and, if so, what rewards are offered. I can promise you that few of your competitors will bother to include this opportunity within a sponsorship proposal, so time spent researching this information could prove very valuable.

How is the company website promoted?

For many companies, attracting people to their websites is of prime importance. If you can find out how they achieve this at present, it will be useful when you come to design your initial approach. Sponsorship can be a very effective platform for the promotion of a company's URL

> **If you research in advance who is important and who isn't, you'll find the knowledge extremely helpful.**

Will any new products be launched in the near future?

This is vital information, but understandably it is well hidden by many companies. If you can do a 'Sherlock Holmes' and find out what's in store, it will add tremendous value to any proposals that you make.

Will any new branches be opened?

It may well be that if a company is opening a new branch, they will be looking at some innovative ways of promoting it and raising awareness. Your sponsorship might just offer some interesting ways of achieving this. If you don't find out this information, you could be missing a great opportunity.

What is the decision making hierarchy?

➔ Who makes the ultimate decision?
➔ Who influences the decision?
➔ What is the decision making process?

This is very important. You can waste a tremendous amount of time and end up being hugely disappointed if you don't check out this information carefully. I don't mind admitting that I've often been guilty of getting quite excited when the person that I have contacted gives out really positive signals, only to discover later that this person counts for very

little in the decision making process, but likes to give the impression that they do.

I've found that there are usually people in most companies who are more than happy to alleviate the boredom of their normal working day by talking about sport to a visitor. If you take their word that they're key to the decision making process, you lay yourself open to a huge disappointment and also some major embarrassment.

If you research in advance who is important and who isn't, you'll find the knowledge extremely helpful. However, the fact that a person isn't the decision maker doesn't mean that you should leave them out of your plans. They may well be part of the decision influencing process. Knowing how decisions are reached and which people contribute to the process is valuable information and well worth considerable effort to obtain it.

Once you have discovered the appropriate people, ideally you need to do some research on them. If you can find some background on these people, such as where they worked previously or their sporting interests, it can help you approach them in an effective way and also help in planning your meetings with them.

As I mentioned earlier in the book, sometimes you will come across opportunities during your research activities to initiate your sales approach. Just be a little careful that you don't get dragged into a decision making process before you are ready. If you're not prepared, you may find yourself face to face with the right person, but because you haven't yet worked out ways in which your property can prove beneficial, you'll quickly end up with a negative response. It's fair to say that the more experienced you become, the better you'll be able to turn such situations to your advantage.

I could go on and on with the list of subjects that I believe are worth researching, but there comes a time when you have to say enough is enough. You can devote too much time to researching.

I recall spending some time in America, helping to train a very hard-working and earnest young sponsorship salesman. He had been employed by a sponsorship agency that represented one of the top American IndyCar teams. His role was to secure sponsors for the team.

He was a very bright lad with a high level of determination. He certainly wasn't scared of hard work, and realised that preparation and thorough research ensured a sound foundation of a good sponsorship sales strategy. I flew over to the States once a month and usually met with him to see how he was progressing. I was always very impressed by the incredible amount of research that he had carried out on a company that had been targeted. I swear that he even knew the birthdays of the president's grandchildren!

The problem was that whenever I asked him how many appointments he had made with companies, invariably he would tell me that he was still waiting to finalise the research before actually getting down to the business of setting up meetings. After six months, it became blatantly obvious that he was burying himself in the research to avoid the task of getting on the phone and trying to establish contact. His research was faultless, but far too in-depth. At the rate he was going, by the time eventually he got to see a company, the research would be out of date.

So keep things in proportion. Research should be a vital part of your sponsorship acquisition strategy, but you must recognise that there has to be a time when you pick up that phone and start acting as a salesperson.

Summary

→ Research is essential if you are to gain a company's interest in what you have to offer.

→ You can avoid a number of pitfalls by researching any previous sponsorship history.

→ If you can find an ally in the company who will help you understand the way in which the company operates and how the management is structured, it can prove invaluable.

→ You need to be able to develop an attention grabbing introduction to your sales approach; careful research can help provide this.

→ If you go about it in an innovative way, your research can help you establish a meeting with the decision maker at the appropriate time. By developing contacts within the company during your research, you can encourage them to introduce you to the decision makers when you are ready.

Look for allies

At the beginning of the book, I explained how I had put together my very first sponsorship deal, enabling me to race in Formula Ford. Following that deal, my racing career had been running quite well, without setting the world alight, for about three years. I'd been competing in Formula Ford 1600 and really needed to take a decision as to what to do the following season.

At that time, I was still competing very much on an amateur basis, being employed as the UK sales training director for the American ITT Corporation. Thanks to a chance meeting, my life was about to change direction in a big way.

Earlier that year, I had negotiated a sponsorship deal with ITT, which would allow the company to promote its in-house magazine, called *ITT Focus*, through my racing activities. This publication was distributed to all of its European employees. In addition, I'd agreed a small sponsorship deal with a garage in Maidstone, which led to its staff preparing my racing car. It was while I was at the garage one day, helping my mechanic load my Hawke DL11 race car on to its trailer, that a driver who had stopped for petrol wandered over to take a look at it.

As so often happens when people see a single-seater racing car close to, he wanted to know how fast it was, what engine it had, where did I race it and so on. He was about to return to his car when I decided to find out a bit more about him and what he did for a living. It turned out that he was employed by a company called SodaStream. Some of you may recall that SodaStream was a kitchen appliance that used a cylinder of compressed air and a range of flavoured concentrates to let you make fizzy soft drinks at home. It's still on the market today.

Sensing that this could be worthwhile, I persuaded him to park his car and have a chat; also I offered him the chance to sit in the Hawke. I knew that once he was in, it would be quite tricky for him to get out of the small cockpit, and I would have a captive audience for a few minutes. A useful ploy!

During the conversation about the SodaStream product, it transpired that there had just been a management buy-out from Kenwood, who had been the original manufacturer of the SodaStream equipment. SodaStream was now a stand-alone company in its own right. We continued chatting for quite a while, until eventually I showed him how to climb out of the car and he was able to escape!

Four months later, I was able to conclude a sponsorship deal that was almost certainly the largest that had ever been achieved within Formula Ford at that time. The deal was worth £25,000, at a time when the typical budget for running a professional Formula Ford team was around £12,000–15,000. I think that I was also one of the very first competitors to arrive at the track with one of the large transporters that are so much the norm these days. Looking back, I'm not so sure that I did Formula Ford any favours in that respect, other than to up the ante somewhat.

Although the SodaStream sponsorship took place many years ago, the way in which I structured and presented the opportunity is as valid today as it was then. It encapsulates many of the points that I have already covered as being vital ingredients if your proposals are to be taken seriously by a company. In Chapter 15, I've detailed the way in which I approached this opportunity. It's based on an understanding of what is often called 'razor and blades' marketing.

The deal that I concluded with SodaStream meant that I had to seriously consider whether I would be able to combine my full-time job with a national racing programme that would take me all over the country. I decided that it was a once-in-a-lifetime opportunity. If it didn't work out, I could always find another job, so I made the decision to leave ITT and concentrate on a full-time career in motor racing.

To help bring in some additional income, I became an instructor at the new racing driver school that had just been started at the Thruxton racetrack in Hampshire.

Sadly, the car that I chose to compete in that year could best be described as an absolute dog! It's little consolation to me now, but that car effectively proved to be the death knell for its manufacturer. The previous season, the Hawke DL15 had been the car to drive, winning just about everything in the hands of two drivers who would go on to grand prix careers, Derek Warwick and Derek Daly. It seemed a logical conclusion to opt for its radical successor, the DL17. This proved to be a disaster, as all the drivers who competed in it will confirm, some of them quicker drivers than me.

One of these fellow sufferers was an infamous celebrity in his own right. It was none other than Roy James, who had been convicted as one of the Great Train Robbers. He was better known as the Weasel.

Prior to serving 12 years of what was a 30-year prison sentence for his part as a getaway driver in the robbery, Roy had been a successful racing driver, competing in Formula Junior. He was a silversmith by trade and while inside, designed and produced several silver trophies, which later he presented to various motor racing clubs.

When he had served his sentence, he decided to try to get back into racing and tested a Formula Atlantic car at Silverstone. The rumour going around the pits at that time was that he was sponsored by British Rail! Such is the black humour in motorsport.

Unfortunately for him, Roy ended up crashing the car and breaking his arm, so he stepped down a category and bought a Hawke DL17 Formula Ford, competing in the same national championship as me. Throughout that season, I found him a very hard and uncompromising racer, but perhaps not surprisingly, an extremely

↗ Brian's high-value sponsorship deal with SodaStream allowed him to become a professional racing driver.

quiet, intense individual. The only time I ever saw Roy become emotional was when he joined with several of us in complaining bitterly to the manufacturer of this unbelievably poor racing car. I think the experience that year put him off racing, and I don't recall him ever getting into a race car again.

The final word on my SodaStream sponsorship is not included in the case study. It concerns a lesson that I learned the hard way. Those of you who have been involved in the sponsorship business for some time may well be able to endorse what I am about to relay, from your own experiences. If you are fairly new to seeking sponsorship, take note and you may avoid what happened to me.

Towards the end of that SodaStream season, I had a long chat with Don Philpot, the man whom I had met at the garage. I had a lot of time for Don, who was an amazing character, full of energy and enthusiasm. I asked

his opinion as to what I should do. It was obvious that the racing hadn't gone as well as planned. We seriously considered changing manufacturer mid-way through the season, but Hawke's promises about improvements that were supposedly in the pipeline stopped us from doing that until it was too late. Don's feedback from the board was that they were very happy with the results of the sponsorship, particularly in respect of a measurable increase in sales activity, attributable to store promotions that we had carried out. He informed me that everyone understood the car problems that year and we started to talk about the possibility of moving up to Formula 3 the following season.

It looked promising, but then I was young and quite naive. It hadn't dawned on me at that time that other people would try to persuade what I felt was my sponsor to direct the money elsewhere.

This is exactly what happened when John Webb, then the boss of Brands Hatch, met with the marketing director of SodaStream. He persuaded him that there would be more merit in becoming the title sponsor of the proposed Sports 2000 Championship that was to be launched the following season, than sponsoring an individual driver.

While I think it was actually quite a good move from SodaStream's point of view, I was very hurt because there was no effort to include me in the new deal in some way, no matter how small. I had worked hard to introduce SodaStream into motorsport and I felt that somehow John Webb could have looked after me. How naive was I? Looking back, I don't blame John. It's a tough business and he thought that what he was doing was the best route for SodaStream. I learned from that experience, however.

Since then, I've witnessed some outrageous behaviour by people whom I had previously regarded highly. Nothing is sacred in the world of motorsport sponsorship. I'm sure it's the same in many other big-money sports.

❝ I come across young people in business who think that it's clever to be rude. Why?

But then when you watch a TV programme like *The Apprentice*, which applauds rudeness, ruthlessness and bad manners in business, it's little wonder that youngsters think such behaviour is clever. More and more, I come across young people in business who think that it's clever to be rude. Why?

As I have already mentioned, I like to treat people in the way that I'd like to be treated myself. It may seem old-fashioned, but by adopting that technique, I've still managed to be successful. It's also far less stressful.

Unfortunately, Don Philpot, the man who had made my sponsorship deal happen, and who had been such a staunch supporter and good friend, died unexpectedly that year, and I lost out altogether. It wasn't long before I'd put another deal together, however, and I was able to sit in a Formula Ford again. This time the sponsorship that brought it about was with Anglian Windows.

My later years in Formula 1 also hardened me to the way in which people in big-time sport operate. Where there is a lot of money, there will always be people prepared to do anything to get their hands on it. My advice to anyone involved in looking for sponsorship is to keep very quiet about whatever leads or contacts you have or are working on. Whatever you do, don't talk to anyone about a possible deal until it is signed, sealed and paid for. You'd be amazed at how many people are out there looking for funds for some activity or another. It may not be for the sport that you are in, in fact it may not even be for sport, but if they hear you mention that a certain company is considering spending some money, they will be in like a shot. Believe me, I now do the same!

I stressed earlier the importance of thorough research. It's worth mentioning that one of the factors that helped me present such a strong sponsorship case to SodaStream was the research that I did on that company, particularly in respect of its specific marketing needs as a new management buy-out operation.

The opportunity to research is so much easier today than it was before the launch of the Internet. That really is an incredible research tool. If you are prepared to use some initiative, you can find out the most amazing amount of information about a company. What I have found, though, is that many of the well-known companies are very cagey about putting people's names and contact details on their sites. If this is the case, you might get more joy by working though a Chamber of Commerce membership list or through a trade association.

↗ Brian on the grid at Thruxton in his Anglian Windows sponsored Van Diemen FF1600 race car.

reporters of the paper, radio and even TV station on your side, they can be extremely helpful.

Another obvious, but still effective source of research information is a company's annual report. If you can't source this online, you'll find that some of the larger public libraries keep these in their reference sections. They can be very effective in providing information about directors and gaining an insight into a company's plans for the future.

No matter how much you are able to find on the Internet and from other sources, sometimes there will still be a need to make direct contact with a company to discover certain information that you feel is important. This can be tricky, as invariably you will be asked why you want the information. In these situations, you have to be a little creative. A method that I find works well is to get one of their secretaries on your side. If you go about it in a professional way, they can be a great source of information about what goes on in a company, but there is a very fine line between patronising them and encouraging them to provide you with information. So, which secretaries and how do you get them to provide you with information?

Their sites can be very useful in this respect. In my experience, very few companies succeed in covering their tracks really thoroughly, no matter how hard they try not to divulge contact information. You just need to use some initiative and try different routes.

"" Keep very quiet about whatever leads or contacts you have or are working on. Whatever you do, don't talk to anyone about a possible deal until it is signed, sealed and paid for.

If you're researching companies that are fairly close to you geographically, it's well worth trying to make friends with someone in the local media. They tend to be a font of local knowledge, and if you can get the business

In terms of initial research, as opposed to making my sales approach, the most successful route for me has been to phone a company and specifically ask for the PA to the CEO or to the sales director. It's my experience that sales department personnel, if approached carefully, will have a little more sympathy for what you are trying to do than people in the marketing department for example. This is probably because they face the same problem themselves, making them more inclined to help you. Sales PAs, in my experience, tend to be fairly open-minded. They have to be, as they are probably dealing with some fairly outgoing individuals.

If you can develop a contact in this way within a company, you can usually find out a lot of the information that you want in terms of target markets, sales incentives, promotions and geographical structures. If you are really persuasive, you can encourage the secretary eventually to use her contacts within the company to arrange a meeting for you with the decision maker or key influencer. What a pleasure! You avoid that difficult job of approaching them from cold.

There is often a network of secretaries within a company, and if you can break into that and make a good impression with one of them, they can make your route through the company so much easier. The real key is the way that you deal with them. If you're over familiar, you have no chance. If you treat them as a junior or an obstacle in your way, you have no chance. Treat them with respect and be aware of the important role they play, and you can make a very good contact.

You are going to get tired of this, but I am not going to apologise for reminding you to thank them. I find that people can be very helpful, and if you take the trouble to thank them and also to let them know what progress you are making as a result of their assistance, they will very much appreciate that. I've asked a number of secretaries if they mind being asked for help in the way that I've outlined. Their reply, almost without exception, has been that they are only too glad to be treated as an intelligent human being, not some mindless barrier who tries to stop people from talking to their boss. Many of them then went on to say that their only criticism is that too often they never receive any thanks from the person whom they have tried to help.

Summary

→ The sponsorship business can be extremely competitive, so it pays to keep all of your negotiations strictly confidential until you have a signed agreement in place.

→ The SodaStream deal that I negotiated came about due to many factors, one being the thorough research that was carried out, which enabled me to make an attention-grabbing approach.

→ It pays to develop contacts while you are researching. These can prove very helpful when you are ready to make your sales approach. With some gentle persuasion, such contacts may be able to arrange a meeting for you with the decision makers in their company.

→ The secretaries in a company are a valuable source of assistance if you go about it in the right way, treating them as individuals with valuable knowledge of what goes on in the company, rather than as a barrier to be overcome.

Creative selling tools

So far in the development of a sponsorship sales strategy, we have covered four important steps:

1. The creation of a sponsorship property that is saleable and priced in a market-related way.
2. The creation of a multi-dimensional sales plan capable of generating interest within companies.
3. The targeting of companies through the use of specific criteria.
4. The research into those companies that have been selected to determine key information.

The next step in your sponsorship marketing strategy should be to decide what sales tools you will need. By sales tools, I am referring to anything that adds weight to your approach to a potential sponsor.

Sales tools can vary enormously. Looking back on my first sponsorship, the Victoria's Night Club deal, I suppose you could say that my racing car was an effective sales tool, because I used it to help me grab the decision maker's attention.

Typical sales tools might include:

→ A visual presentation for use on a laptop.
→ Testimonials from previous sponsors.

→ A DVD introducing the sponsorship opportunity.
→ A hard copy of the laptop presentation.
→ A colour brochure.
→ A Photoshop layout of what the branding will look like on your race car or sponsorship property.
→ A press cuttings portfolio.
→ Case studies of successful sponsorships.
→ TV viewing statistics.
→ Audience demographics.
→ Event video footage.

When I define a sales tool as anything that adds weight to your approach to a potential sponsor, I am not just referring to something that you take with you to your first meeting, such as a brochure or a laptop presentation. You can also use sales tools innovatively to secure such a meeting in the first place. For example, many sponsorship seekers send out a brochure as part of their initial approach. In my book, that's a sales tool.

Over the years, I've seen some very innovative and highly effective sales tools that were used to attract attention, generate interest and secure an initial meeting. Some were very simple, others far more elaborate.

One in particular that I remember receiving, while working for Bath Rugby, was simply a packet of grass seed. It was stylishly presented in silver foil with a see-through front. On it was a label that had been personalised to show a Bath Rugby player and the club's logo. The packet had been sent by a company that wanted to help Bath Rugby develop its brand commercially. It came with a compliments slip, on which there was a message. As I recall, the wording went something like this:

> → We'd like to **pitch** for your business
> → We'd like to help you **grow** your business
> → In the meantime, we hope that this will help you **grow** your **pitch**

Not the most complex sales tool that I've ever seen, but it raised a smile at the club and achieved its aim. A meeting was arranged, probably more out of curiosity as to who could have composed such a naff poem than what the company could offer. It didn't matter what the reason was. The objective had been achieved.

Some months ago, I received a package in the post. On opening it, I found a bar of Kit Kat and a typed letter on high-quality company headed paper. The letter started something like this:

> Dear Brian Sims,
>
> As a busy executive, I am sure that you have little time to read through all of your mail every day. I thought that you might like to 'take a break' and enjoy this Kit Kat with a cup of coffee while I outline briefly to you the services that my company offers.

The letter then went on to explain that this company was involved in creating stylish, eye-catching corporate identities for small- to medium-size businesses.

I liked the approach. I thought that it showed some humour, was different and certainly caught my eye. There was one major problem with it, however.

What actually arrived on my desk didn't look quite like the version shown above. For a start, in the original, my name was spelt incorrectly, as Brain Sins. The address was wrong and there were no fewer than three spelling mistakes in the first two paragraphs.

The name of the company? First Impressions. You couldn't make that up!

It was a great idea, undone by sloppy attention to detail. Would I want my corporate identity handled by this company? I would take some convincing.

Even today, when spell checking is so readily available, I find the lack of attention to detail in communications quite extraordinary. I wish I had a pound for every time that I have seen my name spelt incorrectly, usually with a double 'm' or more often Brain instead of Brian. It's not unusual to find that there are also glaring grammatical mistakes in the main body of a communication.

Sometimes I receive expensive brochures, and I never cease to be amazed at how many are riddled with spelling errors. Proof reading seems to be on the wane. So many websites are full of mistakes, too, even some of those belonging to large, high-profile companies.

You might argue that it shouldn't matter if there are mistakes in your letter, proposal or e-mail, as long as it can be understood. Wrong! It matters very much in this business. There is a very good chance that the decision maker in a company will see it, even if it is sent initially to a PA. It could well be that he or she is a lot older than you and brought up to believe that bad spelling in a communication shows a lack of respect. Why take that chance? It's not worth it. Get it right.

Then there's text or 'Twitter speak'. I receive an increasing number of communications containing examples of this, including job applications and requests for sponsorship. Many of you may be thinking, so what? As I mentioned, to most senior people in business, it shows a great lack of respect. It also indicates a lack of attention to detail and is a great giveaway about you as an individual. Why take the chance of your communication ending up in the recycle bin? You should be looking at ways of increasing your chances, not reducing them by being lazy. Whether it's a job application or a sponsorship proposal, it doesn't matter. Get them right.

> **Don't fall into the trap of thinking that if it's expensive, then it must be good.**

Working in Formula 1, as I have been lucky enough to do, you learn that attention to detail is a crucial attribute. Without it, you won't last two minutes. I recall on one occasion a mechanic being fired on the spot for sending one of the race cars out of the pit with a spelling mistake on the underside of the rear wing. Benneton, instead of Benetton. A photograph of that error appeared in a top motorsport magazine.

While we're on this topic of communication, I want to look at e-mails. The problem with using e-mails is that many people don't consider the impression that their communication sends to the recipient. You might be in a rush to dispatch the e-mail, so you dispense with pleasantries, such as 'Hello' or 'Hi', 'Thank You' or 'Kind Regards'. Too often, the language in e-mails is curt and can easily be misinterpreted by the recipient as being rude or offhand.

If you are going to use an e-mail in a sales situation, take extra care to ensure that it can't be misinterpreted in any way, and that the spelling, grammar and punctuation are all correct. In fact, whenever you make contact with the outside world, whether by letter, e-mail or even a note on a compliments slip, pay attention to detail.

Getting back to sales tools, at the other end of the spectrum from those that I've just described, I've seen sales tools that have cost a lot of money and clearly failed to deliver their objective. These include videos that have been produced at great expense, but that were far too long. Instead of inspiring the audience, they only succeeded in boring them. I've seen brochures that must have cost a small fortune simply thrown in the waste bin by marketing personnel, often because they were bland and didn't grab their attention. Don't fall into the trap of thinking that if it's expensive, then it must be good.

The problem with expensive sales tools is that you feel obliged to use them, even though the situation might not warrant their use. To be really effective, brochures and videos need to be personalised to the company to whom you are presenting. Unfortunately, to secure a good price from a printer, you need to order large quantities. This tends to result in a desire to use them up, even if they are quickly out of date and can't be personalised.

I've explained that some sales tools can be very effective in securing a meeting for you, and I've given you a couple of examples. While I am all for innovation, my advice is that you need to have a talent for creativity if you are going to adopt this approach. If you're not careful, it can easily backfire and look very tacky, or even amateurish. That doesn't mean that you shouldn't be a bit zany if you have the skill to do so, but it might be better to solicit the help of someone who perhaps is better qualified than you in this respect.

Another important point: sales tools are there to use only if you need them to support what you are saying. They should not be a crutch. What I mean by this is don't use them to replace two-way dialogue.

I have always found that my most effective sales tools are my two ears. By asking questions and then listening carefully to the answers, you will learn so much that will help you fit the features of your sponsorship proposal to the prospect's real needs. If you also use your eyes and watch a person's body language, you'll know whether or not you are getting through to them. If you can see that you aren't, try a different route. Don't just plough on regardless because you've practised a script parrot-fashion.

Having stressed the importance of using sales tools sparingly and only at the appropriate time, there is no doubt that they do have an important role to play. What I want to do next is look at how some of them can be designed and used to deliver the maximum impact.

Brochure

A great deal of money can be spent in the design and production of a full-colour brochure. Dependent upon your budget and also the number of times that it will be used, this can be a very powerful marketing or sales tool. I would recommend such an investment, for example, in the case of a sports venue promoter, who needs to sell everything from event sponsorship to corporate hospitality, and from arena to programme advertising. There will be a need for quite a high number of these, so the cost can be effectively amortised.

As with Formula 1, there could be a level of expectation for a quality brochure if you are operating at the very top end of the market. It would look rather unimpressive to distribute something that looks as though it was designed and printed at home. On the other hand, I wouldn't suggest that a young karter, seeking sponsorship to move into a junior formula of motor racing, necessarily needs to spend a lot of money in this way.

One major problem is that an expensive glossy brochure cannot be personalised easily in the same way that a PowerPoint presentation can be. With good-quality colour printers now

available so inexpensively, there is no reason why anyone can't put together a professional looking presentation, personalised to the company to whom you are presenting. You can even bind it yourself, with machines costing as little as £30.

Alternatively, go to one of the many colour print shops that can make the job look very professional, and with digital printing equipment, offer low-volume runs.

I would add, however, that there are no hard-and-fast rules on this. What might work for one person, doesn't always work for another. I'm not saying that you shouldn't use a nicely designed brochure. I just think that unless you have money to spare, you can use it far more effectively.

If you do decide that a brochure is appropriate, I'll give you some guidelines to help make it powerful and dynamic. Unless you are trained in graphic design, you will need to employ a professional designer. Make sure that you brief the person well, so that what is designed is very much sales orientated. Ensure that it contains a range of potential marketing opportunities, rather than simply filling the brochure with lots of lovely colour pictures of competitive sports actions or yourself. You need to demonstrate in a graphic manner that the opportunity can be used to promote many potential aspects of a company's marketing mix. These can include all of the points that we saw in the chapter on creating a saleable property, such as brand awareness, image transfer, case-study development and PR.

In this way, you will be far more likely to sow a seed in the mind of anyone looking at the brochure, as opposed to simply providing them with a collection of pictures that will do little to generate a meaningful level of interest.

A sales presentation

I know that many of you will disagree with my thoughts on what constitutes a powerful, effective sales presentation. You will argue that with modern technology, there are many really dynamic ways of producing an all-singing, all-dancing presentation that has sound, special effects, action and colour. You'll tell me that good old Microsoft PowerPoint has had its day.

You're right; there are many ways of producing a really high-class audio-visual presentation, and there are some circumstances when this is just what's needed. If you are going to invite a number of companies to a presentation, for example, prior to following them up individually, or if you are well into discussions with a company and you have been asked to present to the board, it may well be worth looking at such a personalised, dynamic presentation to really bring the atmosphere of your sport into the formality and tranquillity of the board room.

You might consider distributing a DVD in conjunction with a brochure. I know that this can be very effective. I've also seen some that are far too long and don't allow the prospect to jump backwards and forwards within the presentation to discuss key points. When I talk about these high-powered audio-visual programmes, I will include the production of a DVD presentation within this category.

However, before the majority of you think that unless you spend a lot of money on a presentation, you'll have no chance of competing with those who have the budget to make this happen, don't despair. Even some of the most expensive presentations that I've seen have failed to achieve what they set out to do. On the other hand, I have been able to secure some high-value sponsorship agreements, using what I consider to be powerful presentations, which I've designed and produced myself, using nothing more than a scanner, a PC with PowerPoint, and a little creativity and imagination. The beauty of PowerPoint is that I can be sitting on a train going to a sales presentation when I might suddenly think of an important point that I want to include, and I can add it then and there on my laptop. I couldn't do that with a DVD or some very sophisticated presentation.

Coming back to the point I made earlier, a sales presentation, no matter how costly, is still only a sales tool. It should be designed only to provide support for you in presenting your proposals, not to replace your own input. It is highly unlikely that it will sell your sponsorship proposal for you on its own. Only you can do that. If you remember that, you'll put the role of the presentation into perspective.

If you are going to the expense and effort of producing a really multi-dimensional audio-visual presentation, or perhaps a specially produced DVD, there are a couple of important aspects that should save you from making some of the mistakes that I have made on the occasions when I took this route.

Imagine that you have put together what you consider to be a really interesting, dramatic, colourful, even noisy, DVD presentation. It lasts for ten minutes. You show it to your colleagues, friends and family for their comments. They all like it.

The following day you are in the board room of a potential sponsor. You have your laptop linked up to a projector. Three directors are sat around the table waiting for the presentation to begin. The DVD starts and you watch their reaction.

Unfortunately, what seemed like a very exciting, punchy and short production that was very much to the point when you sat in your own lounge to watch it, cheered on by family and friends, now seems to go on for ever and ever. The noise levels suddenly seem inappropriate. The signals coming from the audience are not good. They start looking at their watches, and you begin to feel uncomfortable. With three more minutes to go in the presentation, it feels as though you have been watching it for half an hour already.

Do you persevere or do you switch it off? You're in a quandary. I know that this is true because

I've made this same mistake myself. You'll find that the majority of senior business people do not have the time or the inclination to sit through several minutes of what I always call a 'scene-setting' movie. When you are sitting in a business environment, watching for even three minutes can seem a long time. What adds to the problem is that it is very unlikely that the DVD will be personalised specifically to that company. Almost certainly its coverage will be of a general nature.

That is one of the reasons why I think you need to be very careful about the format that you use. I like to remain in control of any presentation that I am making. With a DVD, or similar type of presentation, it isn't always easy to do that. With a PowerPoint presentation, you can quickly move forward to a point that is of interest if you feel that you are losing impact. Alternatively, you can go back to re-emphasise a specific point that you want to make. Using a modular approach to its design, it is easy to maintain this essential level of control. If you sense that the audience is familiar with certain information that you are presenting, confirm this with them and move on to the next module.

There is another point that is worth thinking about with an expensive audio-visual presentation – it can date very quickly. Once you have produced your masterpiece, it is usually quite difficult, expensive and time consuming to edit it. Suppose, for example, a couple of weeks after its completion, you manage to secure a sponsorship deal from a high-profile media source, such as a daily newspaper. This can play an important role in any presentation that you make to companies, but if your video is now complete, all you can do is talk about the new deal after the presentation, perhaps losing some of the impact that it would have made if included in your show. With a simpler presentation, you can drop in a couple of new slides as you require them.

To summarise on audio-visual presentations, my advice is to keep them very short. Use

action footage from your sport purely as 10- or 15-second intervals between outlining ways in which the sponsorship is able to provide a range of marketing opportunities. In this way, the audience won't become bored and the action can provide powerful message support. Remember that it won't sell your sponsorship for you, so be very clear as to what its purpose is and why you are using it.

❝ With a PowerPoint presentation, you can quickly move forward to a point that is of interest if you feel that you are losing impact.

Now to the more often used PowerPoint style of presentation.

Although PowerPoint is a fairly basic and simple system, that doesn't mean that it has to be dull, far from it. With some of the money that you save by not going for a costly audio-visual presentation, it is worth investing in some professional-standard photographs from either a good agency or an individual whom you know, so that you can put your message across graphically. Perhaps you will have some of your own, but be careful about copyright infringement. You never know who might see the presentation.

Start the design of your presentation by getting a large sheet of paper and creating a flow chart of the various primary modules (or chapters) that you want to include. Such a presentation for the marketing department of a rugby club might include these major headings:

→ Introduction
→ The Proposal
→ Presentation Contents
→ The Team: Background/History
→ The Team: Future Programme
→ The Sponsorship Opportunity
→ Sponsorship Entitlements
→ Potential Benefits
→ Media Statistics
→ Summary

Secondly, within each of these headings, put down in bullet-point format the main points that you want to put across.

Only when you have done this should you start putting these thoughts on to the computer. In this way, you'll have a good framework on which to build the presentation into a colourful, interesting, yet clear communication of your sponsorship opportunity. It's easier to produce the text initially and then the photographs, rather than the other way around.

I first started working with PowerPoint in 1996. I had just been appointed as head of motorsport sponsorship for Alan Pascoe's API Agency. I had to learn quickly how to put together a computerised presentation of this sort, because it was my job to secure sponsorship in a short space of time for the agency's new client, the Benetton Formula 1 team. I must give credit to a very good friend of mine, Matthew Argenti, another of the Formula Ford racers that I regularly competed against back in my early career, who was managing director of the API agency at that time. He looked at my early attempts to produce a dynamic sales presentation using PowerPoint, and while he liked the graphic style that I had developed, he told me that there were about twice as many words in it as necessary. Time and time again, I would whittle it down until eventually I had a document that he felt was really concise, yet graphically powerful. It is a lesson that has stood me in good stead ever since, and I must thank him for that.

These days, I am shown many sales presentations, and I find that a high number are too wordy by far. All that a presentation should do is support what you are offering, not tell the whole story word by word. You need to provide those words as appropriate during your sales meeting. The presentation should simply be there to help you move through your proposal.

I would never recommend that you send your presentation, as a hard copy, to a prospective sponsor on its own, without you being there to add voice. However, if circumstances dictate that you need to do so, the same still applies. Don't make it too wordy. It's always been my experience that the majority of business people, certainly at the level that you are approaching, will not bother to read through long-winded documents. They will simply put them to one side and almost invariably never get around to looking at them again. They prefer punchy, short, sharp and clearly laid out reasons as to why they would want to find out more details of the opportunity being presented.

I keep coming back to an important point. The presentation will not sell the sponsorship by itself. Its primary purpose should be to provide enough information so that your prospect will want to know more – no less and no more than that.

There is a final point that I would like to make before we look at some of the other sales tools. If you are going to show the PowerPoint presentation on your laptop, or with the aid of a projector, make sure that you don't overdo the use of special effects. By this, I mean that if you want to use the animation facility that allows you to 'fly in' words, or lines of text, don't overdo it. By doing so, you will lose the impact that can be achieved if the animation is used sparingly. A whole presentation in which the audience is faced with every line flying in can be very tedious; when carried to extreme, it can make people feel nauseous.

One more thing: if you intend giving a laptop presentation, always make sure that you have a back-up copy on a Flash Drive or DVD, so that in the event of a disaster with your own computer, you can use a PC at the client's own facility. That may seem common sense, but it can easily throw you completely if you haven't prepared for this eventuality.

Other sales tools

An AA or RAC employee who comes out to fix your puncture at the side of road will certainly arrive prepared for most eventualities. The same should apply to you when you go to your first meeting with a company.

It shouldn't be too difficult to plan in advance for the sort of questions that might come up in the meeting. For example, there is a very good chance that a potential sponsor will want to know the profile of the people who will be watching the sporting event in which you are competing. By this, I am talking about age groups, social rating, gender and so on. It is probable that questions will be asked about the media coverage of the event. If you have to keep replying to such questions with the comment that you don't have that information with you, but that you can send it on, you will lose a great opportunity. By the time the information arrives on the potential sponsor's desk, he or she may well have lost the initial enthusiasm that you had generated at that meeting. You may not get the chance of another meeting, so don't take the risk. It's better to take supporting documents with you, even if you never have to use them.

Similarly, you should always be in a position to support statements that you make in your presentation. Again, if you can't do this while the prospect is seemingly interested and listening to what you have to say, you may well have lost a great opportunity to progress matters. This might well apply to testimonials. If you have some worthwhile letters or documents from a previous contented sponsor, or media sources that you may have worked with within a sponsorship programme, use them. You might include some 'one-liners' from these in your sales presentation, but it will be impressive if you have the full letters in a separate folder that you can leave if appropriate.

The same goes for media coverage. If you have generated an impressive amount of media coverage, a well-presented PR folder can prove very effective. A word of advice on this, however: remember that you are presenting to a business person. not necessarily a sports enthusiast. While they might enjoy sport personally, in their business capacity it may well be the case that they are far more impressed by media coverage in the lifestyle section of a county magazine, than on the sports pages of your local paper. Similarly, generating coverage in the business section of a paper can be quite powerful for the right prospect. Very often, an article about sports on the sports pages will be almost lost. An article that relates to sport, but that approaches the subject from a different angle and that is in the main body of the paper, as opposed to the sports pages, can often be more impressive to a potential sponsor.

As an example, an article about the way that a racing driver trains to cope with the excessive g-forces experienced in a race car has the capability of getting into the lifestyle section of a local paper. You saw earlier how I generated a feature in the South African press on how a competitor goes about finding sponsorship. That got into a Sunday newspaper supplement.

It may be that you are seeking sponsorship for an event. If you can show a range of general-interest media articles about that event in previous years, it will add weight to your proposals. They will help the prospect see what can be created and also demonstrate that you understand the importance of strong, innovative media coverage.

What other sales tools should you consider taking with you?

If you are proposing a sponsorship that includes branding, such as on a car or trackside banners, why not prepare either an artist's impression or a computer simulation of what that company's branding will look like in place. Anything that adds visual impact can only help.

If you are offering the sponsor a significant branding opportunity in sailing, for example, a reasonable-sized model of the yacht, decorated in the company livery, can prove very powerful. If it helps your target individual envisage the impact that it might make, it's worth the effort and expense.

Another sales tool that I've used quite successfully has been to hand the prospect an invitation to an indoor karting evening at a local track, enabling him also to invite a couple of colleagues. I think that this cost me £100, but it was well worth the expense to get the prospect and some business colleagues to spend an evening with me, so that we could talk and develop a better working relationship. With the new bribery Act that I've mentioned elsewhere, you do have to be a little cautious about doing this today. It shouldn't be a problem at this level, but just bear that in mind.

If you are going to do something like this, however, make sure you get the maximum impact out of it. Don't simply drop the invitation into the middle of a conversation. My research had indicated that the person involved was quite into motor sport, so before my first meeting, I bought a model kart in a display box and attached the invitation to it. Only when I knew that the meeting was heading in a positive direction did I bring the model kart into play. I know that as soon as I had left the meeting, he was showing it to his colleagues. Had he not taken up the invitation, it would have only cost me a few pounds, but he liked the idea and eventually we went on to sign a deal. This same concept can be used in any sport and shows, once again, the importance of research.

With a little imagination and creativity, there is no end to the sales tools that you can produce. As long as they have a specific objective and you know how to use them effectively, I am a great believer in them. Just make sure, however, that before going into the realms of creativity, you fully prepare the range of more obvious items that you are likely to need. The TV reports, market research statistics and sponsorship evaluation surveys might not be so colourful, but they can play a vital role in your sales meeting.

One final word on the subject: when you hand an item to a prospect, whether it be a model kart or a press cuttings folder, imagine that it

is very valuable. Don't just slide it haphazardly across their desk. If you give the impression that whatever you are passing across is not particularly important, that will quickly be transmitted to the prospect. You can make a cheap pen seem more valuable by the way you hand it to someone. Throw an expensive pen towards them and it will lose its value in their eyes. It's a small point to remember, but an important one.

Summary

→ A sales tool can best be described as any item that you can use to enhance or support your sales activities.

→ Sales tools can be used effectively to help you secure a meeting with a potential sponsor and also to help enhance or support your presentation at the meeting.

→ Sales tools should not be used as a crutch to take the place of a two-way dialogue with the prospect.

→ Don't equate the likely effectiveness of sales tools to the cost of their production. An innovative sales tool that costs only a few pounds can often achieve more than a high-cost audio-visual presentation.

→ If you are working on a small budget, don't waste money on producing sales tools that can't be easily updated.

→ Personalised presentation material is usually far more effective than that of a general nature.

→ If you are using a video or automated slide presentation, keep it short and to the point.

→ If you are creating a PowerPoint presentation, make sure that it isn't too wordy. Senior business people do not have the time or inclination to read through lengthy documents.

→ Make sure that you take with you documents that support any claims that you will make in your presentation. This can include media coverage statistics, testimonials, press cuttings and case studies of other successful sponsorships.

13

Using selling tools constructively

The course of my life changed drastically in 1980. Some years before, 1975 to be precise, I had decided to take a holiday in South Africa. My parents had lived there for many years and I'd visited them a couple of times previously, finding that I liked the country very much. On this particular occasion, I wanted to combine the visit with a trip to the South African Formula 1 Grand Prix at Kyalami, situated mid-way between Johannesburg and Pretoria.

The most economical ticket was with Alitalia, via Rome. On the flight down, I was reading *Autosport* magazine when the man in the seat next to me asked me what my interest was in motorsport. I explained that I was racing Formula Fords in England; he introduced himself as Max Mosley, who of course went on to become the president of the FIA, the governing body of motorsport worldwide, until his retirement a couple of years ago.

At the time, he was a director and co-owner of the March Formula 1 team and was also on his way to the South African Grand Prix. We struck up a conversation, and while at the race I visited the team.

In 1980, my first wife and I separated. I decided that a complete break would probably do me good. I took the decision to spend a year or two in South Africa. To be able to stay for that period of time, I needed a job, which I managed to find without much trouble; I based myself fairly close to my folks, in Johannesburg.

It wasn't long before I started investigating opportunities to do some motor racing.

↗ FedEx was regularly targeted by most F1 teams. In 1997, a creative business-to-business strategy enabled Brian to negotiate a multi-million-dollar deal, starting with a 'cold' phone call to FedEx HQ in Memphis. It took four months to signature.

Thanks to a sizeable sponsorship deal with a recruitment agency that I was able to put together fairly quickly, I managed to secure a drive in the prestigious Castrol 9 Hours sports car event at Kyalami. During the week of the race, I heard on the grapevine that the Kyalami Grand Prix Circuit was up for sale and that there was a potential buyer in place.

Max Mosley was about to play a significant role in my career. I phoned him in the UK and asked him if he knew who the new owner was. I explained that I'd like to possibly set up a racing driver school there. Max told me to leave it with him. A few hours later, I received a phone call from Bobby Hartslief, the South African who was about to become the new owner of Kyalami. He told me that he had been

contacted by Max, who had suggested that he see me. We arranged to meet that afternoon at the legendary Kyalami Ranch Hotel, just down the road from the track.

When I got there, his accountant and lawyer were there with him, having had an earlier meeting. Two hours later, I left the hotel as the manager of the Kyalami Grand Prix Circuit, having only been in the country a mere five months. It all happened so quickly that I didn't know whether to be nervous or excited. It turned out to be a great experience for me, and the best thing of all was that it still allowed me the time to fit in my race driving.

I learned so much in the three years that I was at Kyalami. Working with an experienced

Taking over at the helm

The man whose job it is to run Kyalami is Brian Sims.

Talking to him at his Parkview home he created an impression of confidence in his own ability to do just that — a mere week after meeting Hartslief for the first time and finding himself taken on full time as manager.

The 34-year-old Englishman has been in South Africa for four months, having been transferred here as part of the Control Data organisation at his own request — attracted to the country as a result of several visits as a spectator to the Grand Prix in previous years.

As a motor racing enthusiast he immediately became involved in racing Formula Fords, but it was his business interest in motor sport that prompted him to contact Bobby Hartslief when Kyalami was sold.

Colin Windell finds out about the new manager.

From their initial meeting things developed rather quickly, says Sims, and he was persuaded by Harslief to join in the various meetings that were being held as an expert to advise the youthful new owner of the track who, by his own admission, knew nothing about motor racing.

The offer of the post as manager developed from that.

"I would like to see Kyalami busy 365 days a year, and I will be going back to England very shortly to take a long hard look at the operation of Brands Hatch and to see how John Webb has developed the place.

"The facilities available to people from all walks of life at Brands Hatch throughout the year for a whole host of diversified activities is the sort of thing I have in mind for Kyalami.

"That Bobby has agreed to keep the track open for the Grand Prix for the next three years does not necessarily mean the Grand Prix will be run, but by the end of November we will know what is to happen with the GP next year."

BACKGROUND TO THE MAN

Brian Sims (34) was born in England near the Thruxton race track and from school moved into sales and marketing becoming the top salesman for Goodyear in England in 1971.

In 1974 he went as a pupil to the Jim Russell racing school, turning his interest in the sport from passive to active and at the same time discovering a strong interest in the business side of motor racing.

Using his experience in sales and marketing he set about finding himself sponsorship and for the 77/78 season turned up the biggest ever Formula Ford sponsorship in England — R48 000.

With a growing interest in the promotional aspects of motor racing he became involved wth Mike Eastick and the racing school he was starting.

Brian Sims became chief instructor at the school working with South African Kenny Gray and current Tyrrell driver Derek Daly, but spent the majority of his time handling the marketing and promotion of the new school.

He slowly phased himself out of the school to go back into business and actual racing, then doing a stint for Radio Victory giving talks on methods of obtaining sponsorship.

The success of these talks gave him the idea of doing something similar as a full time operation, but there was nothing in the offing in England at the time and he decided to come to South Africa, which he did four months ago.

Brian Sims.

Kyalami — ample space for enterprise.

Photograph by Clive Smith.

↗ Brian's first taste of F1 was courtesy of Max Mosley, who helped him to become manager of the Kyalami circuit, then home of the South African F1 Grand Prix.

sales team to secure sponsorship for the South African Grand Prix, each year was a steep, but fascinating learning curve. I recall that in 1981, we faced the prospect of the race not happening. This was due to a fight between Jean-Marie Balestre, the president of FISA, then the governing body of motorsport, and Bernie Ecclestone, then the head of FOCA, the F1 constructors' association. It was a power struggle deluxe, resulting in the F1 teams that supported FISA not coming to South Africa. The race went ahead, but it was decided that it wouldn't count for World Championship points.

As if this baptism by fire wasn't enough for me, the following year saw the much-publicised driver's strike at Kyalami, which involved many of the top F1 stars. All the drivers used to stay at the Kyalami Ranch Hotel, which was situated some 800 metres from the track. Formula 1 was a world apart from what it has become today. For a start, there was far more friendliness and socialising between the teams, and the public could get close to the drivers and crew members, without being treated by the security staff as though they were low-lifes.

During the strike, which was over an issue to do with Super Licences, Alain Prost, Gilles Villeneuve, Ricardo Patrese, Nelson Piquet and many of the other drivers all remained at the hotel pool while the situation was resolved. It was a hard, but useful lesson for me, explaining to the managing director of the grand prix's title sponsor that there might not be a race!

As mentioned, in 1981, I was given the chance to drive in the Kyalami 9 Hours International, a famous sports car race that attracted many of the world's top drivers, including that year Hans Stuck, Jackie Ickx and Bob Wollek. The only problem was that I needed to bring some sponsorship with me, which as you will have gathered by now, is fairly normal in motor racing. In my quest, I found one company that was quite receptive, Churchill Personnel, a large recruitment agency that had branches across the country. I met with their CEO, and he put an unusual proposal to me.

He told me that the previous month, the company had informed all of their staff that they wouldn't be receiving their annual pay rise that year. Business was tough and they couldn't afford to do it. He could see the many benefits of the programme that I was proposing, which incorporated a high level of guaranteed media coverage for the sponsor, as well as a competition designed to attract high-quality potential job seekers. However, he was worried about staff reaction, so he told me that if I wanted to secure the fee that I had proposed, I needed to attend their national sales conference, which was being staged that very weekend.

Nearly all of the branch managers, all of whom were women, would be there. He was prepared to give me 30 minutes to present to these managers and to try to persuade them to support the idea of the sponsorship that I was proposing. If I got the thumbs-up from them, he promised me that he would write a cheque there and then. Some challenge! I can still remember the frosty silence when I was introduced at the conference.

Fortunately, I must have got something right because I did the deal and the CEO was as good as his word. As a result of the sponsorship, I was able to compete in one of the most exciting races that I can recall, albeit that I ended up in hospital an hour from the end of the race, when a rear wheel parted company with my car in the middle of the fourth-gear 130mph Sunset Bend, in the pitch dark.

The Churchill Personnel deal endorsed my belief that for a sponsorship to work well, the company's staff really need to buy into it. Once you've got them on your side, it makes such a difference to the relationship between you and the decision maker in terms of renewing and extending the deal.

What was it that turned those women around and got them on my side? It was very simple. I didn't try to be clever and baffle them with a whole lot of 'marketing speak'.

James Hunt

85 Lillie Road, London SW6 1UD.
Telephone: 01-381 5166
Telex: 8814596 Norman G.

Brian Simms Esq
Kyalami Motor Racing Circuit
Bergviei Bet
Johannesburg
South Africa   11 February 1981

Dear Brian

With my tail firmly between my legs, I write to apologise
for letting you down so badly on Saturday by missing the
charity tractor race.   To make it even worse, the best
excuse I can offer is that I purely and simply overslept
and arrived at the track just as the tractor race was
finishing.   I realise that my failure to appear would
have upset the organisers of the race, the charities
involved and the public who came to see the race, and I
should be very grateful if you would extend my apologies
to the organisers and the charities.   The only loser as
far as the public is concerned is me, but I do hope that
the very exciting motor race in the afternoon gave all
your spectators a good day out.

Your decision to go ahead with the race despite all the
aggravation from FISA was a very brave one, and I hope that
it was financially successful.

Once again, my sincere apologies for my bad manners.

Yours sincerely

James Hunt

As manager of the Kyalami Circuit, Brian organised a charity tractor race for many of the F1 drivers on the morning of the
1981 South African Grand Prix. The race was sponsored by Deutz Tractors. James Hunt, by then a BBC F1 commentator,
was due to race in the event, but failed to show up.

↗ Brian alongside Bob Elliott (in Benetton race suit), FedEx President EMEA, with whom the F1 sponsorship deal was signed.

First of all I explained to them that each branch would be given a supply of tickets for the race, enabling them to bring their friends and families along. This was something that I had negotiated in advance through my contacts at Kyalami. If the sponsorship deal went ahead, it would cost me about 15 per cent of the fee to purchase these tickets, even at a special price. I reckoned that 85 per cent of the fee was better than 100 per cent of nothing! Then I outlined

a competition that I had negotiated with the *Sunday Times* newspaper, at that time South Africa's top selling paper. The competition was designed to generate for each of the Churchill regions a database of people who were in the market for a new job.

Suddenly, I was not quite the ogre that they had expected. They were going to see an immediate, if small, benefit for their friends and family, and secondly, they could see the opportunities that the database might give them to increase their branch turnover. As they could earn bonuses, linked to this, it was of immediate interest. A few other benefits were presented, and the outcome was that they didn't feel left out of a decision making process. The CEO had told them that the choice was theirs. I sweated in a side room for a few minutes while the verdict was reached. Eventually, the CEO walked in, with a grim look on his face. He told me that he had received the reaction of his managers and it wasn't good news. He kept a straight face and then added that it wasn't good news because he was going to have to write me a cheque!

Of course, every sponsorship negotiation is different. That is why it is so important to have as many sales tools as you can devise, to cover every eventuality that might arise in your first meeting. In the last chapter, we saw that sales tools can come in all shapes and sizes. However, I don't want you to go into a meeting armed to the teeth with brochures, presentations, videos and data reports, thinking that you have to make sure that you use them all before you leave. You need to use the minimum that you require to achieve the objective of the meeting. That objective will be covered later in the chapter on your first meeting. The sales tools are there only as back-up to your dialogue with the person or persons whom you are meeting.

Too many salespeople, not only in the sponsorship sector, use sales tools as a crutch, believing that if they go through them all in order, they will have delivered a powerful argument for acceptance of their proposal. That just isn't true!

I recall my very first meeting with FedEx, en route to that multi-million-pound sponsorship deal for the Benetton F1 team. I had arranged the meeting for 2.30pm at their head office in Brussels and had travelled over on the Eurostar from London. I was due to meet their marketing director and their sales director.

At about 2.20, I was told that both men had been called into an unexpected, but urgent meeting and wouldn't be available, although if I was prepared to wait until 5.30, there was a chance that they might be able to see me for about 30 minutes. Not a very auspicious start to my approach for sponsorship.

> **Too many salespeople, not only in the sponsorship sector, use sales tools as a crutch.**

The FedEx European office is situated out of Brussels, on a large business park, not far from the airport, so there was nowhere to go to while away three hours. After about four coffees and a lot of newspaper reading, 5.30 eventually arrived and I was shown into the marketing director's office, where I met the two men.

I had prepared what I felt was an impressive laptop presentation, and after a brief conversation, it was agreed that I would show this to them. I don't know quite what it was that alerted me, perhaps experience, perhaps instinct, but I realised that the presentation wasn't having the desired effect. I quickly pushed it to one side and asked a straightforward question: "That's not hitting the spot, is it?" They both nodded in agreement and one of them went on to explain that they had been approached by just about every F1 team, so they knew all about the subject. He explained that no one had yet convinced them of its merits as far as FedEx was concerned, and they didn't really need to see another presentation showing all of the TV viewing statistics and crowd attendances of Formula 1. They took that for granted. He continued by adding that the reason they had agreed to see me was very simple: I had struck a chord in my approach when I had highlighted the business-to-business opportunities that potentially existed for FedEx within both Benetton and Formula 1.

I really appreciated their openness and desire not to waste either their time or mine. Instead of the presentation that I had prepared, we

Desiré Wilson, South Africa's fast lady, is a possible challenger in a Tyrell.

SUPPLEMENT TO THE CITIZE

Saturday February 7 1981

The Fisa/Foca wrangle has at least made it possible for Desire Wilson to race today in front of her home crowd . . . and we hope she lasts longer than Jody did last year. Kyalami used to be a Tyrell circuit and Desire's expectations will be high today. A good drive may establish her Formula One future for 1981 and it could be THE big break. Desire drives car number 4.

↗ Brian negotiated a deal with Deutz, the German tractor manufacturer, that saw the company sponsor Desiree Wilson in the Tyrell F1 car at the South African Grand Prix in 1981.

had a conversation that lasted for just over an hour-and-a-half. Apart from talking about the type of business-to-business opportunities that would be of interest to them, I asked them a lot of questions about the way in which their company operated; we discussed some of the issues facing them in Europe as opposed to the USA, where FedEx had become synonymous with parcel and letter delivery.

At the end of the meeting, I asked them which had been the main aspects of interest. They told me what they could see working and also where there might be problems to overcome if we were to move forward. I just wish more business people were like these two. They respected my time and I respected theirs. None of us wanted to play games. That meeting was at the beginning of February, and after some really hard and protracted negotiations at both the global headquarters of FedEx in Memphis

and at the Benetton F1 HQ in Oxfordshire, the deal was signed in time for the distinctive FedEx branding to appear on the Benetton F1 cars at the British Grand Prix in July.

The whole point of the story is that if I had persevered with my original plan of running through the presentation, I might have bored both men rigid and quite probably missed the opportunity to develop the areas of the programme that were important to them. It was a crucial lesson for me, and one that I recommend you to take on board.

↗ Benetton F1 driver Jean Alesi at the Silverstone launch of the
FedEx sponsorship.

Summary

→ When you approach a company for
sponsorship, you need to convince yourself
that the company will benefit from
participation. If you are not certain of this,
how can you expect the company personnel
to be convinced?

→ Sales tools can be very effective in
supporting your presentation, but you must
use them sparingly.

→ Don't feel that because you have taken a lot
of trouble to put together such sales tools as
a PowerPoint presentation, a brochure and
a press cuttings portfolio that you have to
use them. They should be there to support
you. You need to bring them in and out of
play to suit your dialogue, not the other way
around.

Loss-leader selling

Originally I had planned to stay in South Africa for no more than two years, but eventually I was there for ten. My role at the Kyalami Grand Prix Circuit was proving to be really interesting and I was learning a lot.

I'd almost convinced myself that I should give it another year before packing my bags and heading home to the UK, and probably I would have done this except for a bombshell that took everyone working at the track by surprise. A high court injunction was slapped on the famous F1 venue.

Kyalami was widely regarded as one of the greatest of the F1 grand prix tracks. In those days, it was right out in the countryside, mid-way between Johannesburg and Pretoria, and there were only a few residences close by. Those that were in the vicinity were beautiful thatched houses on multi-acre plots. The area was a centre of equestrian activity, and for many years F1 and the horses had lived in harmony.

Then a local nurseryman declared war on the circuit, supposedly because of the noise. He claimed that the sound of race cars was upsetting the few cows that he kept on a nearby smallholding. Sadly, this individual had a lot of influence, and after creating a degree of aggravation, he took out the injunction against the owners of the circuit.

To everyone's surprise, the court was bamboozled by the man with the cows. The injunction stopped virtually all activity on the racetrack, even by ordinary road cars, seven days a week. Only a few race meetings were allowed: the injunction restricted the circuit to eight races a year, including the GP, and eight practice days, over and above the normal race meeting practice sessions.

The injunction meant that I couldn't fulfil my role of making Kyalami generate income seven days a week, 52 weeks a year. Despite ongoing discussions and legal moves, there was no end in sight to the dispute, so reluctantly I resigned as manager.

This seemed a good time to stick to my original plan to return to Europe. I wanted to see a bit more of the country first, however, particularly the Western Cape and Cape Town.

To cut a long story short, eventually I moved to Cape Town and ended up racing in the country's new production car championship for the major Mercedes dealer, McCarthy Group – in a Honda. (Mercedes built Hondas in South Africa, the only place in the world where this has happened.) I was delighted to be able to bring some success to the group, winning several races on the way to becoming the champion in my class.

My most satisfying success, however, was in the prestigious six-hour endurance race at the Killarney Circuit in Cape Town. There were many famous names in that race, including a German driver who had raced for McLaren in Formula 1, Jochen Mass. After he left McLaren, he went on to become the World Sportscar Champion, driving for the Rothmans Porsche team. At that time, Jochen was married to Estee, a well-known South African woman who had been an international model. They lived fairly close to me in the Clifton area of Cape Town, and occasionally we would meet for a meal or a *brai*, as barbeques are known in South Africa. Jochen had been contracted to race for VW in a few high-profile touring car events in South Africa.

I was privileged to race against him a second time when I competed in what would be my final race, the Group C international event at Kyalami. He was driving one of those truly awesome Rothmans Porsches. Along with the late Ferrari F1 driver Michele Alboreto, whom I got to know well when he raced for Lola F1 while I was working there, Jochen Mass is one of the most genuine people that I have met in the sport. You always got the feeling with both Jochen and Michele that they would have been quite happy to race for no pay. Racing mattered to them, not the money.

Although I enjoyed a lot of success racing with Honda, including securing the class championship in my first season with the team,

it came as a great surprise when I was offered a full factory drive for the following season with Mercedes SA. Life couldn't get any better, I thought to myself. But it did!

I had met Liz shortly after arriving in the Cape. Due to a strange coincidence, we met again a couple of years later and started dating. It was a relationship that was meant to be, and prior to moving back to Johannesburg to fulfil my new role as a Mercedes contracted driver, we were married. That was nearly 25 years ago; without doubt, it was the best decision of my life.

↗ For once, talent, not sponsorship, saw Brian become a Mercedes works driver – in a Honda! At the time, Mercedes built Hondas in South Africa. He is with team-mate Mike O'Sullivan.

We had a great time travelling around South Africa as I competed in the premier motorsport championship. The country has some of the most amazing scenery in the world and we spent a lot of time discovering it. One of my sponsors owned a huge swathe of land close to the Mozambique border, north of the Kruger Park, and we were able to watch wildlife of all types there in its natural habitat.

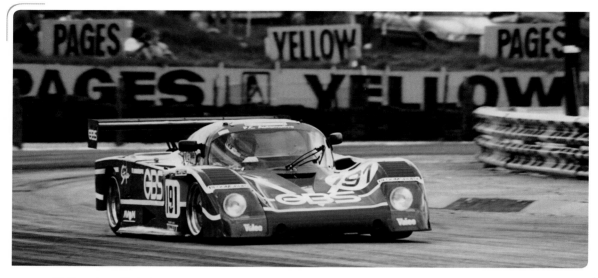

↗ The sponsorship deals Brian secured to race in the international Group C race at Kyalami were yet another example of using media partners to create a saleable property.

I loved the racing, but after a while the testing and endless hotel accommodation started to become tedious. I took the decision to call it a day at the end of the 1987 season.

My last race, for which I had secured the sponsorship deals described earlier, happened to be the last major international event on the original Kyalami Grand Prix Circuit. The track had the longest straight in Formula 1 and was one of the most popular GP tracks among the drivers, being fast and challenging. It also encouraged overtaking.

Sadly, there is no South African Grand Prix today. A combination of currency exchange rate, politics, corruption and the cost of making the revised Kyalami circuit meet modern F1 requirements has made the chances of it happening again very slim indeed.

Having informed Mercedes Benz that I intended to retire from driving, I sat down with Peter Cleary, the company's marketing director, to discuss my options, if any. He came up with what seemed an interesting opportunity.

I was offered the chance to become sales director for a new type of dealership that Mercedes was planning in South Africa, called Silverline. These new franchises would specialise in the exotic car market and were designed to allow Mercedes SA to secure business in a market that was being dominated by many private exotic car businesses.

I decided to give it a try. The dealership would operate in Sandton, the elite northern suburb of Johannesburg, where there was plenty of money and where exotic cars were status symbols. Not only would I be given a top-of-the-range car, in addition to a good salary, but so would my wife Liz. Just over eight weeks after starting, however, I told her that we would have to take the cars back. I'd quit the job!

She wasn't surprised, explaining that it was obvious I hated the job. Well not so much the job, but the people I was working with. It was expected of the senior staff that they would join the dealer principal in the bar most evenings, where it was also virtually compulsory to laugh at his jokes. I couldn't stand the cronyism that was so evident within the company. I knew that it wouldn't change, so I had two choices: live with it or leave. It wasn't a difficult decision. The corporate life wasn't for me any more.

That evening, as we sat by the pool, Liz asked me what we were going to do to bring in some money. She was surprised when I told her what I had been working on. I said that with her help, we were going to start South Africa's first racing driver school.

Just over two months later, the Speed International Racing Driver School was launched at the Zwartkops Raceway, south of Pretoria.

The way that I managed to fund the operation, not having a great deal of spare cash, probably won't come as a surprise – sponsorship, and lots of it!

The method that I used to secure a very high level of sponsorship was one that I have employed more than once with great success. I've never really given it a name before, but perhaps I should call it my 'loss-leader' sales strategy.

It's a method of securing funding that is particularly effective for sponsorship properties that by themselves are not what you'd call particularly high profile. It works very much along the lines used by supermarkets, which will be familiar to many. They will deliberately sell some products at a loss to entice you into the store. Once inside, of course, their hope is that you'll spend a lot more on profitable items. This method worked exceptionally well in enabling me to secure a substantial amount of sponsorship for the racing school. As there had never been such a school in South Africa before, there was no way that it could have been considered high profile, hence the need for some creative thinking.

Having negotiated a deal with the wealthy businessman who owned the Zwartkops circuit, a sort of South African Lydden Hill, I put together an innovative agreement with Toyota that provided me with three Toyota Conquest 16-valve cars, fitted with roll cages, seat harnesses and other racing equipment.

With such a new concept, I realised that we needed something powerful and innovative to attract people's attention to get them to come along to the school. I came up with the idea of a competition that would identify each year's top pupil.

What was needed was a prize that would really capture the imagination of the public. I knew that the school couldn't survive purely on the business that might be derived from young drivers who wanted to become professional racers. It had to have a wider appeal. Moreover, I still needed a substantial amount of sponsorship.

I decided to use the competition as the means of securing a major sponsor, one that would make every one sit up and take notice. It was very difficult at that time for South Africans to travel to Europe, particularly to compete in any motorsport activities, due to the poor exchange rate of the rand. I knew that if I could put together a prize that involved a trip to Europe and that included some motorsport activity while there, I would be on to a winner. So I developed a sponsorship sales strategy around this idea.

As mentioned, what I needed was not any sponsor, but a sponsor that would create a big impact. Why was that so important?

I might have been able to negotiate a sponsorship deal with the local panel beaters, but apart from the money, what would it have done for the school? Not a lot really. It wouldn't have added prestige or image. It certainly wouldn't have given me the platform to attract other high-profile companies.

However, there was a company operating in South Africa that had the potential to do a lot for the school.

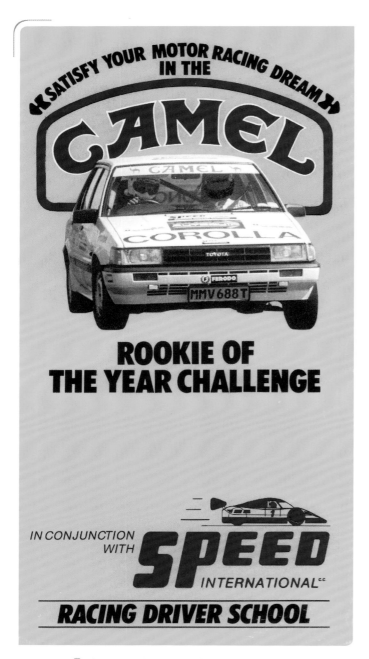

SATISFY YOUR MOTOR RACING DREAM

IN THE

CAMEL

COROLLA

ROOKIE OF
THE YEAR CHALLENGE

IN CONJUNCTION WITH SPEED INTERNATIONAL c.c.

RACING DRIVER SCHOOL

↗ The strategic deal that saw Camel sponsor a rookie competition, at Brian's Kyalami based racing driver school, provided the perfect platform on which to secure many other sponsorships.

The company that I had set my sights on was R.J. Reynolds, the American tobacco giant. The brand that really interested me was Camel. At that time, they were big sponsors in Formula 1, as well as being involved in several other international motorsport categories. I knew that if I could bring them on board as a major sponsor, it would create just the sort of impression that I was looking for. My first step was to secure a meeting with Peter Buckley, who was the South African marketing manager for R.J. Reynolds.

I initiated this by means of a phone call. My objective was very concise. I wanted Peter to agree that it wasn't easy for the Camel brand in South Africa to derive mileage from the parent company's international motorsport activities, such as F1 and Indycar. Then I explained that I was launching a brand-new motorsport concept in South Africa, one that undoubtedly would generate a high degree of media interest and that could provide a link to Camel's international programme. I asked him if I could come and present this to him.

His response was probably predictable. He told me that he did not have any budget for that year or the next and that I was wasting my time, as well as his. Not an auspicious start! My response was to ask him if the concept that I had very briefly outlined appealed, forgetting the cost. Rather grudgingly he agreed that it had some merit. Then I explained that there was a way whereby this could work for Camel at very little cost to the company. He was highly sceptical, but after further discussion, eventually he agreed to see me.

What I presented to Peter Buckley was an opportunity for Camel to sponsor the annual competition that I had dreamed up, designed to identify the school's top pupil. I suggested that it could be called the Camel Rookie of the Year Challenge, which impressed him. Nevertheless, he still insisted that there was one major problem: there was no budget available, since most of it had been committed to the Camel Challenge, a Range Rover trek across the African continent. He accepted that the Challenge could be very successful in generating media coverage, but it would require a lot of budget, he explained.

At this point, I took a calculated gamble. I surprised Peter by telling him that I didn't need a sponsorship fee. He raised his eyebrows at this. I went on to ask him if he would be able to provide the items listed below, in return for the title sponsorship, namely The Camel Rookie of the Year:

→ Two return air tickets from South Africa to the UK for the Camel Rookie of the Year and myself.
→ A test day for the Camel Rookie with the Paul Stewart FF2000 Racing Team in the UK. (This team was run by Jackie Stewart's son, Paul, and sponsored by Camel UK.)
→ 500 Camel T-shirts and caps for the racing school.
→ The services of his PR agency to help promote the Camel Rookie competition.

I also explained to Peter that I had arranged with John Kirkpatrick, the owner of the world-famous Jim Russell Racing Driver School at Donington Park, to provide a week's course for the Camel Rookie winner. This would include a race in a Formula Ford at the end of the course. In return, I had agreed to fly John to South Africa to be one of the judges in the final of the Camel Rookie of the Year competition.

Peter thought it over for a few days before telling me that we had a deal. The Camel Rookie of the Year was on the road!

In the process, I had used the loss-leader strategy. I wouldn't make any money from the Camel deal, but I knew that it would prove invaluable in due course.

There was still a problem, however. Impressive as the name Camel was, it didn't pay for any of the other considerable expenses involved in setting up and running a racing school. These included the design and printing of brochures, track hire, vehicle maintenance, salaries, tyres, fuel, helmets and many other major expenses.

I wasn't too worried, though, as I had achieved exactly what I had set out to do. I knew that the Camel sponsorship would provide the high level of credibility I needed to be able to find the large sponsorship deal that would bring in much of the total budget I needed to run the whole operation.

On top of that, I realised that the fact that every pupil coming to the school would receive a free bright yellow Camel F1 T-shirt and cap would be quite an attraction. Such was the draw at that time of the Camel brand in South Africa.

Within two months of the Camel sponsorship being agreed, I had negotiated a number of meaningful deals, including one with the Luxavia airline, which provided me with free first-class air travel. This meant that not only could Liz and I accompany the Camel Rookie of the Year to the UK, but also that our international judge for the final, John Kirkpatrick, would receive a fully paid return ticket from the UK to South Africa. This was a huge bonus.

Other deals included a year's supply of petrol and oil for the school from Sasol, all of our tyres from Continental, batteries from Sabat, and helmets and overalls from Autoquip. There were many more. I'd even negotiated sponsorship from Safari Plan, a company that owned exclusive wild-game farms close to the Mozambique border. This allowed us to spend a few days of rest and relaxation in the African bush whenever we needed it.

All of this was made possible by one thing: the Camel brand name.

❝ I wouldn't make any money from the Camel deal, but I knew that it would prove invaluable in due course.

I hope you can see why I call it loss-leader selling. Because I realised the power that the Camel brand would give to my new business, I was prepared to sell the deal at a virtual loss. It's a useful strategy in the right circumstances.

That isn't the end of the story. All of the deals that I put together, which came about as a result of that Camel agreement, probably covered about 50 per cent of my running costs for the first year. They didn't cover such expenditure as instructor fees. Neither did they provide me with a salary. I still needed a major sponsor for the school, one that would pay a sizeable fee, in addition to the other deals that provided products or services as payment. Such a cash injection would allow me to move forward with my plans to expand Speed International.

Again, this is where I have to stress the incredible power of the media when you are seeking sponsorship. Because the rookie competition had the name Camel attached to it, everyone assumed that they had put in a lot of money. There was another bonus, however, on which I had based my thinking. I knew that with Camel spending a lot of money in South Africa on media advertising, I should have been able to secure a worthwhile response from the media to promote and cover the Rookie of the Year Challenge. I was confident that in turn this would help me secure a major title sponsor for the school itself

I had no idea of knowing just how much interest there would be, but shortly after announcing the Camel sponsorship, I was able to arrange no fewer than four major TV

↗ The launch at Kyalami of PG Windscreen's sponsorship of Brian's racing school, Speed International, attracted SABC TV News coverage, delighting the sponsor.

RJR

R.J. REYNOLDS TOBACCO INTERNATIONAL

JOHANNESBURG REPRESENTATIVE
HEERENHOF BUILDING, CNR. HENDRIK VERWOERD DRIVE & WILL SCARLETT ROAD, FERNDALE
P.O. BOX 56207, PINEGOWRIE 2123. TELEPHONE: 787-0520

26th July 1989

Mr. B. Sims
Speed International
P O Box 515
PAULSHOF
2056

Dear Brian,

Re: Camel Rookie Of The Year Competition

This is to confirm that I have been very happy with
R.J. Reynolds' association with Speed International
during 1989, and the way you have managed the
Camel Rookie of the Year Competition.

As a result I wish to repeat this competition during
the course of 1990.

Yours sincerely,

P.D.R. BUCKLEY
REGIONAL MANAGER

PDRB/ks

↗ The ultimate goal: a letter from your sponsor seeking to renew the deal. This was for Camel's sponsorship of
Brian's racing driver school in South Africa.

↗ Sir Jackie Stewart's son, Paul, team principal of Paul Stewart Racing, with Brian and Liz Sims during the 1987 Donington Park test drive awarded to the winner of the Camel Rookie of the Year Challenge, held at Brian's South African racing driver school.

In addition to all of these benefits, there was another. I had negotiated a deal with the newly revamped Kyalami Grand Prix Circuit, which meant that I could move Speed International to this prestigious venue. In addition, the circuit owners agreed to allocate a prestigious corporate suite to my title sponsor as part of the deal. Although the South African F1 Grand Prix was no longer on the calendar, this would provide PG Windscreens with an excellent facility for all national race meetings.

I had done enough to generate interest. The managing director referred me to his marketing director, Louis Rosseau, who fortunately had considerable marketing vision. Within a very short time, I was able to bring the negotiations to a successful conclusion, securing a three-year sponsorship agreement, which was worth a lot of money. The media coverage that the school received in that first year of the sponsorship programme was quite exceptional, and the response from all of our sponsors was fantastic.

When the corporate name change came later that year, the company had an innovative vehicle to use for creating awareness. It invited hundreds of media people to the racing school to drive cars painted in the new brand identity. The subsequent media coverage was way above their expectations.

All of this had come about because I was able to see the value of bringing a high-profile brand name, Camel, to the party, even though they didn't provide me with a penny. Had I been greedy, I could have lost everything. Although certainly I wouldn't recommend that you go around offering free sponsorship to all and sundry, the careful and occasional use of this ploy can work very well. If you are seeking sponsorship for a property that doesn't have a high profile, this can be a very effective way of overcoming that problem.

features about the competition, as well as a number of radio programmes, and magazine and newspaper articles. Having gained a commitment from TV, I knew that before these programmes were recorded, I would have to move very quickly to be able to offer a potential title sponsor the opportunity that this media coverage would present.

Through reading the business pages of the main papers, I discovered that a well-known company was planning to re-brand itself. PG Windscreens was a very successful company, with a chain of retail outlets across the country that offered a windscreen replacement service in addition to other glass products. The company was soon to change its corporate identity and name to AutoGlass.

I approached the MD of the company and was able to show him how he could achieve a very high media profile for the new brand by becoming the title sponsor of the racing school. With the guaranteed media attention that I had already put in place, there was an excellent platform for announcing later in the year the change of brand name.

↗ Brian with IndyCar champion Gil de Ferran at the Homestead Oval in Florida, USA.

Summary

➔ If you have a sponsorship property that is not well known, or high profile, it can be quite difficult to capture the interest of a major brand or company.

➔ If you are seeking several sponsors for your opportunity, it can be very advantageous to attract a well-known company as a sponsor. This will add a high degree of credibility to your sponsorship opportunity. It might also provide the potential for business-to-business dealings for companies keen to be associated with that major brand or company.

➔ By adopting a loss-leader approach to the introduction of such a high-profile sponsor, you can attract several other key companies.

➔ The perception that is created by announcing a high-profile sponsor can easily outweigh the loss of income that results from providing some sponsorship entitlements virtually for nothing.

➔ You need to be careful in using this method. Only consider it if you are confident that as a result of using a loss-leader, you will attract fee paying sponsors to provide your full budget.

➔ The risk is that if you commit to a programme with the loss-leader and can't fulfil, you could end up with a legal issue or, at best, a lot of egg on your face.

15

Razor and blades marketing

Having looked at how the loss-leader principle worked for me with the racing school, I would like to examine another very effective way of structuring a sponsorship deal. I'll call this the 'razor and blades' method. By using this method early in my career, I was able to put together the sponsorship deal that allowed me to turn professional and give up my job as the UK sales training director of a global corporation, ITT.

The method is based on a simple fact. Companies that make razors expect to gain their profits not from the razors themselves, but from the blades that users have to continually purchase once they have the razors.

There are many retail categories that work like this. For example, consider the printer connected to your PC. Once you have purchased the printer, the cost of the cartridges becomes an ongoing high expense.

It was this concept that was the foundation of the deal that I put together with the producers of the SodaStream soft drink dispenser. You'll recall that in Chapter 11, I explained how this deal came about following a chance meeting with the company's sales manager, Don Philpott, who told me of the management buy-out from the parent company, Kenwood.

The concept involved in the marketing of SodaStream was very similar to the marketing of razors and blades. In the same way, SodaStream would make its profit from the sale of concentrates used in the machines, not from the sale of the machines themselves. Once a customer had purchased a machine, the expectation was that they would continue to buy the bottles of concentrate. At that time, a choice of eight or nine flavours was offered.

From my research, I was able to identify the major marketing requirements for the new company. The main points were:

→ **Brand awareness** » This was important now that SodaStream would no longer be advertised and promoted by Kenwood.
→ **PR** » The generation of as much media coverage of the product and its advantages was an essential part of the marketing mix.
→ **Database generation** » The opportunity to communicate special offers and promotions to customers, who had purchased concentrate, was seen as being extremely beneficial.
→ **Image transfer** » Although it was largely women who purchased SodaStream machines, the decision was influenced by children and young adults. It was important to create a cool, exciting, colourful image for the product.
→ **Sales promotion** » The opportunity to promote sales of machines in retail outlets was considered a vital part of the marketing plan. The more machines that were sold, the higher the sales of concentrate.
→ **Product sampling** » If people could be persuaded to sample the range of drinks that SodaStream could produce, it would help greatly in encouraging them to purchase.
→ **Staff motivation** » Being a new company, there was a need to introduce team building and incentive programmes to encourage staff motivation and loyalty.
→ **Dealer incentives** » The opportunity to provide wholesale dealers with incentive programmes was considered to be very important.
→ **Merchandising** » The opportunity to develop a themed range of SodaStream branded T-shirts and caps would be helpful.

Having identified these as being the main factors that comprised the marketing plan, I needed to put together a proposal that would show how motor racing could help deliver many of them. This had to be in conjunction with some of the more conventional marketing

GOES RACING

We are entering the fun of Formula Ford and inviting all Soda-streamers to share it with us. Join Sodastream Team Racing and enter a free competition to win the fabulous Sodastream-Hawke DL17.

Sodastream Team Racing will commence in March 1977 and continue throughout the season until November. We will be racing the car in the Townsend Thorensen Championship which is held at a number of venues throughout the country.

Apart from actual racing, the car will be the centrepiece of promotional activities in Stores and County Shows. It will also be featured in special promotional events, e.g. Football Grounds etc.

The support for Formula Ford in the Country is growing at an incredible rate, the enthusiasm for the sport is enormous. It is right that Sodastream gets involved with this sport - and invites all Soda-streamers to share the fun.

Brian Simms, the Sodastream Team Racing driver pictured at the wheel of the Hawke racing car in which he competed last year.

Sodastream Team Racing Kits comprising a Car Sticker, Full Colour Poster of the Sodastream-Hawke DL17, and a Racing Programme will be available at the low cost of 50p. With each Racing Kit will be a FREE competition Form, the prize for which will be the actual Formula Ford Car.

This is a promotion which involves Sodastream, our Stockists and Customers; it will capture the imagination of the General Public and put some excitement and sparkle into 1977.

The Sodastream Team Racing symbol which we hope will be first across the line in every race in 1977.

TEAM RACING

↗ This flyer listed the SodaStream Racing Team membership entitlements, including the chance to win the actual race car.

activities, such as media advertising and in-store merchandising displays.

The idea that I came up with was the creation of an innovative promotion, called SodaStream Team Racing. This would have as its catalyst the sponsorship by SodaStream of a Formula Ford 1600 racing car, which would compete in the high-profile national Townsend Thorensen Championship.

↗ The 'membership' collars on SodaStream concentrate bottles helped provide a useful customer database, a primary sponsorship objective.

→ An A3-size colour poster of the car and driver.
  → A car sticker.
  → A free ticket to watch the team race at any of the national tracks, such as Brands Hatch, Silverstone and Oulton Park.
  → A brochure of SodaStream Racing Team merchandise that could be purchased.
  → A discount voucher for their next SodaStream purchase.
  → A competition entry form, the prize being the actual race car (at the end of the season) and a course of lessons at a racing driver school.

The programme would be designed to deliver all of the major factors that had been identified as being important to the SodaStream marketing plan:

Brand awareness » The car would be painted in the distinctive SodaStream colour scheme and livery. I, as the driver, and all of the pit crew would wear SodaStream branded race suit and uniforms. The car would be moved from track to track in a SodaStream branded transporter. The team would race in the national FF1600 Championship at circuits all over the UK.

PR » Media generating activities were proposed that included launching the team on the pitch at half-time during a Football League Division 2 match at the local stadium, as well as a more formal launch in a top London hotel.

It was proposed that the team would participate in high-profile charity events.

The racing programme would provide a constant source of news stories.

Lifestyle stories were encouraged, based on the personal aspects of the people involved, such as the training regime of the driver, catering at a race track and similar types of story.

Database generation » By completing the applications on the bottle collars, the buyers would provide SodaStream with a national database.

SodaStream Team Racing would encourage the public to take an interest in the racing activities by offering them the chance to become a member of the team. This would be achieved by attaching a collar to every bottle of concentrate that was distributed from the factory. The collar would incorporate an application form, enabling buyers to send in their names and addresses, together with a small fee, which would cover postage and packing. In return, they would receive:

Image transfer » The racing activities would greatly increase the perception of SodaStream as being exciting, cool, colourful, young, daring, extreme and slightly rebellious.

Sales promotion » This was an area where the motor racing programme really came into its own as a marketing tool.

It was proposed that the SodaStream racing car would be made available as a display to major retail outlets, defined by the geographic area in which the team's next race would take place.

The concept was very simple. The car would be positioned prominently in the retail outlet. I would be there in a race suit, together with a promotional girl recruited by SodaStream. As customers entered the shop, it was anticipated that many of them would want to look at the race car. If they wished, they could have a Polaroid photograph taken of themselves in the car. While this was happening, other members of their group would be offered free glasses of SodaStream by the demonstrator and told how inexpensive they were to produce, using the SodaStream machine. There would be a special offer for purchase of the machine at the point of sale. This was expected to encourage a lot of mothers with young children in particular to buy on the day.

Staff motivation » Group visits to race meetings would be organised for the staff.

Dealer incentives » A programme would be established that offered target achieving dealers the chance to bring their families to a race meeting to watch the team in action.

Merchandising » A range of T-shirts, jackets and caps, branded with the SodaStream Racing Team logo would be produced, which could be ordered by mail and also be available in SodaStream retail outlets.

The result was that SodaStream agreed in full to the proposals that I had made.

The success of the programme could be measured fairly accurately through the sales of machines at points of sale in the retail outlets, through the size of the database that was generated and by the return from sales promotions mailed to team members.

At the end of the year, although the racing hadn't been a spectacular success, due to a host of reasons, the programme was judged to have been a definite winner by the management team. It was decided to continue with a motor racing programme the following year, but the form this took changed due to subsequent events.

> " **The programme was judged to have been a definite winner by the management team.**

I hope that this will show you how a programme can be put together to meet the real, not assumed, marketing requirements of a company. It was only through thorough research that these needs came to light. Once they had been confirmed as being important by the SodaStream management, it was relatively easy to create an imaginative programme that incorporated all of them.

16

Getting a meeting

When you have developed your sales strategy, decided on the companies that you will approach and completed your research, there comes that horrible moment of truth. It's time to draw a line under your preparation and start the real business of making contact with the decision makers, with the objective of setting up meetings.

I'm sure that few of you would disagree that one of the most difficult aspects of seeking sponsorship is to establish a meeting at an appropriate level within a company. Some of you might add that it is becoming equally difficult even to get to speak to that person on the phone, let alone arrange a meeting.

There are no hard-and-fast rules for succeeding at this stage of the selling process. A great deal depends on what you feel most comfortable doing and on what you find works best for you.

I know that many of you will really hate using the telephone to try to get that important first meeting. Don't worry too much about that. If you hate what you do, the chances are that you won't be very good at doing it, as in so many walks of life. It's all very well being told that if you practise often enough, you'll eventually become good, but some people just do not

have a telephone voice or manner that works for them. Short of engaging in some in very intense training, that will not change.

If you feel more comfortable making contact with a company by another means, then work really hard at that, and spend time creating effective variations that provide you with the best chance of being successful.

One way of doing this is to try to find someone who can introduce you to a specific company. If you intend approaching a local business, with a bit of initiative, it should be possible to find someone who deals with that company, perhaps a local supplier. Try to find a contact in that business who can give you some information about the company you are targeting. Don't be afraid to ask them if they'd mind you mentioning their name when you make contact, probably by letter or e-mail. This is much more difficult if you are approaching companies outside of your region.

If you're not going to use the phone to secure that important first meeting, then it is quite probable that you will choose to make contact by means of a letter, accompanied by some sort of presentation or brochure. While I am certainly not a believer in indiscriminate mail shots as an effective way of seeking sponsorship, I know that a personally tailored written approach to a company does work for some people.

In this age of digital online communication, there is something special about using a traditional letter as the means of communication. For a start, it will stand out. The number of letters that companies receive today is minimal. For that reason alone, there is a lot to be said for mailing or personally delivering a formal letter.

If you have the ability to write a letter in your own hand, that will be even more of a shock to a managing director or his PA. A word of warning, however: if your handwriting is not very good, don't do it!

A well-laid-out business letter, using a PC and printer can be just as effective, but make sure there are no spelling or grammatical mistakes. Make sure also that you use a high-quality paper and envelope.

If you intend taking this route, there are some important points to remember. As with any approach, the golden rule is that your sole objective should be to secure a meeting, not to try to sell the sponsorship in one step.

Unfortunately, you face one serious problem when you send a letter seeking a meeting. If it is too detailed, the chances are that a decision will be made based purely on the letter's content, without even speaking to you and giving you the chance to expand on your ideas. Whoever reads your letter is likely to look through it quickly, and unless something grabs

their attention straight away, they will put it in a pile along with all the others that generate an "I regret…" response.

On the other hand, if you don't provide enough information to arouse the reader's curiosity, more than likely your communication will generate a similar response. What you need to aim for is the very fine balance between the two.

Remember, your objective is to establish a meeting, or at worst, a phone conversation. It is not to try to sell the whole concept in one go.

When you send a letter, make sure that it's addressed to an individual within the business, not simply to "The Managing Director". If you can't find the correct name of the person to whom the letter should be sent, you really have a problem! If you can, also try to discover who is most likely to open it when it arrives. I have found that in most companies, a receptionist or secretary opens the mail and then sorts it into three piles:

1. Worth her boss reading.
2. Not worth her boss reading, but worth passing on to someone else.
3. For the bin.

This makes your task even more difficult. What you need to ask yourself is what you can do to make sure that the secretary does not put your communication on to that final pile?

It's not that she is being obstructive, far from it. I find that most PAs are very helpful if approached in the right manner. The problem is that the moment the word 'sponsorship' comes into play, mentally she may already be starting to put the letter on to that final pile. Consider why. She might have heard her boss tell colleagues that the sponsorship budget has already been allocated, or he might have told her specifically not to bother him with any sponsorship proposals for a while.

She is only doing her job: there are far more important things for her boss to worry about than yet another sponsorship proposal. Often, if she doesn't recognise the letter as coming from a high-profile club, association or even individual, at best she is likely to put it on the 'pass-on' pile, at worst, into the bin. If she passes it on, it could sit on someone else's desk for the next few weeks and nothing will happen. You may think me cynical, but I know that this is true.

What might stop her in her tracks? Well, there is one thing for sure: a letter that offers her company what is quite obviously a genuine business opportunity.

If the letter gives the impression that you are asking the company to give you money, no matter how you phrase it, your approach won't receive a high degree of interest. If, however, the letter starts by outlining an opportunity for the company to secure some business, there will be a reluctance on the secretary's

part to bin it; she is far more likely to bring it to someone's attention, even if this is done by putting the letter in someone else's in-tray.

The letter below is a hypothetical example of an initial sponsorship approach, aimed at whetting the company's appetite to find out more.

I want to stress that you should not in any way mislead the company. The basis of a letter of this type must be factual and totally genuine:

Fact » The team sponsor does spend that amount on wine for its hospitality facility.

Fact » There is an opportunity for the EURO WINE Company to secure this business.

Fact » It would be possible to arrange sampling and promotional opportunities.

For the attention of Mr Ken Walston

EURO WINES Ltd

Dear Mr Walston,

Last year, the primary sponsors of the Top Man Sportscar Team spent in excess of £120,000 on wine for use in the team's hospitality facility, which is operated at each round of the Le Mans Series. The hospitality is provided to representatives of the international media, to VIP guests of the sponsor and to their own staff attending the races.

I would very much appreciate the chance to meet with you to discuss an opportunity for your company to be the supplier of this wine requirement for next season. In addition, there is an innovative opportunity for you to set up a product sampling and promotional facility at each of the rounds, which take place in the UK, France, Belgium, Italy and Germany.

You will find enclosed some background information on the team, which also illustrates our superb hospitality facilities.

I look forward to meeting with you and discussing in more detail the business opportunities that are available to your company.

Kind regards,

It is also a fact that you want to present EURO WINES with the opportunity to become a team sponsor and enjoy a range of benefits that can be derived from that.

The business opportunity will depend on a sponsorship deal being agreed. However, you have highlighted the opportunity to do business and it is to be hoped whetted their appetite to find out more. Any marketing person worth their salt will realise that you are not presenting this opportunity out of the goodness of your heart. They will expect there to be a 'price' to pay.

Obviously not every sponsorship seeker will be able to provide such a clear-cut business opportunity, but the principle applies in most cases. You need to be creative, and the opening of your letter should present a strong business reason for them at least to want to find out more.

I learned a valuable lesson about writing sales letters early in my business career. In any letter or e-mail that you send, the least used word should be 'I' and the most used should be 'you', or a reference to the recipient's company. If you remember this, you'll go a long way to avoid sending out what I always call the 'gimme' letter. In an extreme form, this can best be compared to young children writing to Father Christmas, conveying a list of all the presents that they would like to receive.

The following example is typical of so many letters that I see. You might think this somewhat simplistic, and it is, but believe me, it is very representative.

Example

Dear Mr Smith,

Last year I won the Formula Ford Zetec regional championship. I was also voted the best young driver in the championship. I am keen to progress my career by moving into Formula 3 next season. I have been offered a drive with

the Radstock Formula 3 Team, considered the best team in the Championship.

I would like to offer your company the chance to sponsor my car. You will get a great deal of publicity in this way, as the Championship is shown on Channel 4.

I need to have a sponsor in place by the end of December, to be able to confirm my drive for next season with the team.

I have enclosed a DVD showing footage of my races this season and also a drawing of what the car will look like with your brand logo on it.

I hope that you find this of interest.

Yours sincerely,

If you count the number of times that 'I' is used and then compare it to the number of times 'you' appears, you'll see what I mean. It's not a healthy balance. As I pointed out, although they may contain a lot more information, hundreds of letters of this type are sent to potential sponsors every week. If it's any consolation, the poor standard of some of the communications and proposals emanating from what could be considered leading professional teams is quite amazing.

It is quite possible that your letter will be accompanied by a sales presentation of some sort, or even one of the innovative sales tools that we have looked at. The infamous bar of Kit Kat that I mentioned in an earlier chapter is a very good example. If you copy this example, just make sure that you don't send it during a hot summer. If you do, it might well undo any possible good effect by arriving as a gooey chocolate mess.

If you send anything, make sure it is in good taste (no pun intended). Remember, too, that what might seem funny to you might be irritating or even offensive to the person to whom you send it.

Another point: your letter should be fairly brief, using bullet-points where possible, as opposed to lengthy paragraphs. I can assure you that most business people do not have the time nor the inclination to read through anything that looks as if it might be tedious.

" A powerful opening paragraph is essential.

A powerful opening paragraph is essential. The difference between the following examples illustrates my point. These hypothetical letters are from the marketing manager of a rugby union association to a potential sponsor.

Letter 1

Dear Mrs Smith,

Last week, I read in Marketing that your company is launching a new product, a coffee drink in a can that can be heated at its point of use. Having seen how many thousands of spectators face arctic conditions on the terraces of the rugby clubs in our championship, week in, week out, your product would seem to have great potential.

I would like to suggest that we meet, to discuss ways in which your brand could be promoted in an innovative way through a relationship with this high-profile, televised championship. This could possibly include the opportunity to sell product at each stadium throughout the season...

Letter 2

Dear Mrs Smith,

I would like to introduce you to the Provincial Rugby Union Championship. This championship is competed for by 20 clubs, with the top four teams at the end of the season playing in a knock-out format to determine the winner. Among the top clubs playing in this championship are Reading, Bristol, Manchester and Portsmouth.

I would like to meet with you to discuss how you could become a sponsor of our championship as a way of promoting your new instant-heat coffee product....

In the first example, Mrs Smith's attention is immediately brought to bear on a potential benefit of an involvement with the rugby championship. It links what is obviously important to her, the new product, with a potential opportunity to promote and even sell it. By setting the scene, a cold day at a rugby match, it is designed to capture her imagination.

Unfortunately, the second example is far more typical of the letters that are sent to companies all the time, and that so often fail to get a response. Consider which you think is the most likely to get a response and then ask yourself why?

The problem with a letter is that unless you are able to follow up on the phone, within a few days, it is highly likely that you will either get a 'Dear John' type of letter in response, or no reaction at all. If you have decided to use a letter for your initial approach, because you don't like using the phone, therein lies a problem. How do you follow up? That is a definite problem.

A final point on letters: I suggested that if you hate using the phone, don't use it to contact companies. Well the same applies to letters. Unless you feel really confident that you can write a persuasive letter, I would strongly suggest that either you enlist the help of someone who can, or that you book yourself on a business letter writing course. There are several available. Believe me, it will be money well spent.

I'm sure you will agree that you don't stand a chance of securing a deal if you can't establish communication with the decision maker. Communication initially can be verbal, telephonic, written or electronic. What is important with any of these methods is that you must be able to grab the person's attention early on and create a desire in that person to want to know more. The idea of sending a packet of grass seeds, described earlier in the book, was an example of how innovative thinking can be used to gain interest.

In considering the best route to take, it may be helpful to look at the advantages and disadvantages of each method of approach.

Letters

If you don't feel confident about using the phone, this is an obvious option. A well-written letter to the correct person might just create the spark of interest you need to be invited to present your opportunity in more detail. However, I want to emphasise the words 'well-written'. If your letter doesn't grab the reader's interest within the first few lines, the chances are that it will go in the 'no thank you' pile.

I would suggest that as much as you don't feel comfortable using the phone to initiate a sales contact, its use in following up your original letter should be slightly less daunting. If you really do have a problem with using the phone, I can't really be of help. Almost certainly you will have to talk to someone on the phone at some stage of the sponsorship process, so I would suggest that either you get someone to help you with this, or go on a telephone sales course to help overcome some of your fears and difficulties.

E-mails

Moving on from letters, we come to the most popular method of communication today, the e-mail. I use this quite a lot, in conjunction with the telephone.

I find that more and more people do not like being bombarded with cold phone calls, which I can understand. An introductory e-mail softens the approach and gives the person to whom you have sent it time to prepare for your call.

Normally I use this method to introduce myself and briefly outline the reason why I would

like to arrange an initial phone conversation with the person. There is an obvious inherent danger that ultimately they might choose not to take the call once they know why you want to speak to them. That is a risk you take. It puts more importance on creating that powerful attention-grabber and on generating a desire to want to know more. If the person still doesn't want to speak to you after you have e-mailed them, then probably you would have had a tough job in securing a meeting if instead you had used the phone to make the approach.

If you have a website that you are happy to use as a reference point, it's always a good idea to provide a link to this in your introductory e-mail. I should add that if your site is not really up to standard, however, then don't draw attention to the fact by providing the link.

> **" A well-written letter to the correct person might just create the spark of interest you need to be invited to present your opportunity in more detail.**

Remember, with e-mails, your objective should be simply to secure a phone discussion or a meeting, not to try to sell the sponsorship.

At the risk of repeating myself, make sure that you use spell check before sending an e-mail, and check that the person's name is correct.

Finally: NO TEXT SPEAK!

Phone

The phone is an amazing instrument of communication. It does pose a few problems, however. As I touched on earlier, one of these is that an increasing number of companies, as well as company personnel, are isolating themselves from having to use it. You must have noticed the rise in the number of people who tend to hide behind voice-mail. In good faith, you leave a message, but how often is a call ever returned?

It's worth looking at the situation from the other side. Put yourself in the shoes of someone working in the marketing department of a company such as Vodafone. Imagine the number of calls that they receive every day, from people seeking sponsorship for one thing or another. Perhaps it's not surprising that they don't want to take them all.

Mind you, before you start getting all teary-eyed about the problems that large companies face in this respect, on the other side of the coin is the fact that we all have to put up with the volumes of unsolicited advertising that they throw at us every day, whether it be in the papers, magazines, direct mail, TV or, most annoyingly of all, on the Internet. So don't feel too guilty about approaching these people and badgering them until you do get to speak to a human being. You're not really doing anything different to what they do all the time. They are trying to sell their products and services; so are you.

> **Phones are notoriously bad at communicating enthusiasm.**

There is another problem with phones. Unless you are able to use a video-conferencing facility, it is impossible to read the body language of the person on the other end of the line, or to know how hard they are concentrating on what you are saying. For all you know, while holding the phone in one hand and carrying on a conversation with you, they could be completing a crossword with their other hand. You're hardly going to get 100 per cent of their attention that way.

Unfortunately, there is not a great deal that you can to about this, other than to ensure that you ask a lot of questions. From their answers, you should be able to get an idea of whether they are really listening to you.

There is another issue with using the phone that you need to be aware of. Phones are notoriously bad at communicating enthusiasm. If you talk on the phone in the same way that you might have a conversation in the street

with a friend, very often it will come across to the person on the other end as being rather toneless. What I mean by this is that when you are face to face with a person, usually you can see emotion in their expression. As a result, it is not necessary for them to make the effort with their voice as well. On a phone, you don't have that luxury, so you must try to put emotion into your voice, emphasising changes in tone and pitch to make it interesting.

It is a good idea to record yourself when you make phone calls and then play them back. If you are honest with yourself, you'll probably be quite surprised at how monotonic and flat you sound. This is an aspect you can work on quite easily to improve your performance.

Finally, don't forget to thank people when you use the phone. I know I'm repeating myself, but it is so important in this business. I never cease to be appalled at the phone manners of so many people who call me to try to sell me something. I'm sure that in most cases they don't mean to sound rude, arrogant or forceful, but that's how they come across. On some occasions, if you're lucky, you get a muttered "thanks", which sounds as though it is costing them money to use it, but there is no sincerity evident.

Put in the effort and practice that is required to make your calls sound interesting, enthusiastic, and sincere, but relaxed, and I promise you that you'll soon see a different reaction from the other person. It might not turn a 'no' into a 'yes', but it will make your calls less fractious, and you will be more relaxed as a result.

We've now looked at the three basic means of making contact. There are others, of course, but I would see them as being variations of the main three.

Let me describe the way of making initial contact that has worked extremely well for me over the years. There is no guarantee that it will work for everyone, however, as we are all very different. It has taken me a while to perfect my system to the point where it works more often than it fails. So if you are going to try it out, don't expect instant results. Almost certainly it will take some time to find out how best to use it to suit your own telephone style.

I put together my first ever sponsorship deal in 1974. Since then, I have lost count of the number of companies that I have approached for sponsorship of one kind or another. I suppose it must be getting on for 2,000, and I'm talking about companies with which I have at least made contact at a meaningful level. That would make my conversion rate about 27:1. In other words, to secure a sponsorship deal, I need to make contact with at least 27 companies.

That's an awful lot of rejections, so if you can come up with a better way of making contact that reduces the ratio, please give me a call. I'm always looking for ways to improve.

I use the following method when I find it difficult to make contact with a decision maker in a company, or when I need to find out who really does make the decisions. It's incredibly simple and straightforward, so obvious in fact that it always amazes me that more people don't use it. When you've read through it, many of you will immediately think that you're already doing exactly what I propose. On the few occasions when I have mentioned it to a colleague, they tell me that they have done exactly the same. It's only when I start to probe a little bit deeper about the way in which they use this method that I find that actually they only scratch the surface.

I suppose that I use this method of making contact in about 65 per cent of my approaches to companies. So what is it?

What I do is make direct contact with the person whom I believe to be the best source of knowledge within the company. That person is the PA or secretary. Before I offend anyone, for literary purposes, I will refer to this person as 'her', although I do realise that there are many excellent male secretaries and PAs.

> **When I call the switchboard of the company, I don't ask to be put through to Mr Prospect. Instead, I ask for his PA, asking her name at the same time.**

Now, I can already hear some of you saying that you always speak to the PA, and that by being really polite in asking her to put you through to her boss, you're already using my method. Please bear with me a little longer.

In most medium- to large-size companies, the decision maker invariably has a PA. It is almost inevitable that you will speak to her before you are able to secure a phone conversation or a meeting with her boss. This is where I go about my task in a different way to many sponsorship seekers. They will usually phone the switchboard and ask for Mr Prospect, the decision maker. If they are lucky, they will be put through to the person's PA. Polite as they may be to her, their objective will still be the same: to speak to the prospect. This is where the difficulties often begin.

Mr Prospect's PA tells you that he is busy and asks if she can help. At this point, some people will briefly explain that they want to talk to him about a really beneficial sponsorship opportunity and ask when he will be free. Some callers don't even do that, taking the attitude that it's none of her business and telling her that they will call back. Some might ask if it is possible for Mr Prospect to call them.

Knowing that it is increasingly difficult to get through to senior personnel within a company, when phoning for the first time, I will take a different tack. When I call the switchboard of the company, I don't ask to be put through to Mr Prospect. Instead, I ask for his PA, asking her name at the same time. The chances are that I would be put through to her anyway, but at least now I have her name, which is important for the next step.

Now, put yourself in the shoes of that PA.

The phone on your desk rings and you answer it. The caller introduces himself or herself. You don't recognise the name. As with most of the calls that you take, you expect the caller to ask to speak to Mr Prospect. As your job is to protect him from unwanted calls, you prepare to go into defensive mode.

What you expect doesn't happen, however.

Instead of the typical "Good morning, can I please speak to Mr Prospect?" when you pick up the phone, there is a different approach:

"Am I speaking to Jo Stevens, Mr Prospect's PA?"

Yes, you confirm, rather surprised that the caller knows your name.

"That's good. You're the very person that I wanted to speak to. May I have a couple of minutes of your time, as I would very much appreciate your advice?"

Now you're thinking that this isn't going the way that most calls go. You agree to help if you can.

"As PA to the marketing director of the XYZ Company, you probably have your finger on the pulse of what goes on in the company better than most people."

A little flattered, you smile and make some appropriate non-committal reply.

"When it is convenient, I would like to present what I hope is an interesting marketing opportunity to Mr Prospect, which has sport as its catalyst. At the appropriate time, I would very much like to meet with Mr Prospect, and hopefully yourself, to identify areas of this opportunity that might be of interest to your company. As his PA, you obviously know the best way of presenting this to him. What I would like to suggest is that I send through an initial e-mail to you, rather than Mr Prospect,

so that you can gain an insight into the opportunity. I'd then very much appreciate your thoughts on the matter. You might also have some suggestions as to how to fine-tune this to make it even more relevant. At that stage, if you could suggest the best way of presenting this to Mr Prospect, it would be really helpful."

What do you think is going through the PA's mind now? For a start, she will probably be quite surprised at your approach. You haven't treated her as an obstacle that has to be overcome, which unfortunately is a fairly regular occurrence in her capacity.

Secondly, you've involved her in the business opportunity that you want to present to Mr Prospect. It's not often that sales people credit her with having the understanding of what their business opportunities might offer her company.

Thirdly, you have treated her with respect and shown that you value her opinion.

Finally, you have shown respect for her boss's time, which is important to her.

It's been my experience that in a high number of cases, if approached in this way, the PA will do whatever she can to help you and bring the opportunity to the attention of her boss. Instead of walking into his office and saying,

"I spoke to a salesman on the phone who is looking for sponsorship for his motor racing. We're not interested are we?"

That is something that happens only too often. If you treat the PA in the manner suggested, she might approach it in a different way:

"I've been in discussion with a person who contacted me a couple of days ago with what looks like an interesting sponsorship proposal. It would give us the opportunity to perhaps launch our new product at a major sports

exhibition that's taking place at the NEC in January.

"I asked him to send the information through to me, which he did, and I think it might be worthwhile you talking to him. Here's the communication that he sent in, which I've marked up with a couple of other points that he added at my suggestion. Shall I set up a provisional meeting with him for you?"

I'm not saying that every PA will be as helpful as that, but over the years I have been amazed at just how many can be of assistance. A lot depends on your sincerity. If you come across as a bit of a 'smoothie', you won't get very far, but if you treat her genuinely as being important within the decision making process, hopefully it will have a beneficial effect. The relationship between a PA and her boss is very often extremely close from a business point of view. If she is on your side, she can prove to be very influential and powerful within an organisation.

Very often, if I don't get any joy within an organisation and can't even get to speak to the marketing or the sales director's PA, I will go right to the very top and ask to speak to the CEO's PA. By adopting a similar approach, I'll encourage her to suggest a person to whom I should be talking. Then she might tell me that the person who handles such matters is Mr Brown, the communications director.

My next step is to ask her the name of Mr Brown's PA. Having discovered this, I will ask the CEO's PA if it would be possible for her to contact Mr Brown's PA and explain that we have had a conversation, adding that I will be phoning her to arrange a meeting. In most cases, I have found that if the CEO's PA, at the top of the secretarial hierarchy, contacts another in this way, it adds great weight to my subsequent phone call.

The network of PAs in a company can be very helpful if you learn how to work it to your

advantage and go about this in a professional manner, not like a 'jack-the-lad'.

IMPORTANT: When you do this, it always pays to go back to the people who have helped you and thank them, informing them of progress.

This all might seem a long-winded way of establishing a meeting, but I can assure you that it has worked for me so many times, that it has to have something going for it. In companies ranging from FedEx to Gillette, and from Marconi to AutoGlass, the help that I have had from PAs has been vital in my success.

> **" In companies ranging from FedEx to Gillette, and from Marconi to AutoGlass, the help that I have had from PAs has been vital in my success.**

Interestingly, when I concluded the deal with Gillette that saw them become a sponsor of the Benetton F1 team, I received a lot of assistance from the secretary to the president of Gillette, Europe. Her name was Barbara Gel and she retired shortly before I wrote this book. I took her out to lunch one day and she told me that she had worked for no fewer than 16 presidents of that company. No wonder she knew her way around the organisation better than just about anyone else. She also told me that I was one of the very few sponsorship sales people who had made any effort to involve her in the process, for which she thanked me. Amazing!

Follow-up

Whichever way you've gone about making contact, the next step has to be a follow-up, hopefully to arrange that much sought-after meeting. Unfortunately for those of you who don't like using the phone, this is another part of the job where use of the telephone is almost mandatory.

One of the reasons I like to involve a PA in my approach to a company is that it provides me with a point of contact to go back to if I feel I am not making any progress. On many an

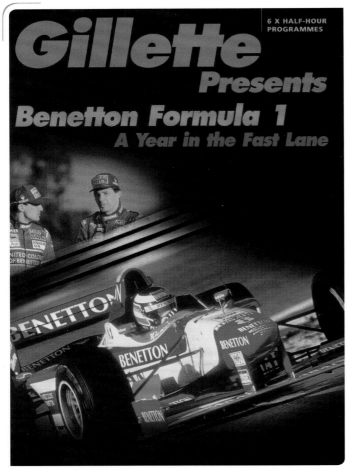

6 X HALF-HOUR PROGRAMMES

Gillette Presents

Benetton Formula 1

A Year in the Fast Lane

↗ Brian secured a high-profile deal for Benetton F1 with Gillette, based on the innovative provision of low-cost TV global advertising.

put through to their PA. If you are, remember that she probably receives a couple of dozen letters, minimum, per day, so don't expect her to remember your name.

When she answers, tell her your name, the date when you sent the letter and a very brief outline of what it was about. Then you need to ask her if she knows whether it has yet been read by the person concerned. If it has, you need to get to speak to that person. If it hasn't, you must ask her when you should call again.

Assuming that you are put through to the right person, if you don't expect a particularly communicative response when they take the call, probably you won't be disappointed. The onus will be very much on you to take the lead.

Before we get to the conversation, as I've pointed out many times, *do not try to sell the sponsorship over the phone*.

If you do, the chances are that you'll receive a negative response. What you should be doing is attempting to whet the appetite of the person sufficiently that they will be happy to meet you to find out more about the opportunity. I know that this isn't an easy thing to do. In fact, it's very tough.

When eventually you reach the person you asked for, it's natural to want to include as many of the potential benefits as possible in the short time that you will be given on the phone. You plough ahead, hoping that one of them might just hit the spot. Soon, you have no cards left to play, so probably the decision will be made over the phone, without you ever getting a meeting. If that is the case, it probably won't go in your favour. Don't give out all of the information over the phone.

So how do you progress the call?

The first rule is to avoid asking direct questions that can be answered with a "Yes" or "No", such as:

occasion, I have phoned the PA with whom I started the process and she has done the chasing up on my behalf. That doesn't always mean that it will be good news, however. A PA will often tell you that the answer is 'no', but even that is better than simply waiting for a letter or a phone call that never comes.

If you've written a letter to the company, or sent an e-mail, obviously you will need to follow up with the person to whom it was addressed. That may well mean that you are

"Did you find the sponsorship opportunity outline that I sent you interesting?"

Rather, ask a question that requires some input. This would usually start with "How", "Why", "What", "Where", "Which" or "When":

"Which features of the outline that I sent through to you particularly appealed?"

"When would be a good time to get together to look at the options in more detail?"

"How would you feel about the potential interest from the education sector?"

Although it is possible to come up with a blunt and negative response to this type of question, that is far less likely. Your intention should be to get the prospect to open up and provide you with an insight into their requirements.

It is very likely that if you do get the conversation moving along, at some stage you will be asked:

"How much are we talking about, cost wise?"

Opinions differ on what your response should be. Do you avoid giving out this information or should you be totally open about it? Much as I would like to give you a straight, uncompromising answer, that's difficult to do. A lot depends on the sponsorship property involved.

Although many people will disagree, I prefer to be quite up-front with a person, even at this stage, because it can save me a great deal of time and effort. I would rather know early on that their budget won't stretch to even the lowest-cost sponsorship option, than go through a long-winded process, only to find out at the end that they can't afford to be involved. Even then, it could be argued that if I were to enthuse them enough, they might find the money. That's true and there may be a few occasions when I will do that, but only when I am very sure that this could be the case. If I

really want that company on board, perhaps to put a multi-dimensional strategy together, I will be more flexible.

Most of the time, however, I choose to be up-front about cost, but only in the broadest terms. I don't get into a detailed discussion about the fee involved and what entitlements they will get for that fee. I am still only trying to secure a meeting, not do a deal over the phone.

If pushed, normally I prefer to outline the approximate starting point financially for a sponsor. First, however, I will explain that as the sponsorship programme will be tailored to suit their identified marketing requirements, it is difficult to put a price on it at this stage until we have selected the range of entitlements that they feel are essential.

❝ It is my experience that if a prospect insists on wanting to know the costs, he will become very irritated if you aren't up-front with him.

If they don't have a problem with that and are happy to move on without pushing the point, fine. Nevertheless, they might still insist on a guideline figure, in which case I will tell them what the lowest and highest fees might be.

It is my experience that if a prospect insists on wanting to know the costs, he will become very irritated if you aren't up-front with him. It will be assumed that you have something to hide and, in many cases, prospects can't be bothered to play games, which is how they see it. Tell them the range of fees, but don't go any further than that if you can avoid it.

How do you bring your phone conversation to a successful conclusion? One way is to provide the prospect with a range of dates when you could arrange a meeting:

"I'm in Chester next week and could be available on either Tuesday or Thursday, or would Monday the 17th be suitable?"

If you come across as though you expect to get a meeting, it will be far better than sounding hesitant and nervous.

You may be asked to provide the person with more information before they are prepared to meet you. Obviously this isn't the ideal situation, as it means that you have lost the advantage of direct communication. You should still push for a face-to-face meeting, however, by explaining that you would like to run through that information personally to avoid any confusion.

If the prospect still won't agree to a meeting, sending the information does provide you with the opportunity to continue your discussion at some stage in the following few days. It's better than being told that the company isn't interested. Try to agree a date with the prospect when you will phone him to follow up on the material that you have sent. Even that is a form of commitment and worth trying to achieve.

In this chapter, we set out to find the most effective ways of making contact with a company. I have outlined the method that works best for me, but there are many other ways of achieving the objective of a meeting with the decision maker. My advice is that, within reason, any innovative way you can come up with to secure a meeting with the appropriate person is worth trying. There are no hard-and-fast rules in this business. In my opinion, if it works, it's good. If it doesn't, at least you have tried.

Summary
→ There are several ways by which you can make your initial sales approach to a company. These include:
  → Letter
  → E-mail
  → Telephone
→ You need to be honest with yourself about the methods with which you are least comfortable. That doesn't mean that you shouldn't try to improve your skills in those areas. It does mean that whatever method

you decide to use, it should be worked on until it is as effective as you can make it.
→ Whatever method you use, it is important to remember that you are not going to sell the sponsorship at the first attempt. Your objective should be to secure either a meeting or a meaningful telephone conversation with a person at the appropriate level within the company.
→ If you decide to communicate initially by letter, you will need to create a powerful, attention grabbing opening paragraph.
→ Make sure that there are no spelling or grammatical errors in the letter.
→ Always address the letter to an individual.
→ If you send e-mails, make sure they are used only to introduce yourself, prior to a telephone follow-up.
→ Take as much trouble to check the spelling in an e-mail as in a letter.
→ Your letter should refer to 'you' more often than 'I'.
→ If you use the phone, it is worth practising with a voice recorder to ensure that you speak with the right level of pitch and tone. Enthusiasm and a smile do come across on the phone.
→ The secretaries in a company can be extremely helpful if you approach them in the right manner. Involve them in what you are trying to achieve and try to excite them about your sponsorship opportunity.
→ Remember to thank people who have helped you and to inform them of progress.
→ Be prepared to answer questions about the sponsorship fee. Don't try to be evasive when replying, as it can irritate the prospect. If you have calculated the fee as shown earlier, you have nothing to feel embarrassed about.
→ Remember at all times that you are not trying to sell the sponsorship over the phone, only the idea of a meeting.

One chance to create a first impression

You might be surprised when I tell you that, in my opinion, we've covered the most difficult steps in the entire marketing strategy. I have always found that the research, preparation and salesmanship necessary to secure a meeting with the decision maker are the hardest parts of the sponsorship sales process.

Once you're sitting in front of the person whom you targeted, you've achieved a worthwhile level of success, because if there had been absolutely no interest on their part in your sponsorship proposal, you wouldn't be there. It is very rare for people to waste their time going through the motions of a meeting unless they have a reasonably open mind about its possible outcome.

When you are face to face with the person whom you need to convince, so many advantages come into play. For a start, you can observe reaction on the person's face. This makes a huge difference and helps you gauge the impact of what you are putting across. Then there is body language. If you can learn to read body language, it can prove extremely useful in this type of situation. In some circumstances,

you might even be able to learn more about the person to whom you are talking by looking around their office. You'll be surprised how many senior executives personalise their office, providing you with great opportunities to store the information and use it when appropriate. You might see that the prospect has several photos of them sailing, or perhaps there is a professional qualification diploma on the wall. This type of information can be very helpful in building a rapport.

Before considering what happens once you're in that first meeting, it's important to understand the need to prepare properly. I know that what I will run through now will seem very basic to many, but there will be plenty of others who haven't had much experience in this area. So I'll go briefly through the guidelines that might stop you from making some of the mistakes that I've been guilty of in the past.

As obvious as this may seem, make sure you know where to go for your meeting. I've arrived at the main entrance of a large company on time, only to find that the marketing department is in a separate building over half a mile away. It was my own fault because I hadn't bothered to confirm beforehand where I should go. As a result, by the time I got to the right office, I was ten minutes late and far from relaxed.

Punctuality is important. It shows respect for your prospect's time. There are few acceptable excuses for being late, because most eventualities can be foreseen. Checking out where to park is one of them; traffic hold-ups are another. You know that there is a good chance of congestion on the roads, so allow for it.

> ## Punctuality is important.
> ## It shows respect for your prospect's time.

Rather, get to the address early and pop into a coffee shop, read the paper for a few minutes and relax. In that way, you'll arrive in the right state of mind.

What to wear for a meeting is a very personal choice, and I wouldn't dream of telling anyone how to dress for the situation. If you're visiting an advertising agency, for example, it is likely that the staff will be dressed very casually. On the other hand, if you are meeting senior personnel in an insurance business, the chances are that they'll be in more formal business attire, such as suits.

However, there is an old, but very well proven adage: you get one chance to create a first impression. Remember that! You're there to present a business proposal, so why not look businesslike? You're not there to make a fashion statement. That doesn't mean that you can't be individualistic, but bear in mind that

you could be meeting people who may be a lot older and have a more formal outlook than yourself.

Whatever your style of dress, there is no excuse for dirty shoes! When you're in a meeting, shoes are very often highly visible, and the good impression given by really smart attire will be ruined by shoes that haven't seen polish for years.

When I've run training seminars based on the contents of this book, I've had several people get a little hot under the collar when we start talking about the way that you turn up for what is effectively a sales appointment. They tell me that today it's an individual's right to dress how they like and that it is discriminatory for people to take offence.

My view is very straightforward. They may be right, but so what if they are? What will it achieve? The person whom they are trying to convince to agree to their sponsorship proposal may also agree with them. Then again, they may not, so why take the chance? I can tell you that I've never lost a deal by turning up for a meeting with a decision maker, dressed either in a suit or a jacket and tie.

It's difficult enough to get a meeting in the first place, so why take the risk that you might upset the prospect by trying to make a statement? The same applies to women: don't overdo the short skirt or low-cut blouse. You might think you're looking a bit special, but will the person whom you're meeting agree? Don't increase the risks, reduce them.

While on the subject of appearance, I used to have a moustache and short beard. I recall having lunch with the president of Gillette after concluding a sizeable F1 sponsorship deal with the shaving division of the company. He told me, with a smile on his face, that I was the first salesperson who had come into his office with a beard, taken a few million dollars off him and walked out, still with a beard!

Beards are okay, but make sure they are well trimmed.

What other preparation can you make? You should have worked out your strategy already, based on the research that you've done, so you need to make sure that you have all of the materials you need, with copies to leave with the prospect. Make sure you have business cards that are clean and not dog-eared, and a notebook and pen. Don't laugh! You'd be surprised at how many people arrive at a meeting and have to ask for a writing implement.

When you get to the company, it's always worth visiting the cloakroom to check your appearance. I remember interviewing a girl who had a large piece of green vegetable wedged firmly between her front teeth. I found it very distracting, and when later she discovered what she had done, she was probably highly embarrassed.

A small tip: if you are really nervous before the meeting, it's a good idea to hold your wrists under a cold tap for a minute or two. It will help cool you down and relax you.

The first couple of minutes of the meeting can easily dictate how the rest of it will develop. It's important, for example, to appear relaxed when you meet your prospect. That doesn't mean a big cheesy grin, but remember that if your nervousness becomes apparent, it might rub off on the other person. It's always a good idea to thank them for taking the time to see you when you first meet.

The most important thing of all is that you need to take control of the way the meeting starts. Almost certainly you will have asked for the meeting, so the onus is on you as to the way it starts. Don't just sit there waiting for the other person to make the running. It may be that the prospect will be keen to put you at ease and will make a few general remarks about the weather, your journey or something of this nature. It's okay to take advantage of this for a

brief period, but be careful not to overdo it. Try to bring it around to business as soon as you feel that it's polite to do so. I always rehearse my opening gambit in the car on the way to a meeting. I put together a couple of sentences that often end with a question. I do this so that I can steer the meeting in the direction that I want it to go. A lot of people whom you meet will disrupt your plans by asking a difficult question right at the beginning. That can easily throw you, so you have to get in first. Here are a couple of examples of the sorts of opening I use:

"First of all Mrs Smith, thank you for taking the time to meet with me this afternoon. I thought it might be helpful for you if I ran very briefly through the background to the sponsorship opportunity that I would like to present to you, and then we could look in more detail at the areas that you feel could be of particular interest."

Or

"Mr Jones, I very much appreciate the opportunity to discuss with you ways in which one of our championship's events might play a role in promoting the launch of your new brand. It would be really helpful if you could briefly outline your thinking on the targeting of this brand. Where do you see the main interest coming from?"

In both cases, what you are doing is taking control and leading the discussion in the way that you want it to go. This will also take away that worry of not knowing how to get the meeting under way.

From this point on, it is quite difficult to guide you through the meeting, because the situation will vary considerably depending upon the sponsorship property that you are selling.

However, there are many points that we can look at that might help you bring the meeting to a successful conclusion. By successful, I don't necessarily mean that you walk away with a positive decision on the proposed deal. It's fairly unusual for that to happen during the first meeting. You should be looking to find out if there are enough potential benefits to the prospect to form the basis of a sponsorship agreement. In effect, your objective is to find enough common ground that you both consider it worthwhile moving to the next step. That next step might well be a meeting with other people in the company, or it might be a visit to your premises, if that is appropriate.

I have always found that one of the best ways to move a meeting along and gather vital information is to ask questions. What you shouldn't do is bore the poor prospect rigid with a long spiel about how good you are in your particular sport, or effectively to tell him how stupid he would be to turn down such a great opportunity. We've seen how important it is to create a situation in which the prospect doesn't feel that he is being sold to, or even told what is going to be good for him.

Think how you feel about being told that something is good for you. What is your reaction when you have been feeling a little unwell and a friend or family member insists that they have just the thing that will make you feel better?

"A sore throat, you say? I know exactly what will make you feel better. It's an old recipe that my grandma swore by. Sit down and I'll make some up and bring to over to you."

Well intentioned as the person may be, you immediately feel a resistance to the solution. Had it been phrased differently, you might have reacted in another way.

"A sore throat, you say? Are you taking anything for it? Would it help if I told you of a remedy that I've been taking for a couple of years now?"

Here is a similar example, but this time in a business meeting.

"A new product launch, you say? This sponsorship opportunity that I am offering you is just what you need to create a high level of publicity."

"Really? So you know more than I do about what I need," mutters the prospect to himself.

Structured in a different way, the response might be more positive.

"A new product launch, you say? That's interesting. From what we've discussed so far, which aspects of this sponsorship opportunity do you feel might be helpful in promoting the brand to your target audience?"

The power of carefully worded questions is immense in a selling situation. But there is one cardinal sin that everyone makes on far too many occasions, and not only in business. We ask a question, but we don't listen to the answer! Instead, we are too busy thinking of what we are going to say next. By doing so, we make two major mistakes.

First, we don't hear what is being said to us, because we only bother to listen to half the answer. Secondly, we fall into the trap of making assumptions in respect of our response. We think we know what the answer to our question is going to be by the time the prospect is halfway through replying, so we base our response on that. In many cases, we assume wrongly.

If you are going to pose questions, you are wasting your time if you don't listen to what the prospect is telling you.

What you should be trying to achieve in this first meeting is to establish a dialogue between you and the prospect, not a monologue from either of you. If you go about this in the right way, you can hold a conversation with the other person that makes both of you feel comfortable and relaxed, without stress, knowing that you are simply exploring opportunities that may or may not be beneficial to their company.

In other words, I put the ball firmly in the prospect's court. Then I do something that doesn't come easily to salespeople. I shut up!

I have talked about the power of questions; the power of silence is also very effective. If you ask a question, wait for an answer. It is easy to wait for a second or two, but it becomes slightly more difficult to sit there for much longer without feeling embarrassed by the fact that no one is speaking. Persevere with it. It is surprising what develops if you are prepared to wait.

Too often a salesperson will jump in just as the prospect is quietly considering his response and make some comment that can change the entire direction of the sales process. That critical moment when the prospect could be coming to a positive conclusion is lost. The pressure that effectively you were exerting has been released. Putting it bluntly, you need to learn when to shut up!

Ask a leading question and then keep quiet. Don't be the first to speak. The pressure on the other person becomes quite considerable. If you use this tactic sparingly, it can be very powerful:

"Mr Brown, is there any reason why we can't move forward on this?"

"Mrs Black, you've agreed that this opportunity can provide you with a great platform for your marketing activities next year. What's the next step, from your point of view?"

On the subject of keeping quiet, we all know people who talk across others when in conversation. They might ask you a question, but mid-way through your answer, they dive in with a comment, or they show through their body language that they can't wait for you to finish so that they can have their say. It is obvious that they aren't listening to what you have to say and are far more interested in their own opinions. It can be very irritating, so don't make that same mistake yourself.

Nearly every question that you are likely to ask within the framework of a sales meeting with a prospect will fit into one of the listed categories. What you need to do is continually practise developing an awareness of the reason why you are asking a particular question. Then you should mentally classify it under one of the categories that I've just outlined. In that way, you will keep control of the flow of the meeting, by knowing just where you are in the logical progress from 'identification' to 'commitment'. You will be able to bring the conversation back to where you want it at any stage of this process should you be taken off-track by a question or opinion that the prospect raises that is out of sequence.

❝ Ask a leading question and then keep quiet. Don't be the first to speak. The pressure on the other person becomes quite considerable.

This might seem a rather tedious process, but it has helped me considerably. It comes back to Michael Schumacher and his ability to win grands prix by implementing a smarter strategy than his rivals. He was always aware during the race just where he was in relation to the planned strategy. If another team disrupted his race by changing its fuel-stop strategy, for example, he was still able to adapt to that quickly, because of the fact that he was in control of his own strategy.

In the same way, you should be able to steer your dialogue with the prospect back on course by asking a question from the category where you feel you should be. No matter how many questions he has thrown at you during the period when the conversation has gone in a different direction, you should still feel confident that you are in control.

Summary

→ It is important to have a strategy for your meeting, so that you know where you are at any time in respect of your objectives.
→ The use of questions will be far more effective if they fit into a 'route map' so that they always have a purpose.
→ Your questions can be categorised under the following headings:
→ Identification
→ Needs awareness
→ What if?
→ Solution
→ Qualification
→ Commitment
→ If you are aware of the category each question falls under, this will help guide you to the final stage, which is the commitment from the prospect to the next step in the sales process.
→ The power of silence can be a very effective way of applying pressure. You ask a question and then you shut up until the other person answers.

19

The lost art of listening

I've gone on at length about the power of questions. I've also emphasised the need to listen to the answers, but it might come as a surprise to you that now I am going to spend some time looking at how you can listen more effectively.

You might wonder how you can learn anything about listening. Surely you just keep your mouth shut and your ears open. What is there to discuss?

Well, for a start, you can hear what is being said without taking on board the information that is being communicated to you. Have you ever sat in a room where the radio is switched on, broadcasting a programme in which people are involved in a conversation? You want to read the paper, so you start browsing through it. The radio is still on and the conversation is in full swing. You become so engrossed in a particular article in the paper, however, that effectively you close your mind to the sound of the voices. Although you heard every word, you didn't actually listen to what was being said.

Think about the conversations that you have in business, or even socially. You ask someone a question. Can you honestly say that you always listen intently to the answer, or are you like most of us, too intent on thinking what

your next question is going to be? If you are guilty of that, then you can't be focusing all of your attention on what the person is telling you. Similarly, you can ask a question, yet be so convinced that you know what the answer will be, that you don't really listen to what is being said.

On another occasion, you might ask a question and misunderstand what the answer actually means. This can lead to major problems further down the road in the sales process.

If you don't believe what I am saying, you need only to listen to other people's conversations, perhaps on a bus or train. Often what you will realise is that actually more than one conversation is going on. Although both individuals might be asking questions, they are so intent on capping what the other person is saying that they hardly hear the answers.

Asking a question, listening to the answer and responding, not to what you think will be said, but to what has actually been said is a very difficult skill to acquire. Few of us do it well. If you can master the technique, however, you will notice that not only does the conversation flow more easily and in a far more relaxed style than previously, but also that people will be happy to talk to you because they realise that you are genuinely interested in what they are saying. That is rare, particularly in the selling business.

As I explained, one of the problems that often arise from not listening properly is that you misunderstand the information that is being fed to you. If you are going to build a strong case for your sponsorship proposals, it must be able to satisfy the needs of the company. If you haven't fully understood what those needs are, as a result of not listening properly, you could find yourself on very thin ice later. If you are given some detailed information, or perhaps a complex opinion on a subject, by your prospect, you need to be sure that you understand not only what they are saying, but also what they mean. You can achieve this by repeating the information, preceded by the words:

"Mr Prospect, if I understand correctly, what you are saying is that…"

Or

"Can I just run through that again with you, to make sure I fully understand what you are saying?"

Provided that you don't do this too often, not only will you have a better understanding of what you are being told, but also you will gain the respect of the other person. They will feel that you are actually listening to them and not simply going through the motions of listening.

The whole point about asking questions and listening effectively to the answers is that it can provide you with some really valuable information. The more relevant information you can extract from a prospect, the greater the chance you will have of matching the features of your property to the requirements of his company. In other words, you will have a greater opportunity of achieving a sale. Unfortunately, while many salespeople will ask questions at first, very often they will fail to keep probing once they receive an initial response.

Here's an example. You are in conversation with the marketing director of a potential sponsor. It is your first meeting with her and you are trying to identify areas of interest:

"Mrs Newcombe, how helpful would it be to use this proposed sponsorship as the basis of a sales incentive programme?"

"Yes, that could possibly work," she responds.

"What about the chance to entertain clients?"

At that point, you move on to seek further areas of interest, thinking that you have gone as far as you need at this stage.

I would suggest that you shouldn't move on after her initial response to your question about sales incentives. Instead, I would probe a little deeper, to see if I can encourage her to expand on her response and to explain why this would be important.

"Yes, that could possibly work," she tells you.

"So how would you go about using the opportunity?"

"Well, I know our sales director is always trying to come up with innovative ideas for creating sales incentives for our sales team."

"Have any of these been based on a sponsorship programme in the past?"

"No, I don't think so."

"How successful have they been?"

"I believe that their effectiveness has tailed off over the last couple of programmes that he devised."

"How might the link to a company sponsorship help improve this?"

"Why don't you tell me?" she asks, providing you with a great opportunity.

In the process, you have discovered something important. Although apparently she agreed that the opportunity to use the sponsorship as the basis for a sales-incentive programme could be helpful, there was an underlying problem. By probing, you were able to discover that the sales director had a problem inasmuch as his incentive schemes obviously weren't working as well as they should. This has given you the chance to demonstrate how your sponsorship opportunity could help change the situation.

Had you accepted on face value her initial agreement, it may not have come to light until it was too late that she was only paying lip service to the potential effectiveness of sales-incentive opportunities. By probing further than you might normally do, you will often find that a person's true feelings will come to the surface. Not only will this help you identify possible problem areas of which you might have been unaware, but also it can often provide a real opportunity to gain a meaningful, rather than a token commitment from your prospect.

It's a tactic that I use a great deal. I find that by probing in this way, not only am I able to unearth a lot more information, but also very often a person's true feelings come to the surface.

You will have gathered by now, that I am a great believer in the power of questions and in the power of listening effectively. These are two of the most important skills that you can possess when you are face to face with a prospective sponsor. There is another aspect of your sales meeting that I want to look at, however, which I feel is also an area that can cause some problems if it isn't handled properly.

When we examined the various items that you can take with you into a meeting to enhance and support what you are presenting, I stressed that they should not be used as a crutch, in place of dialogue or discussion. Sales tools should be there to help you present your case, not to present it for you.

Knowing when to bring them into play is something that is very difficult to learn. It tends to come from experience. You might have spent £10,000 on a CD-ROM video presentation, but if you find that you are in a meaningful dialogue with your prospect, why break that off to bring out your laptop and run the programme? It could easily be counter-productive. If you genuinely feel that the best way to demonstrate a point, or to present your ideas, is to bring that into play, that's fine, but use your judgement on this very carefully.

> **Sales tools should be there to help you present your case, not to present it for you.**

The most likely sales tool that you will want to use is your sales presentation. Perhaps it's a PowerPoint programme, or maybe you have a flipchart style of presentation. Whatever you have decided to use, the way in which you bring it into play can make a big difference to the effectiveness of the presentation.

In my experience, most salespeople use one of two methods. The first is to run through it from A to Z, in the manner that many insurance and financial services salespeople use when they visit people in their homes. Alternatively, you can make the presentation interactive, involving the other person as you move through it.

I prefer the latter style. The problem with the first method is that effectively you are telling the prospect to keep quiet while you perform! The last thing that I want at this stage is quiet prospects. I want them to be doing more talking than me.

I want to hear their thoughts, their opinions, their ideas and most of all I want their confirmation on the points that I am covering. It's only by getting them to talk to you that you will discover whether you are heading in the right direction. Having said that, there is a huge difference between your prospect interacting with you as you move though the presentation, and taking over and interrupting everything that you are trying to say. You still need to be in control.

> ❝ **The last thing that I want at this stage is quiet prospects. I want them to be doing more talking than me.**

The way that I like to handle this situation is by putting questions to the prospect as I move through the slides. We come back to the use of questions again. These are just as important at this stage, as in the dialogue that you have before and after the presentation.

For example, when you get to the point in your presentation that deals with the range of possible entitlements, you might ask:

"How helpful would it be to your sales force to be able to bring potential customers to our Formula 1 HQ to see the use of your software in our design office?"

Or

"How would you use the number of player personal appearance days that you would be entitled to?"

When you are going through the media coverage section, you might enquire:

"Which section of the media is most important for your type of business?"

Or

"How important would regional TV coverage be to you?"

In this way, not only do you keep control of the direction in which you want the presentation to go, but also you continue to build a picture of what is and what isn't important to your prospect. This will help you greatly when you come to putting together a tailored proposal.

Another aspect of the sales meeting that can cause a lot of problems is the question of money. In other words, the time in a conversation when the prospect asks, *"And how much is all this going to cost?"*

If this subject wasn't raised in your pre-meeting phone discussions, which I looked at earlier, you can bet that it will come up in your first meeting with the potential sponsor. I think it is true to say that this is an area that worries a great number of people. You have a natural concern that the moment the prospect hears how much you want for your sponsorship opportunity, they will drop it like the proverbial hot potato. It is very tempting to pre-judge this situation, such that by the time the question comes up, you will have almost convinced yourself that your fee is too high. If this is what you are thinking, almost certainly it will come out in the way that you reply to the question.

The first thing that you need to remember is that if you have done your homework correctly, as we saw earlier in the book, your fee should already be set at the right level for the sponsorship opportunity you are presenting. Naturally, if subsequently you are going to present a personalised proposal based on the specifically outlined requirements of your prospect, that value might rise or fall slightly, but you should still be fairly accurate in your assessment. If this is the case, you needn't feel that you are asking too much for your sponsorship property, and you should have the confidence to be up-front about it. It's at this point that the true value of the preparation that

I covered earlier will become apparent. If you haven't done that preparation, you will have very little confidence in presenting a fee that is based purely on either guesswork or the costs of the project.

Assume that you are in your first meeting with a company. Your objective is to leave with enough information so that you can prepare a detailed proposal based on the identified requirements of the prospect. By arranging to present this at a follow-up meeting, you will have gained the commitment that I stressed is so critical.

When the question about costs is posed, you can explain that you will need to work out the specific cost, based on the range of entitlements that the prospect has agreed are important. You will include this in the tailored presentation that you present at the next meeting. It is a reasonable comment to make.

However, the prospect might persist in asking for an idea of what the final cost could be. If this is the case, you need to give him an indication. You should be able to provide a *"between £x and £y"* response that is reasonably accurate. You can add that it will depend very much on the level of sponsorship that is considered appropriate. If you try too hard to avoid answering his questions on the level of fee, you will create a degree of annoyance and risk losing the person's interest. They will begin to think that you have something to hide. You don't, provided that you have done your homework properly.

When you've given the prospect the figures, it is important to get confirmation from them that this is a realistic expectation. In other words, you want to avoid the situation where as soon as you leave the room, they tear up your proposal and throw it in the bin. You might have been asking for £150,000. They realised that their budget would only stretch to £50,000 and decided not to waste any more time on the matter.

If this is a genuine concern of the prospect, it is better to find this out while you are there and possibly can do something to resolve the problem. It could be, for example, that although this company cannot afford to be a primary sponsor, there could be an alternative option of being a lower-level sponsor. This might involve designing a proposal that offers them a limited range of entitlements, but that includes the main points that were seen as being very beneficial.

Another route that I have taken in this situation involves initially gaining the assurance from the prospect that it is only the price that is the problem. You need them to confirm that they like the concept and the actual proposals, but that their marketing budget will not accommodate them. You need to be very sure at this stage that they're not trying it on, in the hope of benefiting from the opportunity at a knockdown price. If you feel they are genuine, why not suggest that one option perhaps would be to invite some of the company's suppliers to take part as co-sponsors of the programme. This can work very well in practice. Alternatively, you could propose that they help you secure some other co-sponsors by introducing you to some of their business associates.

> **Be very sure at this stage that they're not trying it on, in the hope of benefiting from the opportunity at a knockdown price.**

If you can ascertain that the prospect is telling you he wants to find a way of making the deal happen, usually you can come to an agreement that suits both parties.

When I first started putting together sponsorship deals, I was excited if I got £500. Later in my career, I masterminded deals in Formula 1 that involved many millions of pounds. The strange thing is that when I was sitting in the head office of a company like Marconi, Gillette or FedEx, the way in which the fee was discussed in millions of pounds was very little different to the way that I discussed those very early deals in hundreds. It's all relative. What might seem like a small fortune to you when presenting a sponsorship proposal to a company, may be small fry to them. I know it is easy to say, but try to remember this when you are going through your fee structure. Don't let the prospect see that you are nervous or unsure of yourself. You need to put across the impression that it is the most normal thing in the world to be informing him that the sponsorship opportunity will cost £350,000. Don't sound apologetic when you put it forward.

> **" Provided you know the true value of your property and how you arrived at that value, you are in a very strong position.**

If you get the response that it is too expensive, you need to be absolutely sure that your prospect means that the programme fee is beyond their budget, or whether they mean that they might be able to afford it, but that they think it is too expensive for what is being offered. It's vital that you know this. You will need to handle the objection carefully. Sometimes I ask a question such as:

"Is it only the cost that is preventing you from moving forward?"

Or

"Can I clarify what you are saying? Is it the fact that it is over your budget limit or do you feel it doesn't warrant that fee?"

If you can get confirmation that the programme you are offering is of interest, but that the cost is the issue, you are probably entering the negotiation stage of the meeting. It's important to recognise this. What it really means is that you don't need to defend what you are offering. Instead, you need to start negotiating over what you are prepared to accept and what he is prepared to offer. You've

probably done this on holiday in a market place or bazaar, when you have been trying to buy something. You will have to haggle, but provided you know the true value of your property and how you arrived at that value, you are in a very strong position.

Ideally, you should show that what you are offering is not negotiable. Try to get the full price by going over all the benefits that the prospect has agreed can be accrued. Unfortunately, in such a highly competitive environment, the reality is that the chances of getting exactly what you want will be quite slim. It may be an idea to identify a couple of areas that aren't really vital to the prospect and eliminate them from the proposal, dropping the price slightly to reflect this.

I always try to approach it from the other direction, which is to throw in some extra entitlements that in reality will cost very little: for example, an extra player appearance day or possibly some extra tickets to your event. In this way, you keep the revenue level high, and although you've given something extra away, probably there will be no major direct cost to this.

In the event of the sponsorship fee being a problem, there is another strategy that you can introduce if you've done your homework on the subject. It's known as performance bonus payments.

In Formula 1, it is quite common for a sponsorship fee to include performance bonus payments. What this means is that an agreement is reached with a sponsor whereby they will pay a percentage of the fee asked, perhaps 75 per cent. This will be a guaranteed payment. The balance will only be paid if you attain certain performance-related targets. Normally each target is linked to a fee, which is payable on its achievement. This can provide a worthwhile opportunity not only to reach your sponsorship fee target, but also in some cases to exceed it. The only proviso is that you must have confidence that the levels of performance can be achieved. For their part, companies wanting to consider this method of payment can take out specialist insurance to cover the eventuality.

The following is an example of the way in which performance bonus payments can work in association with a sponsorship agreement.

Suppose you are seeking £100,000 as a sponsorship fee for your powerboat team to compete in a national championship, comprising ten rounds. The sponsor has offered to pay a fee of just £75,000 for the proposed sponsorship package. What do you do?

A compromise might be to suggest that in addition to the £75,000 fee, you both agree on a performance bonus scheme, which usually can be covered by insurance. It might be structured as follows:

→ For each victory that you achieve in the championship, which in the process provides extra media coverage for the sponsor: a bonus payment of £5,000.
→ For each 2nd or 3rd podium position: a bonus payment of £1,500.
→ 1st place overall in the championship: a bonus payment of £15,000.
→ 2nd place in the championship: a bonus payment of £7,500.
→ 3rd place in the championship: a bonus payment of £5,000.

In this way, it is conceivable that you could earn £65,000 in addition to the £75,000 sponsorship fee, by winning the championship and every race. Even if you won three races and secured four third places, finishing outside of the top three in the championship, you would earn £21,000 in addition to the £75,000.

Perhaps you are a cricketer. A personal sponsorship programme might include a payment every time you hit a half-century or take four wickets in a match.

There are many ways in which you can structure an attractive performance bonus scheme that works for you and for the sponsor. It doesn't just have to be related to performance on the track or in your particular sport. It can also be linked to business performance. Let me explain.

If you have put together a proposal to a company and it's based on a business development opportunity, there is a lot to be said for telling the company that you are prepared to share the risk with them.

Suppose that you have proposed an agreement along the lines of my first ever sponsorship deal with the nightclub, as described earlier. I told them that I believed they could generate more membership subscriptions through an association with my team and the use of the race car in shopping centres.

The deal that I structured shared the risk. I asked for a basic sponsorship fee and proposed that in addition I would be paid a 'performance bonus' if they reached certain targets in subscription sales. If the sponsorship worked, we both benefited; if it didn't, we needed to look at what we could do to make it more effective.

> **If you have put together a proposal to a company and it's based on a business development opportunity, there is a lot to be said for telling the company that you are prepared to share the risk with them.**

In general, potential sponsors feel comfortable with this type of deal because you are seen to be putting your money where your mouth is. If it doesn't do what you are suggesting, you don't get the money.

Multi-dimensional selling

It may well be that your initial proposal was designed to offer a multi-dimensional method of selling, of the type that we looked at in some detail in Chapter 7. If it did, you would have discovered by this stage whether the idea is feasible and of interest. However, if you didn't, but now have identified such an opportunity, it is still not too late to incorporate this. You need to be very alert to an opportunity for presenting this type of strategy. It will depend very much on the feedback that you have received from your line of questioning. If you begin to sense that such an opportunity is opening up, it might be worth keeping the possibility up your sleeve for the time being. By all means, put out a few more feelers to test the potential, but rather wait until you are able to incorporate it into the tailored presentation that you will submit at the follow-up meeting.

If, at that meeting, you can produce a surprise element that will demonstrate a possible route for the sponsor to generate additional, measurable business as a result of your sponsorship proposals, it will be even more impressive than trying to explain this at the end of the first meeting.

Measurement of sponsorship performance

If you can build into your sponsorship proposals a degree of measurement of performance against agreed objectives, I can promise you that you will be head and shoulders above most sponsorship seekers.

If you can build into your sponsorship proposals a degree of measurement of performance against agreed objectives, I can promise you that you will be head and shoulders above most sponsorship seekers.

What do I mean by measurement? Anything that will help the sponsor answer two very important questions:

➔ *"Am I getting value for money?"*
➔ *"How do I know that the sponsorship is working for me?"*

Measurement of sponsorship performance is a highly controversial subject, and opinions vary enormously on effective measurement techniques. As I mentioned in my opening chapters, there are specialist companies that can provide levels of measurement for a sponsor. The problem is that, at the present time, there is no universal standard of measurement. Many supposed experts on the subject will have their own views, but what is needed is a method of measuring achievement that is accepted by everyone involved with sponsorship.

The big problem is that sponsorship performance is not always easy to measure in strict terms. It is easier, for example, to measure the impact of a sponsorship that is based on the amount of brand awareness achieved in specified media sources. By measuring the number of seconds that a brand name appears in an event, a comparison can be made with other methods of achieving similar exposure.

On the other hand, managing a sponsorship that is based on image transfer is far more difficult to measure.

It could be argued that measurement of hospitality effectiveness should be based upon the amount of business that is derived from guests, perhaps measured over the six months following their participation in the event. But how can that be accurate? For a start, you will never know whether or not that level of business might have come in anyway, without the expense of the sponsorship and hospitality.

You might be able to generate a business relationship between two sponsors of your team. Then you can show that as a result of meeting through the sponsorship activities, they did £X of business with each other. In other words, that success is measurable.

Sales-incentive programmes based on the sponsorship can provide a good form of measurement. It might be possible to show that sales during the incentive period were up by an above-average amount.

PR is another area in which measurement guidelines can be introduced. The number of column inches of editorial coverage that were achieved by your sponsorship property will provide a measurement tool for you. This can be compared against the targeted amount.

The most important thing to remember is to show your prospective sponsor that it is not your intention to take the money and not worry about delivering results. The very fact that you are prepared to raise the subject of measurement of performance against the sponsor's objectives will add to their respect for you.

If you can afford it, retaining the services of a sponsorship evaluation agency to measure the performance of the sponsorship can be very effective. For a start, this shows your sponsor that you want the agreement to work for them. By offering to pay for the service, you also demonstrate confidence in the property's ability to deliver what you are promising.

Even if you can't afford to do this, don't be afraid of suggesting to your sponsor that they might like to consider doing so for themselves. This is quite a normal practice.

If, on the other hand, you feel that this might show that the sponsor is not getting value for money, you really should not be approaching them in the first place.

Closing the meeting

There will come a point in the meeting when you realise that it is time to wind up. Perhaps the prospect is starting to glance at their watch, or perhaps has indicated to their secretary that the meeting will be over in a few minutes.

Be aware of these signs and don't overstay your welcome. That doesn't mean that you should get up and walk out straight away. It's better to indicate to the prospect that you are aware of

their time constraints and wait for a reaction. It may be that you'll be told you can have another few minutes, or you may be asked to wind up.

❝ Move into a summarising mode and then gain a commitment in line with your objective.

What is important at this stage is to move into a summarising mode and then gain a commitment in line with your objective. I don't mean that you should simply run through every major part of the proposals you have made during the meeting. What I normally do is simply highlight the main points that I feel are important, confirming as I run through them the prospect's previous agreement that they were important to the company. Here's an example:

"We looked at the opportunity that this programme offers your company to develop a powerful and innovative sales-incentive scheme, based on the calendar of events. You mentioned to me that you were looking for a new format and this could provide the answer.

"You also pointed out that this programme could provide your company with an excellent opportunity to develop a relationship with the local community.

"Finally, the opportunity to use some of the players for your company golf days would, as you agreed, add greater value to them."

When you have done this, it is vital that you gain a commitment in respect of the next step in the process. There are many ways of doing this, which are dictated by what you want to achieve. Perhaps, for example, you want to invite the prospect and his colleagues to an event in which you are competing. Alternatively, you might want to arrange a meeting where you will present a more detailed and tailored proposal, based on your findings in this meeting. Whatever it is, make sure you get this commitment.

"So, having agreed that there is the basis of a workable sponsorship programme that meets your marketing requirements, would it make sense to invite you and your CEO to our next home match to sample some of the hospitality facilities and meet some of our directors?"

Or

"Having agreed that this sponsorship programme can offer you all the points that we've just covered, what's the next step from your point of view?"

At which point, you should not say anything more until he has answered.

Summary
→ Listening is a very rare quality among most salespeople.
→ To listen properly, you shouldn't be thinking of your next response.
→ Only by listening carefully and asking another question based on the previous reply will you uncover the real reasons for a prospect's opinions and reactions.
→ You will be surprised at the reaction of people to you if you are prepared to listen carefully to what they are saying. You will go up in their estimation quite considerably because it doesn't happen too often.
→ The way that you use your sales presentation in a meeting can be very influential. You don't want to lose control of the meeting, but equally you don't want to stop the prospect from asking questions or making observations. The way in which you keep to the middle path is by the careful use of questions that encourage the prospect to confirm those points that they see as being beneficial.
→ At some stage, you will be asked about the fee involved. It is better to be up-front about this than to keep trying to avoid the matter.
→ If genuinely you haven't worked out a fee because you will need to put together a tailored proposal, be open with the prospect and explain this. If the prospect persists in wanting a ball-park figure, you should provide a likely maximum and minimum fee, so that you are not seen to be avoiding the issue.
→ When you have done this, you need to find out whether both amounts are within his budget range This will avoid wasting his time and your own
→ If the cost is raised as an objection, you need to find out whether that is because the amount is actually outside his budget or he feels that it is just too high for what is being offered.
→ By introducing a performance bonus scheme, sometimes you can solve the problem of the fee being considered too high by the prospect.
→ If you can introduce a system that will help the prospect measure the effectiveness of the sponsorship, you will stand head and shoulders above the majority of sponsorship seekers.

20

Gaining a commitment

Usually I have found that if you achieve a second meeting, there is more than an even chance that your prospect is looking for a reason to enter into an agreement with you. It may not be the precise deal that you wanted, but for the sales process to continue in that way, there has to be a reasonable level of interest.

The ideal situation is to gain a commitment for a second meeting while you are still in the first. You may gain agreement for a follow-up meeting where you will submit a personalised and more detailed proposal, based on everything that was agreed in the initial discussion. Whatever the commitment you obtain, I cannot overemphasise the importance of maintaining communication with the prospect beyond the first meeting.

To design and produce a tailored presentation should be a great deal easier than the original. If you went about that meeting in the right way, you will have come away with a list of all the points that need to be included. Eventually this proposal will form the basis of an agreement between you and the sponsor, so it is important to include everything that your prospect agreed would be beneficial. If you want to include your multi-dimensional plan,

as we discussed at the end of the last chapter, you should do so now, but be careful not to contradict anything that has been agreed already, otherwise you might have to go back to square one to gain their commitment all over again.

It's always my aim to arrive at a situation where the prospect feels that they are developing the sponsorship programme themselves. As you have seen, I do this by the careful and planned use of questions, encouraging them to agree on the areas that would work well and discarding those that wouldn't. Then it is not so easy for them to turn down a tailored proposal that has been structured around all of the points that they agreed were important and beneficial.

The time for the follow-up meeting has arrived. You should be a lot more relaxed for this meeting than you were for the first. You know that there is a level of interest and you have met the prospect before. However, it is still important to prepare as well as for the previous meeting. It's a good idea to take some spare copies of the presentation or proposal, as there may be more than one person present at the meeting. Also you should set yourself an objective. Ideally, this should be to obtain a positive decision in principle before you leave the meeting. Often, however, this will depend very much upon the size of the company in question.

If you are presenting to a large multi-national corporation, for example, the decision process could be quite long and not possible to achieve in one more meeting. The FedEx deal that I put together took me a total of four months and about 12 meetings in total. On the other hand, with a privately owned company, you might even get a firm decision there and then. The higher your prospect in the company pecking order, the faster a decision is likely to be taken.

Even if you don't get a decision in principle at this second meeting, it's important to get some form of commitment. This might be a further meeting, or it might be that you will be asked to provide some additional detailed information, endorsing TV viewing figures for example. In one case, I had to prepare an internal proposal for the directors, which in turn they would send to their American bosses at the company's global HQ for approval.

Usually I find that the second meeting is very different from the first, normally moving along quite well on its own, although it is still important to be in control. As I said before, you wouldn't be there if there wasn't a reasonable level of interest within the company. What you need to do is maintain your level of enthusiasm and a healthy dialogue so that it reaches a successful conclusion.

By now you should be at the stage where opportunities to close the deal start appearing. This is an area about which a great deal has been written. Closing the sale, as it is called, is perhaps the most difficult part of the sales process. I suggest that you read some of the many books on selling that fill the shelves of bookshops today. These will provide you with a range of methods that different sales exponents will use. As I keep saying, there is no right or wrong way. All that matters is that it works for you.

All salespeople have their own way of going about the task. Some simply like to ask a direct question when they feel that the time is appropriate, such as:

"So Mr Davies, having agreed that the opportunity presents so many beneficial entitlements, are you happy that we go ahead with the agreement?"

Another way of closing is to obtain a response on a relatively minor point of detail, which effectively will show agreement overall. Often this can help a prospect reach a decision without too much heartache. Remember, you might be nervous at this stage, but so might your prospect. If the sponsorship goes wrong, he could be in trouble. Instead of asking him the big question, *"Do you want to go ahead?"* ask him a question that is more concerned with a point of detail:

"Where would you like to hold the launch party?"

"Which of the two colour schemes are you going to adopt?"

"Which stage payment suits you the best?"

I should stress yet again that at this stage you should keep quiet and wait for the prospect to answer.

By responding to these questions, the prospect effectively is agreeing to the proposal without facing the 'Yes' or 'No' situation that a direct question would necessitate. Another possibility is to pose a question that provides the prospect with two options, neither of which is to respond in the negative:

"Would you prefer to start the agreement on the 1st September, or would you rather have it commence in your new financial year?"

"Which of the two options makes the most sense for you, the title sponsorship or the co-sponsorship programme?"

It is quite normal to have to attempt your closing process several times. However, it is better to do this than to leave the meeting without trying at all. In selling, asking for the order is something that a lot of people find very difficult. It comes back to the point that I raised right at the beginning of the book: the fear of rejection. You worry perhaps that if you try to close the deal, you'll get a firm *"No"*. You might feel that if you keep the discussion going, you won't get a rejection.

The thing about closing is that it will tell you whether you are heading in the right direction. If you have been doing a good job of gaining commitment all along the route, a positive close should almost come naturally. If you find, however, that the prospect raises an objection, the nature of that objection will indicate whether you are near to a positive close, or whether you need to go back to your questioning process and uncover the underlying problem area.

If you have been successful in obtaining a positive response to your close, you need to confirm the fact as quickly as possible, ideally by means of a document called a Letter of Intent. I'll explain what this is shortly.

It is quite likely, at this stage, that you won't be able to secure a response, either negative or positive. On many occasions, you'll be told that the prospect intends to discuss matters with his colleagues and then get back to you. Some salespeople might try to push the point by asking what they need to discuss. It's my experience that if you are not careful, you can irritate people in this way. What is being suggested is normal practice. Usually, in this situation, I will ask the prospect if there are

any particular points that they would like me to clarify further before they do this. I will also ask if it would be helpful for me to be at that meeting. If the answer is *"No thank you,"* I don't push my luck any further.

If you get to this stage of the sales process, it becomes much more difficult to advise you. If you haven't reached a specific conclusion in the meeting, but have been asked to wait for a response, usually one of two things will happen:

1. You receive a letter or phone call, which informs you that after careful consideration, the company has decided not to move forward. Then you have to make a decision. Do you accept this negative response and plan a different way of attacking the issue, or do you decide to cut your losses and move on to the next prospect? That is a personal decision and will depend on how many other companies you are talking to at the time. It will also depend on what you believe the reason to be and whether you can come up with an acceptable solution. If you feel that you can, then you should go for it, but be careful not to waste a lot more time unless genuinely you think that you can turn it around.

2. You get a positive response from your contact. This might mean that a decision has been made to accept your proposal. More often it will mean that the company wants to continue with further discussions. Normally in this case, I find that the sales process starts to gather a momentum of its own. To a certain extent, the way in which it does this will be dictated by the actions and requirements of your prospect.

You might be asked to present your ideas to the board of the company at yet another meeting, or the prospect might want to involve the CEO and financial director for an informal discussion on the plan's implementation. Very often it can be that the prospect wants to go ahead with the proposals, but tells you that the fee is too high. This will mean that you are entering the negotiation phase of the sales process.

The art of successful negotiation is a complex subject that would require a book on its own, but much of the process comes down to common sense. The higher the fee that you are demanding, the more negotiation will be required. If you are very inexperienced in doing this, and you are talking about a sponsorship fee in excess of £100,000, I would strongly recommend that you take a lawyer or even your accountant with you to help in the process. A show of strength doesn't do any harm, as long as you decide with this person in advance your limits of negotiation.

Once you have reached this stage in the sales process, you will need to consider how you will go about finally closing the sale and getting

a commitment in writing. This is important, because life has a horrible knack of throwing up unpleasant surprises. Imagine if your contact suddenly decides to leave the company, or is knocked over by a bus. If you have nothing in writing, there is a strong chance that the sponsorship could be postponed or, even worse, cancelled. It's very important not only to gain approval for your proposals, but also to get that approval in writing as soon as possible.

The easiest way of doing this is to prepare and have with you a Letter of Intent. While this isn't a legally binding document, it will be a major step in the process of securing a signed agreement and will give you more protection than a verbal assurance that a deal has been reached. It is well worth asking your solicitor to draft such a document. This example will give you an idea of what is required:

THIS IS A LETTER OF INTENT BETWEEN

(SPONSOR) HIGHLANDS FLIGHT SERVICES COMPANY

OF

37/45 AYR ROAD
DUNDEE
SCOTLAND

AND

(YOU) JETLINE RACING LTD

OF

UNIT 7 PARK INDUSTRIAL ESTATE
NORTHAMPTON
NORTHANTS

DATED THIS

3RD DAY OF SEPTEMBER, 2011

Dear Mr Smith of Jetline Racing,

Following meetings on the 23rd April and 4th July, 2011, at which proposals were put forward by Jetline Racing to Highland Flight Services concerning possible sponsorship of the team in the 2012 National Powerboat Championship, it is hereby confirmed that Highland Flight Services intends to accept these proposals and enter into a three-year sponsorship agreement with Jetline Racing.

This acceptance is conditional upon the terms and conditions of any subsequent legally binding contract being acceptable to the directors of Highland Flight Services.

It is understood that the agreement will be based on the points outlined in the attached document and contained in the proposal dated 29th July. [Attach a copy of the proposal.]

I look forward to receiving a draft copy of the contract from your lawyer in due course.

Yours sincerely

On behalf of Highland Flight Services.

This is a normal business practice. Although it isn't legally binding in itself, it will speed up the eventual process of having the contract drafted by your lawyer, and it should provide you with some peace of mind. Such a letter will confirm in writing the main points on which the subsequent legal agreement will be based. As a guide, it will include the entitlements that the sponsor will receive and the fees to be paid for those entitlements. It will not include all the normal legal information about termination, breach of contract and so on. That will only appear in the legal document. The Letter of Intent will make it much easier for the two parties' lawyers to reach an agreement and will help keep your costs down.

It's well worth mentioning the duration of an agreement. It is always best to push hard for a long-term agreement with a sponsor. By this I mean typically a three-year deal. The reason for this is that it genuinely benefits both parties.

For a sponsor, there can be a problem with a one-year agreement. It can be argued that the first year of a sponsorship is very often the most expensive. This might be because of the one-off costs involved in branding vehicles or producing promotional and advertising materials. To recoup the full value of this will not be so easy if it will be measured over a single year. Most sponsorships only become really effective in their second and third years. Unless there is a high level of previous experience, it often takes a sponsor the best part of the first year to tune the programme to gain maximum impact.

From your point of view, a long relationship will give you the chance to prove to the sponsor just what you are capable of delivering on their behalf. It will also relieve some of the pressure that you are bound to feel, knowing that halfway through the agreement you will need to start looking at a possible renewal.

Once you have obtained a signed Letter of Intent, the next step is to ask your legal representative to draft a formal and legally binding agreement, based on the contents of the proposal that has been accepted. Unless you already have a lawyer who understands the subject, my advice is to go to one of the many lawyers who specialise in sports sponsorship contracts. You can obtain the names of those in your area from the Law Society. It will save you a great deal of hassle, because he or she will know just what should go into the agreement, unlike a lawyer looking at this for the first time. It will also save you money in the long run. Some lawyers will have standard agreements already prepared, which can be personalised to your particular deal.

> **From your point of view, a long relationship will give you the chance to prove to the sponsor just what you are capable of delivering on their behalf.**

If the sponsorship is very small, you might feel that it's not worth the trouble and expense of having a formal contract drawn up. It's up to you, but my experience is that while usually they are put into a drawer and forgotten, if something goes wrong you will need one.

Moreover, in most sponsorship agreements, the sponsor will insist on a legally drafted contract. Although this can involve you in some expense, it does give both parties full protection. The more complex the deal, the greater the requirement for a formal agreement. Similarly, the higher the sponsorship fee, the greater the need for a legal agreement.

Sometimes your sponsor will insist that their lawyers prepare the sponsorship agreement. This is often the case with a company that is an experienced sports sponsor. I wouldn't be too concerned about this, but make sure you have your own lawyer check it through. That might even save you some money.

The last point, but most certainly not the least important, is that before you sign a sponsorship agreement, you must be 100 per cent certain that you will be able to deliver everything that you have committed to. If you're not sure, don't sign until you've sorted it out. It's no good signing the agreement and then, when a thorny issue is raised, saying that you didn't fully understand it. Neither is it any use assuming that if you can't deliver entitlements to the absolute letter of the contract, a company won't really mind. Normally they do mind. They mind very much!

Summary

→ If you are able to secure a second meeting, the likelihood is that your prospect has a genuine interest in trying to reach a successful conclusion.

→ It is quite likely that you will use the second meeting to present a tailored sponsorship proposal that is based on all the points that the prospect agreed were important at that first meeting.

→ Almost certainly this will form the basis for your eventual sponsorship agreement, so make sure that you include as many entitlements as you feel necessary, but try to keep some up your sleeve as a negotiating tool.

→ When it comes to negotiating, it is better to add extra entitlements that do not have a real cost to you, to keep the fee at the same level, rather than to exclude entitlements and reduce the fee.

→ At the second meeting, you should be thinking about gaining a commitment. A Letter of Intent can prove very helpful in this respect.

→ It pays to go for a three-year agreement or, at worst, a two-year period. Both parties will benefit from this.

→ The Letter of Intent is not legally binding, but it does act as the precursor to a full sponsorship agreement. It lists what both parties have agreed will be the basis on which the sponsorship deal is to be structured.

→ It is worth involving a lawyer in the process of drafting the actual sponsorship agreement. Try to find a specialist in sports sponsorship, as this will save you time and, therefore, money.

→ Never enter into a sponsorship agreement unless you are confident that you can deliver all of the entitlements that you have agreed.

21

The most significant deal

When I started out in my motor racing career, I was no different to many other drivers in wanting to climb the ladder to the very pinnacle of the sport, Formula 1. I realised early on, however, that it wasn't going to happen as a driver, for two reasons:

➜ I had started too late, at the age of 28.
➜ I wasn't determined enough to give up everything else in life.

By recognising this, I was able to capitalise on the skills that I did possess and build a career, which eventually led me to Formula 1, but not as a driver. I remember the excitement that I felt when I secured my first ever Formula 1 sponsorship deal with Gillette, on behalf of the Benetton F1 team. Although there is nothing that compares with the adrenalin rush that you experience at the start of a race, the phone call that I received from Gillette, informing me that the deal was going ahead, came pretty close.

When I speak to business audiences, usually about the business of international motorsport and how it operates, I'm often asked what I consider to be my most significant sponsorship deal. This question really made me think, the first time I heard it. After all, I secured my first ever deal in 1974 and a lot of water has passed under the proverbial bridge since then. When I

mentioned it to Liz, however, she identified the right answer immediately.

It wasn't the most valuable deal, which would have been the Marconi sponsorship that I negotiated for Benetton F1, nor was it my first ever deal, the one with Victoria's nightclub in Maidstone. Other deals that came to mind were those that enabled me to launch and build my racing driver school at the Kyalami circuit in South Africa, and one with the private bank Arbuthnot Latham, which helped me secure a publisher for the first edition of this book in 2005.

The deal that Liz helped me recognise as being the most significant in my career was one that I secured with a company known as Andersen Consulting. Since then, it has become Accenture, and it can best be described as a global management consulting, technology services and outsourcing company.

There's a new team servicing your interests - this is your chance to sign up

MOTORSPORT INDUSTRY ASSOCIATION

Motorsport is a growth industry - the MIA can help you grow with it

MOTORSPORT INDUSTRY ASSOCIATION

The MIA, PO Box 1240, Marlow, Bucks SL7 1WD
Telephone: 01628 487085 Fax: 01628 487001

SPECIAL OFFER SUBSCRIPTION RATE FOR NEW MEMBERS details inside

↗ In 1994, having secured Andersen Consulting sponsorship, Brian founded the Motorsport Industry Association (MIA). Today it is one of the motorsport industry's most powerful representative organisations.

Those of you who are long-term followers of F1 will probably be aware that they were sponsors of the Williams F1 team from around 1996 until very recently. It was a deal in which I played an introductory role, but for which I would never claim responsibility.

As Andersen Consulting, the company had also sponsored the Newman Haas IndyCar team in the USA.

To explain the significance of the sponsorship deal and how it came about, I need to go back to the days when I was the marketing and PR director for Lola F1 in the early 1990s. Lola Race Cars, based in Huntingdon, was then the most successful race car manufacturer in the world in terms of revenue. The company had been started in the 1960s by Eric Broadley, who along with Colin Chapman and John Cooper formed the nucleus of a new breed of innovative engineers who designed and built the vehicles that would put Britain on the map as the world leader in race car design.

Colin Chapman arguably became the most famous of them, thanks to his Lotus race cars and sports cars. Broadley and Cooper were as talented, but probably not quite as commercially astute as Chapman.

However, Lola Cars gained a tremendous worldwide reputation for building carbon-fibre race car chassis (tubs) for the very popular Formula 3000 series in Europe, Formula Nippon in Japan and most importantly the IndyCar (CART) series in the USA. In 1991, every race car, bar one, on the grid of the world-famous Indianapolis 500 was a Lola, built in Britain. At upwards of $250,000 per chassis, it was a lucrative business, employing around 140 skilled staff at its Huntingdon HQ.

In 1991, Eric Broadley decided that, after years of supplying teams around the world with various types of race car, he wanted to set up his own Formula 1 team. He had worked closely with the French Larrouse F1 team, supplying them with a chassis in 1990, but that wasn't the same. He wanted a Lola F1 team, using Lola-built cars. The immensity of the task was not to be underestimated.

Eric's managing director at the time was Mike Blanchet, whom I'd had the pleasure of meeting when I started my race career. We'd both competed in that incredibly competitive Formula Ford era of the mid-1970s, which produced the likes of Mansell, Warwick, Daly and many other future F1 stars. Mike himself had had the ability to make it to the very top, but unfortunately, as is the case with so many race drivers with great talent, probably wasn't in the right place at the right time.

In January 1991, I returned to Britain after spending ten years in South Africa and met up with Mike Blanchet again. For me, the outcome was a dream come true: he offered me the role of marketing and PR director for the new Lola F1 team.

It had taken 17 years, but I'd made it. I was in Formula 1, not as a driver, but in a role for which undoubtedly I was far better equipped.

The three years that followed my appointment with Lola were quite incredible and would warrant a book of their own. Sadly, my very good friend Mike Blanchet was taken seriously ill during my second year at Lola. In fact, he became so ill that at one stage there were fears that he wouldn't survive. I'm delighted that he did pull through, and today he is a highly respected and popular player within the British motorsport industry.

> **It had taken 17 years, but I'd made it. I was in Formula 1, not as a driver, but in a role for which undoubtedly I was far better equipped.**

Mike's problems, however, meant that he was away from the job for many months, and along with other colleagues, I was asked to undertake some of his duties. This involved playing a role in the negotiations between the Italian F1 team BMS Scuderia Italia and Lola with the aim of forming a joint venture for the 1993 Formula 1 World Championship. The idea was that the race car would be designed and built by Lola in Huntingdon, the engine would be an ex-works unit from Ferrari (albeit to the previous year's design) and BMS Scuderia Italia, headed by Italian steel tycoon Beppe Lucchini, would run the car and supply the necessary personnel.

With Lucchini based in Brescia, near Milan, Eric and I spent a lot of time flying back and forth to Italy while we negotiated the deal. It was fascinating to be a part of this whole process.

The two drivers who were selected for the team were the former Ferrari F1 star Michele Alboreto and the young Italian Luca Badoer, who eventually would become Ferrari's F1 test driver for many years.

Suffice to say, the outcome of the Lola/BMS union was somewhat disastrous. The car proved to be totally uncompetitive, much to the frustration of the two drivers. At the time, there were more teams trying to enter F1 than there were spaces on the grid, so teams had to pre-qualify, and on several occasions Lola F1 missed the cut. Imagine trying to explain that situation to sponsors who had invited a host of VIPs as guests. In our case, it was Chesterfield, one of the Phillip Morris cigarette brands. It was a lesson in managing sponsor expectations, believe me!

All I could do that year was watch a crisis develop. It was Eric's business, and he had every right to run it his way. The problem was that while he saw the setbacks as being mechanical in nature, the Italians and the two drivers felt that they were aerodynamic. The situation grew steadily worse until at the end of the year, the plug was pulled on the project. It was sad to see such a brilliant and likeable character as Eric find himself out of his depth in the world of F1 technology.

❝ This meant that just one race car manufacturer, one engine supplier, one tyre producer, one brake manufacturer and so on would be selected to build all of the cars for the series.

Another result of taking over some of our MD's responsibilities while he was in hospital was that I spent quite a lot of time in America. With Lola selling so many race cars into IndyCar, the USA was a very important market for the company. Our US agent was Carl Haas, who ran Newman Haas Racing, then the leading CART team. Mario and Michael Andretti were the team's driving duo at the time, but in 1993 Nigel Mansell went straight from having been the F1 World Champion in a Williams to driving for Newman Haas in the USA. He took the CART title in his first season. Most of his victories came on the high-speed oval tracks that were so unfamiliar to him. If ever there was an underrated race driver it was Nigel Mansell.

From the sponsorship point of view, the time that I spent in the USA was a great learning curve. In particular, I had a great mentor. His name was Barry Chappel, and he had been a sponsorship agent for Carl Haas's team. It was Barry who was responsible for selling the Kmart multi-dimensional sponsorship programme that first appeared on the Newman Haas cars. You'll recall that I explained how this worked so well that it lasted for well over 15 years.

I will never forget Barry meeting me at Kennedy Airport whenever I went to the States. He drove a Rolls-Royce Corniche, and there he would be, pinstripe suit, bright red braces and sometimes a leather cowboy hat. What a character!

To return to the story of my most significant sponsorship deal, 1993 was a very tough year for Lola. The F1 season had been a disaster and the plug had been pulled on the joint venture with the Italians. Eric Broadley was very downhearted, as you can imagine. His mood wasn't helped by an incident that took place towards the end of September that year.

I was chatting with him in his office one morning when his PA walked in and suggested that we look at an article in the latest *Autosport* magazine. I can't recall the exact headline, but it was along the lines of 'Bernie and Max to make F3000 a control formula'.

This came as a bombshell. The International F3000 Championship was the last step on the ladder to Formula 1, and the article spelled out how it was to be drastically changed in an attempt to cut costs. At the time, there were several different car manufacturers in F3000 (Lola being one of the leaders), not to mention engine suppliers, tyre producers, brake manufacturers, battery suppliers and so on. What was being proposed by Max Mosley, President of the FIA, the sport's governing body, and supported by Bernie Ecclestone, was that the series should become what is known as a 'control series'. This meant that just one race car manufacturer, one engine supplier, one

↗ Brian was invited to launch the new Lola IndyCar at the 1991 Autosport Show.

tyre producer, one brake manufacturer and so on would be selected to build all of the cars for the series.

The concept might have been sensible in many ways: the costs of participating had been spiralling. There were two significant problems, however.

Firstly, timing. The announcement came just as Lola and all of the other constructors were selling new cars to the teams for the following season. The result was that within hours of the article appearing, the phones were abuzz at Lola, their competitors Reynard Cars and several other constructors. The teams no longer wanted to order new cars that would be obsolete within a few months.

Secondly, potential loss of jobs. If the new regulations were imposed, all of the many companies that made cars, engines or other

parts for the current series would be invited to submit tenders to become the sole supplier of such items for the new format. This would be fine for the winning companies, but what about those that weren't successful in their bids? The subsequent loss of business could lead to the loss of jobs. It would also impact on the hundreds of small businesses that supplied parts and services to each of the race car constructors.

Eric Broadley was stunned by the potential consequences of the changes that were being proposed.

As Mike was still away from his job, recuperating from major surgery, Eric asked me for my thoughts on what we should do. I suggested that as I knew Max Mosley reasonably well, it might be an idea if I called Adrian Reynard, the boss of our major competitor, Reynard Race Cars, and arrange for us both to meet with Max and put forward our concerns.

Adrian and I did meet with Max, and it came as no real surprise when he told us that if we weren't happy with the new proposals, we should get all of the businesses involved in F3000 to meet and come up with alternative cost cutting proposals of our own, which he would consider.

Trying to set up such a meeting was a nightmare. Nearly all of the people who needed to be there were so busy competing with each other on a day-to-day basis, that trying to get them to forget their differences and look at the overall picture was nigh on impossible.

It was widely accepted at the time that Britain was the world leader within the international motorsport industry. The majority of the F1 teams were based there, and young aspiring drivers from all over the world came to Britain to make their name. From a technical point of view, Britain was the place to work.

Bearing that in mind, it seemed very odd that there was no mechanism for lobbying the governing body of the sport over major issues of the type that companies like Lola were now facing. There was no organisation to promote and protect the interests of businesses, many of whom were very small, that comprised the motorsport industry in Britain.

> ❝ **The more I thought about it, the more I realised that there was a long overdue need for an organisation that could provide a voice for the businesses that comprised the world leading British motorsport industry.**

In those days, if you were a young person wanting to work on the technical side of motorsport, there was no structured career entry route for doing so. If you rang a team and asked for advice as to how you got into the industry, the typical response was to suggest

that you found a weekend role with a club-level racing team, perhaps helping to polish the car or sweeping the workshop, and then to work your way up from there.

This seemed to be totally at odds with the rapidly increasing level of technology that was being used within motorsport at all levels. I thought about the range of skills that would be needed by the growing motorsport industry: from composite materials technology to telemetry, from digital instrumentation to aerodynamics.

The more I thought about it, the more I realised that there was a long overdue need for an organisation that could provide a voice for the businesses that comprised the world leading British motorsport industry. It could also promote and protect their interests while creating meaningful career paths to ensure that the growing need for technical skills could be met. Another point also struck me. Where were the motorsport industry specific qualifications that would recognise skill levels? There were none as such.

My mind raced on! How big was the British motorsport industry? How many people worked in it? What types of business comprised the industry. The questions just kept coming.

I spoke to several figures within the industry and received a similar response from most of them, which was that they hadn't really thought much about the matter. Their businesses were successful, the industry was successful, so what was the problem? Why did they need to change anything?

I was quite shocked by the lack of vision these people displayed. Hadn't they seen the dramatic decline of the British motor and motorcycle industries, and asked themselves if such a fate could befall the motorsport industry? In Japan, America and South America, there were already signs that these growing motorsport markets were developing their own support industries.

To my friend Brian many thanks

↗ Brian considers the late Michele Alboreto to be one of the most likeable people he has met in F1. The former Ferrari star
drove for Lola F1 in 1993, when Brian was the team's marketing and PR director.

Andersen Consulting sponsored the inaugural MIA Awards event in 1994. Award winner David Richards of Prodrive is shown next to the Andersen Consulting marketing director and Brian Sims.

I decided to take the bull by the horns. I made a list of six of the most influential figures within the British motorsport industry whom I knew personally. I went to see each of them and presented the idea, in principle, of establishing what effectively would be a trade association to represent the industry. I called the proposed organisation the Motorsport Industry Association, MIA for short.

Contrary to the response that I had received when I had mooted the idea of a trade association before, this time I received a positive reaction. I think the difference was that each of these people was at the top of their game. They saw the benefits that such a new body could deliver, and they also realised the perils of ignoring the threats that the industry would face in future years. While there was a

high level of support from them, however, they all pointed out that it would be very tough to get such a concept up and running, as the industry tended to be rather cynical in nature. They also asked who would be prepared to take on this role. I responded by asking them if I took on the role of the driving force behind the initiative, would they support me and serve on an inaugural steering committee? They all agreed to do so. We were on our way.

Now, this is where the sponsorship angle comes into play. I know it's taken a while, but I hope you'll agree that I had to provide the background for it to become relevant.

I realised that for the MIA to become a reality and to convince businesses to join the organisation, I would need to add a vital ingredient into the mix.

During my sponsorship acquisition activities at Lola F1, I had approached a high-profile company that was a sponsor of the Newman Haas IndyCar team, Andersen Consulting. That particular deal had been negotiated with the American head office of the company. To discuss the Lola F1 opportunity, I had arranged a meeting with Rob Baldock, a senior partner of Andersen Consulting in the UK. As it turned out, we weren't able to agree a sponsorship deal for Lola, but we still got on really well.

I decided to call Rob and ask if we could meet again. This time, I outlined my ideas for the formation of the MIA. My research had shown that Andersen Consulting liked to create case studies of how they consult with a large business or corporation to show how they

helped that business grow or perhaps become more profitable.

I put forward a very simple proposal to Rob. Here was an opportunity for Andersen Consulting to do just that, play a role in growth and development, not of a business, but of an industry, an exciting, sexy, high-profile industry: the British motorsport industry.

He liked the idea very much and, in turn, put a proposal to me. He asked me to invite the six influential industry figures I mentioned to the head office of Andersen Consulting. I was to make a full presentation to them and him. If they supported my ideas, he would agree to my sponsorship proposals.

So who were those six people?

↗ John Kirkpatrick, Brian's instructor at the Jim Russell Racing Driver School. He later became one of the Motorsport Industry Association's founding committee, which Brian established in 1994.

→ **Richard Scammel, MBE**, managing director of Cosworth Racing Engines, whose engines were being widely used in Formula 1.

→ **Ralph Firman**, managing director of Van Diemen International, the world's largest-volume race car manufacturer, in terms of numbers of vehicles sold.

→ **John Kirkpatrick**, managing director of the world-famous Jim Russell Racing Driver School.

→ **Tony Schulp**, publishing director of Haymarket's motoring and motorsport publications.

→ **Tony Fletcher**, managing director of Premier Fuel Systems.

→ **Tony Panaro**, managing director of Euro Northern Travel, specialist in motorsport travel.

I still recall that meeting in London. To my amazement, every one of the seven people present agreed that a representative organisation for the industry was way overdue. They felt that while it would be of value to all businesses within the industry, probably it would benefit most those of small to medium size.

↗ Brian with his school friend Ian Gillan, lead singer of Deep Purple, at the Autosport Show. A one-time Formula Ford rival of Brian's looks on.

They all confirmed their previous commitment to become members of the steering committee, and most importantly of all, Rob Baldock agreed that Andersen Consulting would play an active role from day one.

There was one proviso from everyone there: I was to resign from Lola and be appointed the new organisation's CEO. They felt that without a driving force on a permanent basis, the Motorsport Industry Association wouldn't ever get off the ground.

As part of their support, Andersen Consulting agreed to fund the launch of the MIA. This would be held at their head office in Arundel Street. London. It would be held in April of that year, 1994.

I had achieved my primary objective. By bringing Andersen Consulting on board as the corporate partner of the MIA, I had secured the stamp of credibility that was so important for the new association.

My worry had always been that the first response of so many people to the MIA's formation would be that it was just another motor racing 'club' designed to attract sponsorship. However, the connection with one of the world's most high-profile business corporations would help people realise that the MIA was first and foremost about the development of businesses that comprised the British motorsport industry. It was not about racing drivers as such.

The other major benefit that I knew would accrue from the new relationship with Andersen Consulting was the PR that would be generated within the business media, as opposed to the motor racing press. In my opinion, this type of coverage would be far more important in creating awareness of what the MIA was all about.

I will always be grateful to Rob Baldock, to Andersen Consulting and to all of the original steering committee, with one notable exception, for the support that they provided, both on a personal level and to the MIA. Rob went on to become the chairman of the MIA and is one of only three honorary life members of the association. The one exception shall remain nameless, but he used his position on the committee to try to undermine the new association for his own personal reasons in a most disruptive and unpleasant manner. There always has to be one!

It was Rob Baldock who introduced me to James Kelly of Rawlinson and Hunter, an international grouping of professional firms that specialised in financial and taxation advice. James agreed a partnership deal with the MIA that saw his firm provide our auditing and accountancy requirements at no cost for the first two years, in return for becoming our auditors on a commercial basis after that period.

Law firm Norton Rose entered into a similar partnership to manage the MIA's legal incorporation, while a colleague of Rob's, Ian Spencer, brought his advertising agency on board to handle our brochure designs and production.

The MIA launch in April 1994 was a great success, generating a high level of media coverage. Within a year, we had 25 businesses as members, including the Benetton F1 Team and TOCA, the company that runs the British Touring Car Championship. Interestingly, in 2007, Alan Gow, TOCA's owner, was appointed chairman of the MSA, the governing body of motorsport in Britain.

Having launched the MIA, I realised that we needed a 'quick win' to get members on board. We also needed to create even more awareness of the aims and objectives of the association.

I came up with the idea of creating an industry awards programme, recognising outstanding business and technical achievement within the British motorsport industry. There was a great annual event in place for the drivers and teams, the Autosport Awards, but little recognition of the industry per se.

We needed something special to generate that interest. Sponsorship came into the equation once again. I was able to secure another sponsorship deal with Andersen Consulting: this time the company would provide the top award at the proposed event. We had drawn up a list of the award categories, which included:

→ Small Business of the Year
→ Service Business of the Year
→ Exporter of the Year
→ Media Business of the Year

The Andersen Consulting Award would be for outstanding achievement within the British Motorsport Industry. The prize would include an Andersen Consulting consultancy programme, hopefully an attractive opportunity for companies seeking expert assistance in business development activities.

There was another person without whom the MIA wouldn't have got off the ground. My wife Liz worked full time to allow me to leave Lola and start building the new association on a permanent basis. In addition, she helped in the evenings and at weekends with admin and other important support work.

Between us, we arranged and managed the inaugural MIA Business Achievement Awards dinner. It was held in November 1994 at the Rothley Court Hotel in Leicestershire. We sold 100 tickets at £40 each to break even. That night, one of the worst storms to have hit Britain for some years did its best to ruin the occasion. It failed and we had a 100 per cent turnout.

" None of them would have believed that within a year they would be attending the 1995 MIA Awards at a different venue, the House of Lords.

The Andersen Consulting Award was won by a well-known company, Prodrive. Located at

Banbury, Prodrive was a successful race and rally car preparation business. Its CEO, David Richards, was there to receive the trophy and the consultancy programme prize.

Several senior VIPs were present from Andersen Consulting as David collected his award and gave a short speech congratulating the committee for the MIA initiative. Then he came out with a real classic line, which caused me to think that we were about to lose the Andersen Consulting deal! He referred to the consultancy that was a part of the prize, then suggested that Prodrive could probably teach Andersen Consulting more than Andersen Consulting could teach Prodrive.

A brief shocked silence followed, then came a great round of applause. Grins on the faces of the Andersen Consulting VIPs showed that they probably thought there might be some merit in David Richard's words.

When the guests departed after a superb evening, none of them would have believed that within a year they would be attending the 1995 MIA Awards at a different venue, the House of Lords.

22

Tea at the House of Lords

Without the sponsorship that I was able to secure from Andersen Consulting, the MIA would never have been launched. I've included the details of how the association came about because it illustrates that sponsorship can play a very different role in business to what I suppose you would call the traditional function.

Sponsorship is the process that allows a business to achieve pre-agreed objectives through a commercial relationship with another party that charges a fee for the provision of specified commercial entitlements. As you will be aware, sponsorship is not limited to sport. In nearly every walk of life, sponsorship is an accepted way of achieving a mutually beneficial commercial relationship.

Important aspects of a commercial relationship, such as that we achieved with Andersen Consulting in establishing the MIA, are the importance of delivering what you promise and the building of personal relationships.

As I explained, the deal with Andersen Consulting was negotiated in 1994. Little did I realise that 12 years later, I would be entering into another sponsorship deal with the same

company, but this time in South Africa, albeit that Andersen Consulting had changed its name by then to Accenture.

Before concluding the new deal, Accenture carried out due diligence on my original relationship with them back in 1994. Had we not delivered on that deal, there was no way that they would have entered into another agreement.

The message is very clear. Look after your sponsors and build relationships, because you never know when you might want to approach a company again.

At the end of Chapter 21, I mentioned that in 1995 the House of Lords became the venue for the MIA Business Achievements. How did this happen?

There is a saying that you make your own luck. Securing this extraordinary venue for the MIA awards presentation was just such a case.

Richard Scammel, then managing director of Cosworth, was on the inaugural steering committee of the MIA. Early in 1995, he invited me to be the guest speaker at a function Cosworth was hosting at Silverstone for an all-party group of MPs and peers. It was a great opportunity to partially pay back Richard for his tremendous personal support in setting up the MIA, so I accepted the invitation.

After my talk, during which I spoke in some detail about the MIA, I found myself chatting with Lord Astor of Hever, who showed a lot of interest in this world leading British industry.

When next I met with my committee members, I suggested that it might be a clever move to have a figurehead for the association, someone who could help us penetrate the corridors of government. I suggested that Lord Astor might be that person and agreed to make contact with him.

Following a phone conversation, I was invited by Lord Astor to the House of Lords. After a fascinating behind-the-scenes tour, we sat in the peers' tea-room and discussed the possibility of him becoming our honorary president. His response was quite straightforward. He said that he would be interested, but only if he could actually do something practical to help us, rather than just being a figurehead.

↗ The 1995 MIA Awards at the House of Lords: Honorary President Lord Astor of Hever (seated), MIA founder Brian Sims (in Jordan F1 car) and event sponsor Geoff Banks of Hewlett Packard.

I still don't know quite where it came from, but an idea formed in my mind. I asked him if it would be possible for the MIA Business Achievement Awards to be presented at the House of Lords that year. He thought it highly unlikely, as it would be deemed a commercial event, but he promised to make enquiries.

Within a fortnight, he invited me to the House of Lords again. At that meeting, he told me that he'd spoken to Black Rod, the official responsible for the day-to-day management of the House of Lords. To his surprise, Black Rod had given his approval for the event, to be held on the Monday evening in July after the British F1 Grand Prix. We could use the riverside Cholmondeley Room and terrace, and to crown it all, we could have two F1 cars on display.

The response from the motorsport industry was fantastic, and the awards reception attracted an amazing combination of government and motorsport industry VIPs.

That was 1995. The reception has been held every year at the House of Lords since then and undoubtedly is the motorsport industry event of the year.

Three years after starting the MIA, I felt that I had gone as far as I could with the running of the association. I felt that a different set of skills was required to take it to the next level. It wasn't an easy decision, as Liz and I had put so much effort into reaching that point. I was a salesman and had not only sold the concept for the MIA in the first place, but also, together with the committee, had worked hard to develop the foundations on which the organisation could grow. However, the time had come to find someone who could take it forward.

Committee member Ralph Firman introduced me to Chris Aylett, who had a background with the Sports and Allied Industries Federation. We needed someone with that level of experience, so I interviewed him. He came on board in 1997 and I stood down to leave him free to get on with his new role.

History shows that it was a good appointment; Chris Aylett has taken the MIA to exceptional heights of success.

As the MIA's founder, I was delighted to be appointed the first ever honorary life member of the association, an honour that subsequently has been deservedly bestowed upon Rob Baldock and Lord Astor of Hever, who remained honorary president until 2009.

> **❝ What started out as a two-man band... has become one of the most effective motorsport industry bodies in the world.**

I said in the previous chapter that the sponsorship deal that I secured with Andersen Consulting was the most significant of my career. Not only did it bring about an organisation that has gone on to help hundreds of businesses within the British motorsport industry, but also it has made the motorsport industry an achievable career goal for so many young people. The creation of the world's first ever motorsport engineering degree course, in association with Roger Dowden at Swansea Institute, has resulted in well over 20 universities in the UK, and many internationally, offering similar courses, and expanding them to include marketing and other related skills.

What started out as a two-man band, Liz and myself, working from the spare room of my house in St Ives, Cambridgeshire, has become one of the most effective motorsport industry bodies in the world.

Having resigned from my CEO role at the MIA in 1996, it's probably not too difficult to guess what I wanted to do – get back into the sponsorship business! As you will have read earlier in the book, I became head of motorsport for Alan Pascoe's sports marketing agency, API, which had just negotiated the worldwide rights to be Benetton F1's sponsorship agency. I was back doing what I do best – sponsorship acquisition.

Not all sponsorship properties are saleable

We've covered a lot of ground, looking at the steps that are necessary to secure a sponsorship deal. One of the most important elements, you may recall, was ensuring that you have a saleable product. If it's priced incorrectly or not structured to meet the needs of the market, you'll always have a tough job on your hands trying to find buyers.

In 2005, this is exactly what happened to me. I received a phone call from John Surtees, the only man ever to have won the World Motorcycle Championship and the Formula 1 World Championship. He explained that he had been appointed the team principal of the British team in the new A1 Grand Prix series, which had been set up by Sheikh Maktoum Hasher Maktoum Al Maktoum of Dubai.

The A1 Grand Prix series was called the World Cup of Nations and would comprise teams from individual countries competing against each other during the months of September through to April on a number of international racetracks. The ownership of each national team was offered as a franchise, costing several million dollars. The cars were all one-make, one-engine-manufacturer single-seaters, designed to ensure close racing. They would be painted in colour schemes representing the nationality of the team. Every driver had to be a national of the country for whom they were driving, either directly or indirectly.

A1 GP was a great concept, and to start with there was no shortage of money behind the project.

John Surtees asked me if I would consider becoming marketing consultant to A1 Team GBR, helping the new franchise holder design and implement a sponsorship strategy for the team. It was a role that excited me, and I gladly accepted the offer. It was a decision that I would regret.

The first season started off in spectacular fashion with the British A1 Grand Prix, which was run at Brands Hatch in Kent. A crowd of around 80,000 turned up to watch this new type of racing. I remember the lavish hospitality entertainment centre that had been set up by the organisers. Created to emulate and even surpass Formula 1's exclusive Paddock Club, it was called the Pangea, the Latin name given to the continental land shifts millions of year ago.

The marketing people involved in promoting the A1 GP series spent a small fortune on brand identity, marketing and promotional material. They also set out the most effective way for each of the franchise holders to secure the high levels of sponsorship that would be needed to cover their outlay and move into profit.

In the process, they committed a cardinal sin. They generated the belief that not only would sponsorship pour into the teams, but also that the levels of sponsorship revenue would be in the hundreds of thousands to millions of dollars. In my opinion, however, this would never happen until the series had built a reputation and following.

poor. Sponsorship decals on the race cars of nearly all the teams were conspicuous by their absence.

From my point of view, looking at how we could generate sponsors specifically for the British team, I realised that we had a very tough job. The product itself wasn't right.

For British TV viewers who wanted to watch races, the difference in time zones meant that many events were run in the middle of the night. They were also shown only on Sky, not free to air. Print and online media coverage of the series was also very poor after that first event.

Another issue was the fact that the majority of the drivers were relatively unknown to the general public. This didn't help create high-profile lifestyle or motorsport coverage.

All in all, it very quickly became clear that, along with most teams, we were going to struggle to find the level of sponsorship that was said to be realistic by A1 GP's own marketing team.

> **"** **The sad reality that eventually led the A1 GP series into liquidation was that the business model didn't work in practice.**

The sad reality that eventually led the A1 GP series into liquidation was that the business model didn't work in practice. Once the series left the UK after the great success of the Brands Hatch race, it went to a number of countries around the world where it was badly promoted and spectator numbers were almost non-existent. I think it fair to say that only the superb street race that was run along the waterfront in Durban, South Africa, generated any sizeable attendance.

Another factor that led to its decline was that TV audience viewing figures were very

In the case of the British team franchise holders, there was another problem that I faced. They knew absolutely nothing about motor racing and motorsport marketing. That wasn't the problem in itself. I had expected that. What I didn't expect was an attitude that refused to recognise the difficulties of attracting meaningful sponsorship. I don't know why I didn't. After all, so many people in motorsport follow the same example: they see sponsorship as their right!

There was also an impatience that failed to accept that it would probably take an absolute

↗ A1 Grand Prix at Brands Hatch, 2005: (Left to right) MIA's Chris Aylett, MIA founder Brian Sims, Lord Astor of Hever, Minister of Sport Richard Coburn, CEO of UKT&I Sir Stephen Brown.

minimum of a year or more for the series to start gaining some level of interest, both from the public in Britain, which had a surfeit of motorsport activities to choose from, and from the business sector in terms of using A1 as a cost-effective marketing tool.

We had a problem. Little did we realise at the time, but so did the A1 GP series.

I came up with what I hoped might be a solution. I met with the head of Sky TV's own sponsorship sales team, Peter Dair. His team was responsible for securing the broadcast sponsorship necessary for Sky's coverage of events across a wide spectrum of sport. The Sky database of potential sponsors was highly attractive.

I succeeded in getting Peter to agree to work with me to see if we could secure some much needed sponsorship for the British A1 team. He was very enthusiastic and was instrumental in setting up some very promising meetings. We presented the opportunities to many high-profile companies, but without success.

The TV viewing figures for Sky's coverage of A1 were unbelievably poor. There was hardly any print media coverage in the mainstream press or dedicated motorsport publications. Attendances at races were going from bad to worse.

Eventually, after a great deal of hard work, Peter was forced to admit that there was no market for the programme that we were trying to sell.

Then I had a stroke of much needed luck. I was approached by a company in High Wycombe, whose owner wanted to ask about the cost of hospitality at an A1 event. The company, AC Lighting, specialised in the provision of lighting equipment for a range of activities, such as the Rolling Stones' world tour, the outside of the BT tower in London and the exterior of the Natural History Museum. AC Lighting had been built from scratch by its owner, David Leggatt, and after 20 years it had become a very successful small- to medium-size business.

I met David and, after several discussions, was successful in encouraging him to come aboard A1 Team GBR as a corporate sponsor, albeit in a small way. The primary objective was to provide AC Lighting with an innovative platform for entertaining staff and clients. The sponsorship suited what he was looking for, providing an association with the team and thereby adding value from a guest's point of view.

The AC Lighting deal offered a real opportunity for growth during and after the two years of the initial agreement, if both the partnership and the series proved successful. At around $2,000 a ticket for admission to the luxurious Pangea at each race circuit, I also realised that this would bring in some much needed revenue to the team.

AC Lighting came to several races that year, and I guess their total spend, including the sponsorship fee, would have been in the region of $135,000.

25

The role of social responsibility

The lessons I'd learned in establishing the MIA in 1994 came in very handy when I started the daunting task of repeating the process, some 6000 miles away in South Africa. Most importantly, I knew that unless we had a solid financial platform on which to build and develop the new association, it wouldn't be able to achieve the objectives that we'd set for it.

I realised that there was a huge need for sponsorship. This time, however, it would be very different from the sports sponsorship that I had spent so much of my career negotiating. This time we were looking for companies to see the benefits of sponsorship from a social responsibility point of view. It was a fascinating challenge.

All too often, social responsibility sponsorship has been confused with social responsibility donations. By this, I mean that people write to companies asking for donations to good causes, whether they are representing a local charity or even a national organisation. They are not offering any commercial returns, simply the opportunity for a company to be seen to have a corporate sense of social responsibility.

Social responsibility sponsorship, on the other hand, is very different. This involves a company entering into an agreement to provide funds, services or products to what it might believe is a good cause, but being offered a commercial benefit or entitlement in return. As such, it may be that the company will decide to provide some of the fee from its marketing budget, as opposed to its social responsibility budget. The result for the recipient is more or less the same, but there is the added burden of having to provide a return on the company's investment. The main advantage is that company marketing budgets tend to be a lot larger than social responsibility budgets.

As we saw earlier, if you can add a relevant social responsibility entitlement to a more traditional sponsorship deal, sometimes it can prove a vital ingredient.

While I was on one of my feasibility trips to South Africa, I started to look at potential sponsorship opportunities. One area where I knew we would need a lot of help was in IT, both hardware and software. I spoke to one of the support team that Accenture had provided for Liz and me at their head office in Johannesburg, where we had based ourselves on these visits. Accenture, I was told, did a lot of business with Dell Computers. They gave me the name of Dell's SA marketing director.

This highlights another aspect of sponsorship acquisition. Don't forget that your existing sponsors may be able to introduce you to companies that you would like to approach. Don't be afraid to ask if they can help in this respect.

" Persistence is a key part of the sponsorship acquisition job.

I set up a meeting with the Dell marketing director to present the opportunity of becoming SAMIA's official IT partner. On arrival for my appointment, I was greeted with the news that due to the arrival of a foreign VIP, he wouldn't be able to meet me. I tried again before I left the country, but without any success.

When I moved back to South Africa in January of the following year, I made contact with a few other IT companies, without generating a lot of interest from them. Moreover, despite my efforts, I still couldn't get a meeting with Dell. I kept trying to make contact until eventually I did manage to speak to the marketing director, Rob Nunn. He apologised profusely for what had happened at that original meeting, then told me that he would be in Cape Town the following week. We met and I presented my ideas. He was cagey about his feelings, but a week later he called to ask me to meet with the head of their social responsibility organisation, the Dell Foundation.

The eventual outcome was a two-year deal that saw Dell become SAMIA's IT partner: the Dell Foundation provided us with all of our hardware requirements, and Dell's marketing division with the financial balance of the proposed deal. It proved to be a great relationship, and I know that both Dell and the Dell Foundation gained a significant return from it. Dell effectively got a foot in the door of a new business sector, the motorsport industry, while the Dell Foundation saw it as being in line with their aim of helping previously disadvantaged youngsters into an industry that was very much IT orientated.

If there is a lesson to be learned from this story, it's that persistence is a key part of the sponsorship acquisition job. I have been called the proverbial 'rat up a drainpipe' on more than one occasion and consider it a great compliment! Before we could move forward in setting up SAMIA, however, we still needed a major partner to provide the majority of the substantial funding requirements. This was where another aspect of the sponsorship acquisition role came in.

When I was working in Formula 1, I did a lot of speaking at business functions on behalf of the team. Normally this was to groups of sponsors and their guests at races. Not only did I enjoy this task, but also I seemed to be generating a good response from those listening. It gave me an idea. Why not register with a speaking agency and do this professionally?

I sourced a few agencies and eventually signed with one. I saw two advantages. Firstly, it would provide some additional income. More importantly in many ways, it would also put me in front of companies. Normally at sales conventions, conferences, product launches, sales training seminars and the like, a company will invite a motivational speaker. Invariably the senior executives will be present, and if you are that motivational speaker, you will be given the chance to meet them.

When I arrived back in South Africa to establish SAMIA, I signed with an agency immediately. My first booking turned out to be very significant in my search for sponsorship. I received an invitation to speak at the Cape Town University Business School's monthly business lunch. My chosen subject was the business of international motorsport, and there was an audience of around 125.

During my 45-minute talk, I also touched on the reason for my being in South Africa, SAMIA. The talk seemed to go down well and everyone departed.

One of the delegates had arrived too early. I didn't see him, but he left his card with Liz, who was sitting outside selling copies of my book.

A few days later, I phoned him. Gareth Shaw turned out to be a senior chemical engineer with PetroSA, the government owned oil and petroleum corporation. PetroSA has a massive refinery along the coast to the east of Cape Town. It has offices in Europe and America, and is a huge organisation. I suggested that Gareth and I should meet, which we did.

He liked the SAMIA concept and suggested that I should try to get a meeting with the PetroSA vice president, Dr Nonpumelelo Siswana, to see if they might be interested in helping in some way. Two weeks later, the three of us met for breakfast at the Radisson Hotel in Cape Town, at a table overlooking the ocean. You couldn't wish for a more beautiful place to have a business discussion.

Two hours later, Dr Siswana, who eventually went on to become the acting president and CEO of this huge organisation, and a personal friend, agreed to a two-year high-value sponsorship of SAMIA. PetroSA would become the association's founding partner. When we created the SAMIA Business Achievement Awards in the first year, PetroSA became a primary sponsor, along with Dell. Thanks to additional sponsorship, I was able to bring the Ferrari F1 designer, South African Rory Byrne, from Maranello as our special guest.

What can you learn from this? Well, although this wasn't the most difficult sponsorship 'sell' that I've ever experienced, it resulted from one factor: I put myself in front of a business audience. If I hadn't done that, I would never have met Gareth Shaw from PetroSA, and probably the deal would never have happened.

❝ It was time to adopt my previously successful and well utilised idea of securing a media partner to help generate sponsorship.

You might say I was lucky. My view is that you make your own luck. I had taken the trouble to increase the chances of meeting key business contacts. That's not luck. That's planning.

The SAMIA Business Achievement Awards were more difficult to establish than the MIA Awards. SAMIA was a brand-new concept, and motorsport in South Africa is relatively small compared with Britain. We needed to get the message out to the business world and government that although it had never been formalised, there was indeed a successful South African motorsport industry.

It was time to adopt my previously successful and well utilised idea of securing a media partner to help generate sponsorship.

As with the launch of MIA in Britain, I was very determined that SAMIA would not be seen just as some type of motorsport club. I wanted to make it clear that SAMIA was all about business development and technical/business skills training.

If there was one publication in South Africa that seemed an obvious choice, it was *Business Day*. This was a daily newspaper dedicated almost entirely to business and finance. The *Financial Times* would be a similar paper in Britain.

Every Thursday, the paper published a motoring supplement, which was highly regarded. The same company also owned a TV channel, which broadcast *Ignition*, a weekly look at the automotive industry, through the eyes of businessmen.

I was able to convince the editor of *Business Day* of the merit of becoming SAMIA's Business Awards official media partner. The opportunity to be in on what effectively was the launch of a new industry in South Africa, a rather sexy one at that, was too good for the paper to turn down.

It was an interesting deal. The payment was made through the provision of extensive full-colour advertising of the awards reception, as well as a guaranteed double-page editorial spread in the main body of the paper, following the reception.

Such was the extent of the deal in attracting ticket sales that we didn't need to look for another sponsor for the event. In addition, with Rory Byrne, Ferrari F1's chief designer as our special guest, we had to turn away quite a few people who wanted to book.

The power of the media must never be discounted in supporting sponsorship acquisition strategies. If you structure the right partnership, it can add huge value for you.

As you will have seen, in so many of the deals that I've put together over the years, the role of key media partners has meant the difference between success and failure to attract meaningful sponsorship fees.

26

Still learning and still doing deals

After running SAMIA very successfully for four years, Liz and I eventually decided that it was time to hand over the reigns to a South African. This is a necessary step at some stage in the growth of a business in South Africa, due to the Black Empowerment requirements, so it was something that we knew would be required eventually.

In addition to the business decision that we made in stepping down, both of us wanted to leave South Africa and return to Britain. We had enjoyed some great times, but found the stress of living behind electric fences and constantly being on the lookout for intruders a little too much. This was not an easy decision for Liz, in particular, as she would be leaving behind family in Cape Town, but there was no doubt in our minds about the decision.

I feel that in SAMIA we started something very special. South Africa's governing body of motorsport, the MSA, had been obsessed with finding the next Jody Scheckter, ideally in the guise of a young Black driver. They saw this as a route to securing large amounts of sponsorship within the sport. In my opinion,

↗ (Left to right) Gareth Shaw, PetroSA Vice President Dr Siswana, Brian and Liz Sims at the launch of the corporation's sponsorship of the South African Motorsport Industry Association (SAMIA).

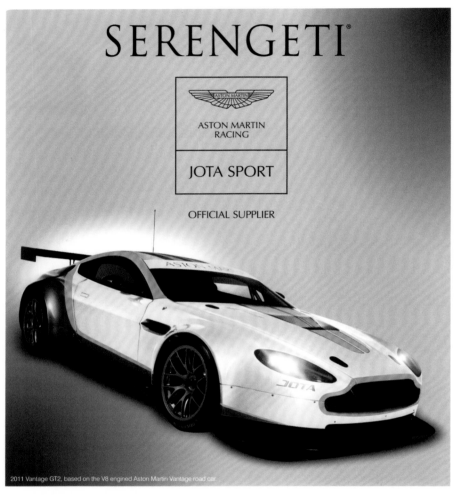

↗ Following the deal that Brian negotiated for Jota Sport, the Aston Martin Racing partner, Serengeti, promoted the partnership in retail outlets across the UK and Europe.

however, they had done very little to bring about real change.

I made my feelings very clear. I tried explaining to the MSA directors that in my 37 years in motorsport, I had never seen a job advertised for a racing driver. However, I had seen thousands of ads seeking people to work in what was an attractive industry to young people, the motorsport industry. Unfortunately, my words fell on deaf ears.

What we saw originally in setting up SAMIA was a great opportunity for motorsport to be the ideal catalyst for attracting youngsters into engineering and technical skills training, for providing jobs and encouraging people to start small entrepreneurial businesses, and making it possible for some of those youngsters eventually to gain valuable experience internationally.

Sadly, at many levels of government, motorsport administration and education, we found too much self-importance, too many political shenanigans and, on more than one occasion, blatant corruption. Far too often, the objectives of what we were trying to achieve were forgotten in the rush to secure political points, personal gain or simply to stop an idea that didn't emanate from a particular individual. A few weeks before we left South Africa, the CEO of PetroSA was fired at very short notice.

In October 2010, we returned to Britain. While still in South Africa, I had made a couple of approaches to motorsport operations in the UK and had been offered the role of commercial director of the Jota Group, based in Tunbridge Wells. Among the company's many activities are motorsport, aviation, and automotive design and engineering. On the motorsport side of the business, Jota is an official Aston Martin racing partner team, running a GT2 in the 2011 Le Mans Series. The company also operates Mazda Motors UK's motorsport programme.

As this book took shape, we were busy preparing for the Le Mans 24 Hours with

↗ Brian concluded a sponsorship deal to support Jota Group's Le Mans activities in 2011 with specialist insurance company Hiscox. It was announced on seven-metre-wide posters at London mainline stations.

the GT2. In support of the programme, I put together three highly significant sponsorship deals with Serengeti (driving sunglasses), Canon (through their distributor Systems Technologies) and Hiscox, the specialist insurance group. All three were based on business-to-business principles.

> **The deal with Hiscox, was launched and publicised by means of seven-metre-wide posters in Waterloo and Liverpool Street stations.**

In a very innovative step, the deal with Hiscox, was launched and publicised by means of seven-metre-wide posters in Waterloo and Liverpool Street stations in London, which were expected to turn a few heads!

From a sponsorship acquisition point of view, I suppose you could say that there is life in the old dog yet!

27

Levels of expectation

In the process of writing this book, I've recalled a lot of things that over the years I'd almost forgotten about professional selling and about my career. I'm still securing sponsorship deals and have been doing so now for 37 years.

Writing this book has been a great help to me, reminding me of some of the basics that tend to be forgotten. It has also endorsed my belief that, no matter how much experience you may have and no matter how successful you may have been, in this business you never stop learning.

My objective in writing this book was to help you increase your chances of securing sports sponsorship. Right at the start, I emphasised that I can only provide you with a guide to the sponsorship selling process. I can't hold your hand and take you through very step, because each meeting will be different and every person you meet will have their own way of progressing matters with you.

It's rather like learning to drive. I could teach you the basics and give you a good grounding in the subject, but only experience will turn you into a good driver. Despite having been in this business for a long time, I still read as many books as I can on selling techniques and

practices. I would recommend that you do the same, if you're serious about improving your performance when you're face to face with a prospect.

Keeping up with modern marketing trends, particularly the explosion in online marketing, is essential if you're to present a realistic opportunity to companies for generating the return on investment.

If this book does nothing more than provide you with a platform on which you can build and develop your skills to a much higher level, then my efforts will have been worthwhile. I have almost achieved what I set out to do when I started writing it. Almost, but not quite!

What I haven't yet done is highlight one of the most important aspects of the sponsorship process: how to keep your sponsor on board. Although this book is aimed primarily at helping you secure new sponsors, I can't complete it without a brief look at this important topic.

Finding new sponsors is one of the most difficult of all sales activities. The task is getting tougher by the day as more and more individuals, teams, clubs, associations and organisations enter the market, all wanting their slice of the sponsorship cake. Consequently, it's far more cost effective to look after the sponsors you have managed to secure than keep looking for new ones.

By developing a long-term relationship with a sponsor, you'll both derive increasing benefits. You'll learn just what is important to the sponsor and therefore should be able to modify your programme when necessary to suit their specific requirements. Increasingly, the sponsor will come to understand the sport and how it can be exploited to provide a meaningful commercial return. If you have done your job properly, the sponsor will come to trust and rely on you to help make the programme even more successful as it develops.

If you work hard at developing a good two-way communication with an existing sponsor, there is every reason to believe that you will be able to increase the scope and size of the agreement that you negotiated initially. Very often, long-term major sponsorship programmes have resulted from a small initial involvement.

It's not unreasonable to expect a company entering the world of sports sponsorship for the first time to be reluctant to commit to a big spend until it has fully understood what sponsorship is all about. You need to take responsibility for helping its personnel realise the full potential of the sponsorship. If you can show them what can be achieved by expanding their involvement, you may well end up with a long-term major sponsor, way beyond your initial expectation.

The key to sponsorship development is to make sure that you deliver more than your sponsor expects, not less. It's all too easy to

be fired up and enthusiastic in the early days of a sponsorship, when everyone is excited about the prospects that lay ahead. When you are mid-way through the season, it can become more difficult to maintain this early enthusiasm.

Perhaps results haven't gone your way. Maybe a couple of events have been rained off. It could be that you've realised you are spending more than you budgeted for, and on top of that, you're beginning to get fed up with the sponsor's increasing demands. This is the testing time in the relationship. It can easily go 'belly-up' from this point on, and all that will be left is for both parties to finish the season as quickly as possible and part company. On the other hand, it can be the turning point in strengthening the association and building a solid foundation on which a long-term relationship can be developed. The route you take is very much up to you.

One of the most common complaints from sponsors is about lack of communication from the sponsored party. During the build-up to the agreement being signed, they will have received a string of phone calls and occasional visits to check that everything is still okay. Once the first stage payment has been made, however, the communication will dry up suddenly. Occasionally a press release will find its way on to the sponsor's desk, but that's all that will be heard from the sponsored party. In such a situation, is it surprising that the sponsor becomes somewhat concerned and even annoyed?

One way that I used to ensure that this didn't happen was to instigate a procedure aimed at maintaining communication. I did this right at the beginning of the sponsorship. I would recommend to the sponsor the establishment of a small working group within the company, to be given the day-to-day responsibility of managing the sponsorship. Depending on the size of the company, this might include a representative from financial control. Then I would have regular meetings throughout the period of the sponsorship with this group. In this way, we built up a relationship that was capable of working through both difficult and good times, with a level of understanding of each other's requirements.

The decision maker with whom I had negotiated the deal rarely took part in this group, but appointed someone suitable to represent them. By having this regular meeting, I found that if there were any problems, they were not allowed to fester and become really serious. Instead, they would be spotted early on and action taken to manage the situation. It also provided me with a chance to make further proposals as to the way in which the sponsor could get even more out of the arrangement. It's a method that I would strongly recommend.

It's important to avoid burying your head in the sand if there is a problem on the horizon. In my experience, problems seldom go away and have a habit of growing in importance the more you try to ignore them. Most people in management will understand that problems occur with any business, no matter how large or how efficient it might be considered. What they will be more concerned about is the way in which the problems are handled. It's like being served a meal in a restaurant when the meat hasn't been cooked in the way you requested. Provided someone apologises and does their best to rectify the matter by bringing a perfectly cooked replacement meal, probably you will be satisfied. If they start arguing with you, or the second meal is no better than the first, you are likely to become irritated.

It's the same with problems in sponsorship. As an example, if you learn that a particular round of a championship may be cancelled and you know that your sponsor is planning major hospitality at that event, don't leave it until the last minute to inform them of the imminent problem. You may hope that it will resolve itself, but very often it won't. Rather, approach the sponsor straight away and tell them about the situation. Also try to develop a contingency

plan, which you can suggest at the same time. If you only present the problem, without a possible solution, it won't be as well received as if you had given some thought to ways of dealing with the matter.

Something else that will help you maintain a good relationship with your sponsor is what I refer to as the 'management of expectation'. This ensures that both parties going into a sponsorship agreement have a similar level of expectation. A good example of this is to consider anticipated performance levels. You might fool a sponsor at the beginning of the relationship into believing that you are going to clean up in your championship. If you know that this isn't likely to be the case, you're doing yourself no favours. It can work in reverse, however.

I recall that when I put the FedEx deal together, Benetton F1 was going through a very lean period, following the departure of Michael Schumacher, who had won the world title for the team. I deliberately played down to FedEx the level of expectation, in terms of likely results for the 1997 season. Their sponsorship started mid-way through the season, at Silverstone. Results to that point had been very poor. To everyone's amazement, however, the team achieved second and third places in the British Grand Prix. Then we went to Germany, and Gerhard Berger, who had missed the previous three races, won the grand prix at Hockenheim. By now, the FedEx directors were asking me why I had been so pessimistic about potential results!

The next race was in Hungary, and unfortunately the results went back to a more realistic level with eighth and eleventh places.

Controlling the level of expectation of a sponsor is a very important aspect of managing a sponsorship. If they expect too much, because of the build-up that you have given them, and the results don't match their expectations, it can prove an embarrassment. You need to work hard at creating the right balance.

Another important part of maintaining a good relationship with your sponsor is to ensure that the company's own staff are involved from the outset. It's worth raising this with your new sponsor early on in your discussions. This applies equally to small companies and large corporations. I've seen several sponsorships die a death because of the internal politics that can arise from a lack of staff involvement in the new programme. I have often suggested to sponsors that they have a proper staff launch of the programme to tie in with the media launch. If their own people understand why the company is involving itself in the sponsorship, they will be less likely to see it simply as a great expense with little return.

Innovative staff-incentive programmes can be based on a sponsorship, with special trips to events for staff and their families. Regular online newsletters for an internal readership are rarely a waste of time. You also need to make yourself or, if applicable, perhaps your team's players available to visit staff functions, or maybe a charity event that the staff have organised, such as a sports day, a children's party or even a golf tournament. Even if it isn't written into your agreement, make that extra effort. It will pay dividends later when the time comes to assess and renew the agreement. The more effort you put in, the greater the chance of the deal being renewed or expanded.

I've found that nothing is appreciated more by a sponsor than your continual efforts to help that company develop new business relationships. It pays to take an active interest in the business growth areas that they are targeting. If you try to come up with new ideas as to how they could use the sponsorship to help achieve introductions or meetings, you'll be well looked upon. Perhaps you could suggest that in your search for co-sponsors, you might approach some of the companies on their own target list. In the process, you can suggest potential multi-dimensional alliances that might work for your existing sponsor and that could help them gain a foothold in the new business sector.

It's all about helping the sponsor achieve and surpass the objectives that you both set at the outset of the sponsorship. If you show a genuine interest in making sure that the sponsor gets every last ounce of value out of the agreement, you are far more likely to renew the deal.

For sponsorship to be successful, it has to be a two-way relationship. If it only works well for one of the parties involved, it cannot be classed as anything other than unfulfilled potential.

Summary

→ Obtaining sponsorship is an extremely difficult task. Once you have secured a sponsor, it makes sense to put a great deal of effort into keeping the company happy and eager to renew at the end of the initial sponsorship period.

→ One of the main complaints from sponsors is that the level of communication between the sponsored party and themselves declines rapidly once the deal has been signed.

→ It is worth structuring a communication channel, so that you can regularly meet the key people who will be involved in monitoring and managing the sponsorship programme. At these meetings, you can advise them of opportunities that might arise and also of any imminent problems.

→ It is always better to draw any likely problems to the attention of the sponsor before they grow in importance. If possible, when you present the problem, try to offer some possible solutions.

→ If you can develop a relationship with the sponsor whereby you try to help them develop new business, using the sponsorship as the catalyst, you will be well looked upon.

→ It is important to convince the sponsor of the need to ensure that the majority of his staff buy into the sponsorship by involving them in activities and keeping them informed of progress within the sponsorship.

28

Make it happen

We've covered a lot of ground together. While I was considering what should be included in this book, I spent a substantial amount of time trying to identify my likely target audience. Many of you may be experienced sponsorship seekers, flicking through the pages to see if there is some new approach that you can adapt for your own use.

If that is the case, I hope you're not too disappointed to find that there is little new in this tough business. Mostly it's a case of sticking to the basic principle of selling, which is to ascertain just what it is your prospect is trying to achieve and then to help them identify ways in which your sponsorship property can assist them in that task. Sometimes even the most experienced salespeople forget that simple philosophy.

Others may admit to being very inexperienced in the skills of seeking sponsorship. Some of you may even be parents of youngsters involved in various sporting activities, a number of which have become so costly that they necessitate commercial sponsorship. It may be that lots of you have never had to look for sponsorship before and have bought this book because you really had no idea of where to start.

I hope, too, that there will be some readers who are just embarking on a career in sports marketing or in related areas. Perhaps you have gained a degree in a sports-related subject and you are seeking that all-important first job in the sports sector. I was astonished to learn that there are over 1,500 degree courses at British universities that relate to sport in some way. If you fall into this category, I really hope that you get as much enjoyment out of your future career as I have had during mine.

Whatever your level of experience, I hope that you have found this book to be both interesting and helpful. Sponsorship is not an easy subject to write about because every situation you face will be different. You're all individuals with varying skills and desires. Unfortunately, there isn't a set format that will take you through a sales meeting, unless you have the ability to programme your prospect so that they ask the right questions at the correct time!

Training someone to be a salesperson is very different from training a plumber, or even an accountant, where there are specific right and wrong ways of handling most situations. In selling, there are few black or white areas; most are different shades of grey. It is difficult to teach empathy, for example. Empathy is defined as the ability to sense the feelings of another person as though they were your own. It is a vital skill within the sponsorship sales process, but one that I believe only comes with experience. In effect, what you are doing is putting yourself in the position of the other person, so that you can see things from their perspective. Few of us manage to do that in everyday life, let alone in a business meeting. If you make a genuine effort to do this, however, I can promise that it will make a huge difference to the way that you come across to your prospect.

Learning how to obtain sponsorship, whether for a one-off activity or for a career in sports marketing is very much about gaining experience. If you can put in place a strong foundation on which to build that experience, you will be far more successful. A good comparison is someone who wants to learn to play golf. Give that person a set of golf clubs and the use of a golf course, and eventually they might find a way of achieving a score that is not too embarrassing. It's almost certain, however, that they will make a lot of mistakes and develop many bad habits along the way.

On the other hand, had they been taught by a professional, who showed them the basics of the game, undoubtedly they would have saved themselves a great deal of time and effort. More importantly, they would still have been able to develop their own style of playing. By knowing what they should be doing at any particular moment, gradually they can introduce their own style. They would be far less likely to develop any bad habits, which

become more difficult to iron out the longer they are left.

That really sums up the purpose of this book. It is intended to provide you with a solid foundation on which to build your own style of selling. It should help you identify your own strengths and weaknesses, and work on them to develop an individual, yet effective, style that works for you.

I hope that you will decide to try out some of the ideas and suggestions that I've included, but please don't be too disappointed if they don't bring about the results you want immediately. It will take time to perfect the ways of delivering different strategies. Also you will need to mould them to suit your own style of presentation.

> **Learning how to obtain sponsorship, whether for a one-off activity or for a career in sports marketing is very much about gaining experience.**

As I said right at the very beginning of the book, everyone can sell. However, some people find that it comes more easily to them than others. If you decide that sponsorship is important to you, for whatever reason, you have two choices. You can either find someone to act on your behalf or you can set about the task yourself. I would like to think that after reading this book, you'll realise that if you have the enthusiasm, as well as the confidence that comes from thorough preparation, you can be as successful as anyone else.

Go for it and make it happen!

Summary

1. You need to fully appreciate the number of reasons why companies use sports sponsorship as an important part of their marketing programmes. There are many more than most people realise. Although brand awareness and hospitality are perhaps the two most common uses of sponsorship, the more possibilities that you can identify within a company, the more successful you will be in matching your sponsorship property to its marketing requirements.

2. You need to create a sponsorship property that is saleable and priced at a realistic level. You can do this by identifying as many of the features that your property can deliver as possible. The more options you have at your disposal, the more likely that you will be able to tailor a proposal to fit the real, not assumed, needs of your prospective sponsor. You should be able to justify the fee level that you have placed on the property by knowing that you arrived at the figure in a logical, calculated manner.

❝ Use the media as a powerful marketing tool by building strong media partnerships, which will help you attract commercial sponsors.

3. Use your creative powers and business acumen to devise an innovative sales strategy. One way of achieving this is to use the sponsorship property as a catalyst around which to build multi-dimensional, business-to-business relationships. Another way is to use the media as a powerful marketing tool by building strong media partnerships, which will help you attract commercial sponsors. The more effort and imagination you put into conceiving really creative options at this stage, the easier you will find it to gain interest and secure meetings.

4. If you have put the effort into devising an innovative sales strategy, it will make the task of selecting companies to target a great deal easier. It's important to prepare a list of criteria that will help you narrow your choice. It can prove very advantageous to target companies by business sector. In this way, you will learn a great deal about the industry sector and just what is important to companies within it, from a marketing point of view. It will help you identify the major players and whom the companies are targeting for new business.

5. Research is a very important aspect of the sales process. If you approach the task in the right way, you can find a great deal of information that will help you build a picture of the company you are approaching, including its aims and objectives. It can help you avoid possible minefields if you discover a past sponsorship history. Research should indicate the decision making hierarchy and help you understand the geographical

operation of the company. Used effectively, it can even help you secure a meeting with the decision maker at the appropriate stage of the sales process.

6. Having prepared a sales strategy and knowing which companies you will contact, you can design and create effective sales tools. These include your sales presentation. Selling tools can be used to achieve your objective of securing a meeting as well as adding support to your sales dialogue in the meeting.

The sales presentation is the most important of all your sales tools. It needs to be flexible and easily updated. It should not be too wordy, but it must be designed as a sales presentation, not simply as a showcase for past sports performances. It needs to demonstrate graphically the potential effectiveness of your property at providing the prospect's company with a cost-effective marketing platform. Finally, sales tools should be used to support you, not to replace you. It's important to know when to bring them into play and when to push them aside.

7. There comes a time when you have to stop planning and research in favour of making contact with the companies that you have targeted, for the purpose of securing a meeting. Whichever method you use, remember that your objective in making contact is only to secure a face-to-face meeting, not to try to sell the sponsorship in one go. It is important to find the method that works best for you, then focus on improving and fine-tuning it until it becomes really effective.

You need to use every ounce of initiative to find your way through the barriers that increasingly are being put in place in the corporate world to protect their marketing staff. This is where the research that you have carried out will stand you in good stead. You need to grab the attention of

companies in a way that makes the right people want to find out more. It's a fine balancing act between giving them too much information, which will allow them to make a premature decision, or not enough to whet their appetite.

> **Set the tone by asking the right questions and listening to the answers, gradually steering the meeting in the direction you want it to head.**

8. Once you have secured that first meeting, you need to prepare carefully and to be able to lead the meeting in the direction you want it to go. Don't go into a meeting and just hope that it will go in the right direction. You have worked hard to get that meeting, so you don't want to waste the opportunity by not being prepared. You need to take the lead from the earliest moments. That doesn't mean that you should dominate the meeting by talking over your prospect; it means that you should set the tone by asking the right questions and listening to the answers, gradually steering the meeting in the direction you want it to head.

It is important to obtain some form of commitment before you end the meeting. This might be that you set a date for a follow-up meeting, or that you arrange a meeting at your own premises to show the prospect the facilities available. Whatever you achieve, it is crucial that you don't walk away without that commitment.

9. If you have done your job properly, you should have gained a firm commitment at the first meeting. Even if this involved setting a date and time for a second meeting, you still need to follow up on that initial meeting. Apart from anything else, you need either to write to, or e-mail the person with whom you had the meeting, thanking them for their time and interest. If a meeting has been arranged, confirm that in the communication.

If you left the meeting without any form of commitment, it's important to follow up directly with the person you met, to try to determine their reaction to your proposals. If you can make contact, you need to do everything you can to get a commitment at this stage. If you don't, you are in danger of losing the momentum that you have built up. Remember, the commitment doesn't have to be for the deal itself, although that would be great. It needs to be a commitment to the next step in the sales process.

10. Eventually you will get a feel for the way that the situation is progressing. When you believe that you are getting close to the decision stage, you should prepare a document that can be signed at the time of that decision. This should confirm the main points that you have agreed with the prospect and will form the basis of the sponsorship contract. A Letter of Intent, as it is called, is a valuable document, although normally it is not legally binding.

11. Having had your Letter of Intent signed by the prospect, you need to draft a legally binding agreement, ideally with the help of a solicitor who specialises in sports sponsorship contracts. This will be submitted to the company, which almost certainly will make some changes. Without the help of a legal representative at this stage, you might end up signing an agreement that isn't necessarily in your favour, so I would suggest that the money you spend on seeking professional advice is money well spent.

12. Once you have achieved your objective of securing a commercial sponsor, you are only at the beginning of your task. You need to make sure that you keep your new sponsor happy and help the company achieve the agreed objectives. The first step in this process is to maintain regular communication and identify in advance any problems that may arise. By dealing

with these early, you will save yourself a great deal of trouble. If you allow them to fester, however, they could cause a major altercation. It is far easier and less expensive to put in the effort to retain a sponsor than it is to keep searching for new ones.